PLAY THE MUSIC, PLAY!

Joy! joy! joy! there is joy in The Salvation Army,
  Joy! joy! joy! in the Army of the Lord.
Sing to God, sing to God, with loud joyful songs of praise;
Beat the drums, beat the drums, while salvation music plays.
Play the music, play, sing the happy song,
Loud hosannas shout with the happy throng,
To the happy land we'll march along,
  And be joyful all the way.

William Pearson (1832–92).

PLAY THE MUSIC, PLAY!

BY
BRINDLEY
BOON

the story of
Salvation Army
bands

LONDON:
Salvationist Publishing and Supplies, Ltd.

Early chapters originally published in ' The Musician '

First produced in book form 1966

© *The Salvation Army*

Major BRINDLEY BOON, author and composer, is the editor of *The Musician* at International Headquarters. He has also served in Canada.

*Made and printed in 11 point Bembo type
by The Campfield Press, St. Albans,
Great Britain*

CONTENTS

Page

1. FOUR MEN IN A MARKET-PLACE 1

2. ON THE MARCH 5

3. KINGDOM OF BRASS 12

4. ALONG THE QUEEN'S HIGHWAY 21

5. THE INTERNATIONAL STAFF BAND 29

6. ASSOCIATED HEADQUARTERS BANDS 39

7. STARS OF THE STATES 47

8. IN THE LAND OF THE MAPLE 54

9. SOUTH OF PANAMA AND THE CARIBBEAN . . . 62

10. IN THE ANTIPODES 68

11. ACROSS THE CHANNEL 78

12. MID-EUROPEAN MELODY 84

13. SKIRTING THE SKAGERRAK 93

14. BOTH SIDES OF THE BALTIC 98

15. AFRICAN VARIETY 105

16. EASTER INTERLUDE 117

17. MUSICAL AMBASSADORS 130

18. BEHIND THE NOTES 145

19. ADMINISTRATION AND MISCELLANY 166

20. MUSICAL MILESTONES 193

21. UNIQUE FELLOWSHIP 207

BIBLIOGRAPHY 227

INDEX 229

CHAPTER ONE

FOUR MEN IN A MARKET-PLACE

THE respectable citizens of Salisbury had had enough. For six months the quiet atmosphere of that West of England city had been disturbed by a group of 'hooligans' who, 'under the cloak of religion', had dared to sing and preach in the market-place and afterward march in procession to a former joiner's shop which they used as a mission hall, there to conduct services which to passers-by sounded not far removed from the 'rowdyism of a travelling menagerie'.

These people, who called themselves Christian Missioners and were led by a man and woman who went under the title of 'Evangelists', had made their first appearance in March of that year, 1878. Less than a month later the *Salisbury and Winchester Journal* published a complaint. It was written over the pseudonym, 'Disgusted', and called the attention of the readers to the disgraceful scene which took place in the city every Sunday when 'disorderly characters' paraded in the streets singing revivalist hymns, which were freely interspersed with yells, whistling and comic songs.

Through that summer an outraged public, brought up under the shadow of the stately cathedral, actively opposed the 'invaders'. In July a man was fined twenty shillings for assaulting a Christian Mission convert, Austin Grant.

By the autumn Mrs. Sayers, who had been in charge of the work, had moved on to Merthyr Tydfil and had been replaced by Captain Arthur Watts. The Christian Mission had by now become The Salvation Army, hence the military title of the new Commanding Officer.

One Sunday evening the crowd gathered in the market-place received a shock. With the Salvationists stood four men, each playing a brass instrument—two cornets, a valve trombone and euphonium. The onlookers could not believe their eyes or ears. Those who imagined that this innovation would drive but another nail in the coffin of The Salvation Army spoke without knowledge, for from that quartet of musicians grew the world-wide fraternity which now numbers tens of thousands.

The instrumentalists were Charles Fry and his three sons, Fred, Ernest and Bert. Their appearance was not part of a preconceived plan of William Booth. They had not been sent from the London Headquarters; there had been no order that brass bands should be formed. The first Salvation Army band came into being at Salisbury because the

Fry family responded to the need for a bodyguard to defend the pioneers from rough handling by the supposedly respectable citizens. That the father and his sons played musical instruments was not of paramount importance. The fact that they were militant Christians was of far greater consequence. Thus the pattern and priority of Army banding were established.

Charles William Fry was born on May 29, 1837. His mother was formerly Miss Hardiman, whose father kept 'The Green Dragon' at Alderbury, near Salisbury. His father, a builder and the son of a builder, spent too much time in the tap-room. It was when Mrs. Fry, Charles's mother, saw the Wesleyan Methodists going to their eight o'clock Sunday morning prayer meeting, while she was cutting cabbages to sell on the Sabbath Day, that she became convicted of sin. Dropping the cabbages, she went indoors and began to search the Scriptures. This led to her attending services in the village chapel. She was converted through hearing a local preacher line out the Wesley hymn, 'Weary souls that wander far'. Following the incessant prayers of his wife, Charles's father was converted and the boy grew up in a hallowed and helpful atmosphere.

When he was quite young, the boy, with his brothers, became fond of music and learned to play one or more instruments. The singing at the chapel in those days was led by an orchestra, of which Charles Fry became the leader.

At the time of his marriage, Charles played first cornet in the band of the 1st Wiltshire Volunteer Rifle Corps. His three sons were taught to play brass instruments almost as soon as they could hold them. The eldest, Fred, was installed as second cornet in the chapel orchestra and, when this was abandoned, was appointed organist—at the age of eight.

Charles Fry, by this time leader of the choir, arranged sacred concerts and on many an occasion the small village premises were full for 'Elijah', the 'Messiah' or Mozart's 'Twelfth Mass'.

As the sons became of age to earn their own living, they left to work away from home and the family was split up. At the end of three years Charles Fry had become a master builder and the sons were recalled to help in the business.

In May, 1878, the family attended a Christian Mission meeting conducted by James Dowdle, the 'Hallelujah Fiddler'. Fry, a well-respected local preacher of the Salisbury Circuit, was impressed by the evangelist's holiness teaching and his sympathies were with the missioners from the first encounter. The rough treatment they received deepened his regard for them and he quickly reached a decision when Captain Watts suggested that he and his sons should bring their musical instruments to the market-place to assist with the open-air meetings and help quell the disturbances. For such a well-known and respected person as Fry and his three teenage sons to identify themselves with the much-abused and generally-despised Salvationists was a bold step. After a while the family decided to become Salvationists and were sworn-in as soldiers of the Salisbury (No. 33) Corps.

Although the honour of being the first Bandmaster in The Salvation Army rightly belongs to Charles Fry, and his eldest son is recognized as the first bandsman, individual brass instrumentalists had taken part in Christian Mission events some time before. In August, 1877, the Rev. William Booth paid a brief visit to a northern station and reported: ' The last Sabbath we had a little novelty, which apparently worked well. Among the converts are two members of a brass band. One plays a cornet, and to utilize him at once Brother Russell (in charge of the station) put him with his cornet in the front rank of the procession from South Stockton. He certainly improved the singing and brought crowds all along the line of march, wondering curiously what we should do next.'

Even before the advent of the Fry family as the Army's first brass band, a ' musical service ' had been held. This was on Wednesday, August 7, 1878, in connection with the annual conference, renamed war congress, of The Christian Mission. The event was well announced and members possessing a musical instrument of any description were invited to take part. Reporting the festival rather apologetically, *The Christian Mission Magazine* said: ' It was our first. We could not be expected to perfect everything at once. . . . We were rather disappointed in the number of instruments, but the fiddlers and concertinists and clarion sounders of the evening showed an example.'

Colonel Robert Sandall, in the first volume of *The History of The Salvation Army*, identifies one of the ' clarion sounders ' as George Leedham, who represented Hammersmith at the war congress and of whom Bramwell Booth said that he was the first man to play a cornet in a Salvation Army meeting.

*   *   *

Salvationists would not claim to be the first to use musical instruments in a religious service. For two hundred years church bands had fulfilled a useful purpose. Perhaps Salvation Army bands stem from the same stock. Both demand our attention.

Before 1660 church music was supplied by organs. When these instruments were abandoned by the Puritans and the priest or minister was left to give the key note for singing, the help of vocalists and instrumentalists was enlisted. It is said that during this period professional exponents of the violin, lute and flute who had performed in the theatres and at Court, wandered away into the villages, and in the taverns and ale-houses taught the local inhabitants to play the instruments, which they bequeathed to them. The rural orchestras were formed in this way and were ready-made to answer the appeal for church bands.

There were usually about half a dozen instrumentalists perched in the choir gallery each Sunday, all looking very smart in their Sunday best or in embroidered smocks. The girls wore attractive dresses and poke bonnets. The leader was either the parish clerk or the schoolmaster, and the instruments included flute, clarinet, cello, violin, bassoon, oboe, seraphine (an early form of harmonium), Kent bugle and the triangle. The most popular was the bassoon. So important was this wood-wind considered that the player who manipulated it was the only one who received payment for his services.

From the church bands sprang the town and works bands. As early as 1818 the famous Besses o' the Barn boasted a reed band, while the first all-brass bands to be formed were those attached to ironmorks in South Wales—at Pontybydurum and Blaina. That was in the 1830s.

By 1860 the brass was firmly established and all over Britain musical groups rose Phoenix-like from the ashes of the string, reed and drum and fife bands. In 1853 the Besses o' the Barn was converted to all brass. Two years later Black Dyke Mills was formed from a remnant of a reed band. Within ten years Irwell Springs had been commenced by six villagers of Weir, near Bacup, Lancashire, as a result of a conversation they had whilst returning from a contest. John Dennison, a young South Shields musician, was approached by a deputation of pit workers and requested to form a brass band. St. Hilda's Colliery was the outcome. Wingate Temperance Band was begun by scholars of a Methodist Sunday-school class. The once-famous Morriston Band was founded in a village near Bristol by an English family; it moved bodily into Wales during the 1860s.

The brass band is an accepted British institution, the delight of the working man, born out of the industrial revolution and introduced in many instances by mill-owners and factory managers to provide agreeable relaxation during new-found leisure time. Little wonder that the idea caught on among Salvationists! Brass banding was a medium they understood. How natural that it should become the basic unit of the musical forces of an organization which exists to meet the needs of the ' man in the street '!

The sociological soundness of this approach is realized when one becomes aware of the phenomenal growth of Army bands, both in numbers and in artistic efficiency.

CHAPTER TWO

ON THE MARCH

'MR. BOOTH! A brass band! I don't think I should like it in connection with religious services!'

The speaker was Marianne Faulconbridge, the youthful evangelist in charge of the Seaham Harbour Corps. General Booth sat watching her from across the room in the humble dwelling which was her quarters. On the way to another appointment in the north of England he had broken his journey to pay a surprise visit to the girl whom, six months before, he had accepted for full-time service in the rapidly growing Movement of which he was the Founder.

After inquiring how she was progressing spiritually and praying God's blessing upon her consecrated service, the General made the unexpected announcement: 'I am going to take you away from here and send you to Salisbury, and there you will have a brass band to help you.'

Captain Faulconbridge's reaction to this offer of musical support was not surprising, for news of the Fry family's activities at Salisbury had not won universal approval. But the young woman's gravest fears were quickly allayed. Soon after arriving in Salisbury, in April, 1879, she was reporting that the 'Hallelujah brass band' was doing good work and rendering appreciated service.

General Booth himself had not been easily convinced that the innovation of a brass band was a good thing. After the appearance of Charles Fry and his sons on the streets of Salisbury, James Dowdle, then in charge at Plymouth, conducted week-end meetings at the '33rd', heard the band in action, foresaw the great possibility provided by the experiment and recorded his impressions for the benefit of the General.

This resulted in William Booth paying a hurried visit to see and hear for himself. While he immediately realized the potential value of bands to the Army, he was not the kind of person to be hastened into a decision affecting an Organization which, by this time, was operating in more than fifty centres in Great Britain.

The Founder moved cautiously. He decided to place the family band 'on trial' by using it in several campaigns. In March, 1879, the sons, without their father, assisted Captain Ted Irons at the opening of a theatre at Portsmouth, which had been taken for Sunday meetings. Two weeks later they were at Manchester (Grosvenor Street) giving musical support to the Founder's second son, Ballington, who had been

5

'Happy Eliza' in the Edgware Road area of Marylebone, London

sent to open the corps. The brothers remained for a week and then went on to Bolton.

During the August bank holiday week-end that year Charles Fry joined his sons for a campaign. Mrs. Sayers, who had pioneered at Salisbury, had been appointed to ' open fire ' at Stroud. When her efforts to attract the crowds into the hall failed, she appealed to the family for help. The venture stirred the quiet little Gloucestershire town, congregations increased during the Sunday and twenty-three seekers knelt at the Penitent-form at the close of the night meeting. Next day a further thirty converts were added and three people were converted at dinner time in the house where the Frys were billeted.

Thus, at the beginning of the Army's musical activity, the divine seal was placed upon the soul-saving endeavours of men who, first and foremost, were concerned with the spiritual welfare of those to whom they ministered through the medium of consecrated music. That desire is still predominant among Salvation Army bandsmen.

In March, 1880, the ' Salisbury Brass Band ', as it was referred to in the pages of The War Cry, accompanied the General to South Wales to take part in the great Council of War gatherings, visiting Tredegar, Merthyr, Pentre, Aberdare and Brynmawr. At Tredegar there was a crowd of three thousand Salvationists to meet the band at the station (states a War Cry report). Windows were thrown open and the inhabitants of the Welsh mining town lined the streets as the band, playing ' Soldiers fighting round the Cross ', headed the procession to the hall.

A Council of War in the Midlands followed the successful Welsh revival campaign and the Frys were present throughout. On their way home they called at Marylebone for the opening meetings in an old theatre in Church Street, just off the Edgware Road. The officer appointed to lead the salvation onslaught on this notorious area was Captain Eliza Haynes, known far and wide as ' Happy Eliza '.

In Nottingham her unusual methods of attracting the attention of the citizens were successful. When attempts to begin operations had left the people unmoved, Lieutenant Haynes, as she then was, decided to create interest by dashing through the streets with a banner, ' Happy Eliza ', streaming from her hair. Later she was marching along the same streets beating time with her ' fiddlestick ', as the Army's early writers preferred to call a violin bow, while a procession of converted ruffians sang the songs of salvation.

It was no surprise when, to draw a crowd at Marylebone, ' Happy Eliza ' appeared in the Edgware Road neighbourhood sitting on the box seat of a four-wheel cab attracting attention by playing her fiddle. On the roof ' Welsh Tom ', a fearless revivalist who also played the violin, banged the big drum and from the inside an officer distributed handbills announcing the arrival of 'Happy Eliza'. The 'Happy Band'—the Frys enjoyed a variety of descriptions—followed in, and on, a second cab.

The fame of 'Happy Eliza' spread. She became the subject of music hall songs, comedians in Christmas pantomimes, dressed for the part, mimicked her, and dolls, toys and sweets were named after her.

When the Fry family was invited to assist in the Whitsuntide meetings to be led by General Booth at Whitechapel, Charles had to make a decision. A successful building business would not thrive or even continue to exist with the firm downing tools at frequent intervals to embark upon an evangelical adventure, however commendable the action and pure the motive. If the business was to be maintained, future invitations to campaign would have to be refused. If the band was to go on travelling, the business would have to be sold.

The Founder was acquainted with the problem and promptly advised the family to make it a matter of prayer. The answer was not long coming. The business was disposed of, and on Sunday, May 8, 1880, the Frys farewelled from Salisbury, the father preaching in the morning and night meetings. Six days later they arrived in London, where they participated in the Whitsuntide Council of War and remained at Whitechapel for two weeks before travelling north to assist William Booth in similar gatherings in Grimsby, Bridlington, Hull, Whitby, Sheffield and Rotherham.

Charles Fry and his three sons thereby became the nucleus of the first 'staff band' of The Salvation Army. They spent their time assisting at new openings, encouraging corps where the activity had reached a low ebb and at centres where storms of persecution had broken out. Their apprenticeship at Salisbury stood them in good stead when it came to that! When 'Gipsy' Smith was in charge at Hanley he asked for help. The Frys were sent. 'Gipsy' never wanted for a congregation after that.

The boys often assisted in making seats for circuses, skating rinks and other buildings in which meetings were held, and devoted their spare time to arranging and copying music. They learned a system of shorthand writing and, whenever a new song was sung, would take down the words in shorthand and the music in tonic sol-fa. The father wrote words to popular songs and the four sang together with marked success.

The presence of the Fry brass band in the towns and villages of England and Wales in those days proved an incentive to the early converts and caught the imagination of great numbers of young people who fancied themselves as star performers on the cornet, trombone or euphonium.

After barely two years of travelling in this way Charles Fry was taken ill and, after recovering sufficiently to sing a solo at an Exeter Hall meeting on March 27, 1882, went to stay at the home of the Livingstone-Learmouths at Polmont, Glasgow, from which he was promoted to Glory on August 24, 1882.

A monument to ' The First Bandmaster of The Salvation Army ' was unveiled over Charles Fry's grave in Glasgow on New Year's Day, 1884. The stone is inscribed with some verses written by this good man who, at the age of forty-five, after but four years as a Salvationist, left so great an influence:

> The former things are past
> And ended is the strife;
> I'm safe at Home at last,
> I live an endless life.

'As Richard Slater was the father of Salvation Army Music, C. W. Fry was its grandfather!' wrote Colonel Robert Sandall. Of the ' grandfather ', the ' father ', who never knew him, said: ' I have never known a man who left behind a better report of the saintly life. Everywhere people could testify to his unqualified obedience to the call of God and consecration to His service. Hundreds of people were led to salvation in his meetings, and the Holy Spirit put His unquestionable seal upon all his labours. . . . How gracious God has been by putting at the head of our musical forces a man so good, so gifted, so triumphant in a holy life of splendid service in the Army!'

The band was dissolved after Fry's death. The youngest son, Bert, migrated to Australia; Ernest became secretary to Colonel Henry Edmunds, then in command of Scotland, and Fred was appointed secretary to Mr. Herbert Booth, the Founder's third son, at that time in charge of the men's section at the Training Home.

From time to time during its campaigns the Fry Brass Band was augmented by other instrumentalists, and at one time numbered seven —three cornets, baritone, valve trombone, euphonium and bass drum —being dubbed the ' Hallelujah Minstrels '. At times ' Welsh Tom ' was the drummer, but the name of Jack Wilson has also been mentioned in this connection. Johnny Clifford must have played the baritone, presuming that the Frys remained on their original instruments. ' Welsh Tom ', Griffith by name, later served as an officer in Canada, where he was known as the Welsh Minstrel, and became the father of Lieut.-Commissioner Richard Griffith.

The third cornetist was Arthur Sheard, an engineering apprentice from Attercliffe. He was attracted to Christian Mission meetings in

his home town early in 1878. He had been converted in the Methodist
Church and had learned to play a cornet in the Methodist Brass Band
which, apart from its name, had no connection with any religious
endeavour. When he became a Salvationist his cornet was pressed
into Army service and when the Attercliffe comrades marched three
miles to attend a meeting led by William Booth at Sheffield, Sheard,
providing martial strains on his cornet, headed the procession.

As the company neared the hall, the Founder, already in the
building, asked: ' Who is that young man with the cornet? Send him
to me.' The nervous lad was shown into the presence of his General,
who demanded: ' Now then, let's hear what you can do '. Young
Arthur raised his cornet and played ' We're travelling home to heaven
above, Will you go? '

' That will do, my boy,' was the Founder's reaction. ' Be ready to
come to me when I send for you.'

A few weeks later a letter arrived from Bramwell Booth, then
Chief of the Staff, appointing him an officer. In January, 1880,
Lieutenant Sheard was sent as second-in-charge to Manchester Temple.

Sheard was recalled from Manchester and appointed ' The General's
Trumpeter '. For two years Trumpeter Sheard, as he was known,
travelled with the Founder, taking part in the great Councils of War
in Cornwall and South Wales, and at the opening of such centres as
Scarborough, Bristol and Regent Hall.

He was with Elijah Cadman at the opening of Heckmondwike
Corps. There was so much opposition that when the crowd became
too demonstrative Cadman commanded: ' Here, Sheard, escape with
your life and my bag to the railway station; I'll join you there later on.'
The ' Trumpeter ' made his way to the station without any further
instruction. After a while Cadman arrived at the head of a howling
mob. Friendly hands helped him through the barrier and closed the
gates on the angry crowd.

At Derby, Sheard appeared in court for playing ' You must be a
lover of the Lord ' on his cornet in the market-place. Forty years later
he was again in Derby. By that time both corps in the town possessed
a band of some forty instrumentalists. He played the same tune on the
same cornet in the same market-place. Next morning the local
newspaper reported: ' Trumpeter Sheard has returned to Derby and
got his own back.'

Later, Trumpeter Sheard relinquished his officership and returned
to his apprenticeship. For many years he was Bandmaster at Hanley.

Just after the First World War his name suddenly hit the Army
news headlines once more. Retired from corps musical leadership, he
began to travel again to conduct spiritual campaigns in many parts of

the British Isles. The white-bearded veteran, with his cornet, was a welcome visitor wherever he went, and his link with the past made him a romantic personality, especially to the younger generation.

In 1940, at the age of eighty-two, the 'Trumpeter' announced his retirement from campaigning and wrote a final message in *The Musician*. He died two years later.

CHAPTER THREE

KINGDOM OF BRASS

AT Christmas time, 1879, four soldiers of the three-year-old Consett Corps, County Durham, braved the seasonable elements, on which hardy Northern Englanders could depend in those days, to play appropriate music on brass instruments.

The idea did not originate with Edward Lennox, George Storey, James Simpson and Robert Greenwood. A former colleague, Captain (later Commissioner) Isaac Unsworth, who by this time had taken command at Salisbury, had written home with news of the Fry band, to which had been added a drum played by Austin Grant. He suggested that Consett should follow Salisbury's example. The Christmas playing adventure was the outcome and marked the beginning of the first corps band in The Salvation Army.

This claim was hotly contested by Salisbury and Northwich. The Wiltshire corps may be forgiven for its pride in being the cradle of Army bands. When the Frys left for full-time service in London— there is no doubt that they were the Salisbury Corps Band until that time—the corps was left without an organized band, though there were individual players. When William Booth presented Charles Fry with a cornet, the old one was sold to Stephen Fry, a local baker and no relation, and this cornetist, with Drummer Grant, carried on the good work until more instrumentalists were added.

The Northwich claim was based on the fact that a *War Cry* report of September 4, 1880, stated that this corps had a band of twelve brass instruments and big and small drums, and that arrangements had been made whereby—without any question of personal ownership—the bandsmen should purchase the instruments by weekly instalments over a period of six months. The first reference to Consett Band did not appear in *The War Cry* until November 17, 1881. Lieut.-Colonel Richard Slater always supported the claim of the Northwich men.

The matter of the disputed honour led to an official inquiry being held in 1906. In *The War Cry* dated April 14th of that a year, a notice said:

THE FIRST BAND
INTERESTING QUESTION TO BE
SETTLED
Which was the first corps brass band in The Salvation Army? Some doubt having arisen on the subject, a special inquiry is to be instituted in order to ascertain and settle beyond dispute this interesting question.

Bands which claim to have been in existence in or before 1880 are asked to give full particulars as to the date upon which the band was formed, the number comprising the band, instrumentation, etc., accompanied by documentary proof of the evidence they adduce.

Soldiers and bandsmen whose experience goes back as far as 1880 are also invited to co-operate with the Board of Inquiry by giving any information they may have on the point in question.

Three months later, on July 21st, a further statement was issued:

Among British Salvationists, and especially in Army band circles, much interest has been excited over the question as to which corps is entitled to the honour of having been the first to possess a properly organized band.

The inquiry was set on foot by the Chief of the Staff and, acting upon his instructions, the officers appointed for the purpose—Commissioner Carleton, Colonel Hay and Brigadier Powley—have made strict investigation into the matter and arrived at a definite decision.

Hitherto, a certain corps in Cheshire has been regarded as having the chief claim to the distinction of being ' the first '. It is found, however, that whereas their claim dates back to March, 1880, a small band had been started and was in active operation with the Consett Corps during the latter part of 1879.

With the complete evidence before it, therefore, the Board of Inquiry has no hesitation in awarding the palm to Consett—to which corps we extend our sincere congratulations.

The four gallant pioneers of Consett must have been quickly augmented, for the now famous photograph of the first band shows fourteen instrumentalists. The men followed the example of the local iron works band and sported uniforms that included pill-box hats with large metal badges on the front, and small bow ties. ' Ned ' Lennox became the first Bandmaster and many early-day bandsmen were taught to play instruments in his one living-room in Puddler's Row.

One of the bandsmen of those days, Sam Carruthers, was probably the first Salvationist to play a slide trombone. Another feature of that pioneer group was the circular bass played by James Simpson. He became a Major and was the father of Mrs. Commissioner William Grottick.

*　　　*　　　*

Although the Founder was impressed by the efforts of the Fry pioneers and was convinced that the playing of instruments should be added to the methods already in use to attract people to the meetings, it does not appear to have been his intention at the beginning to utilize brass bands only, or indeed bands at all in a strictly organized sense.

An order in *The War Cry* dated March 27, 1880, and repeated at frequent intervals throughout the summer, said:

Whereas, during the great Welsh and Cornish Councils, and before that time at Plymouth, Nottingham and elsewhere, we have proved the great utility of musical instruments in attracting crowds to our open-air and indoor meetings, we do here express our desire that as many of our officers and soldiers generally, *male and female*, as have the ability for so doing, shall learn to play on some suitable instrument.   And as in many instances the obtaining of an instrument is a difficulty, we shall be glad if any friends who may have such instruments lying idle will consecrate them to this service and send them to Headquarters.   This includes violins, bass viols, concertinas, cornets or any brass instruments, drums, or anything else that will make a pleasant sound for the Lord.

It does not require a great deal of imagination to picture the result. At Bradford the band consisted of two violins, a banjo and a brass whistle; at Mexborough, a violin, a flute, bell and huntsman's horn; at Grimsby, four violins and a piccolo.   Such musical groups must have

Whitechapel Corps marching in Ratcliff Highway, in the early 1880s

proved a novelty to the eye, especially when utilized for open-air meetings as well as indoors.   But would not the string instruments prove awkward to manipulate on the march?

While these nondescript musical groups were making the most of their quickly fading existence, the brass bands were increasing in numbers and popularity.   Hull, to which corps Captain Unsworth had been moved from Salisbury, was among the earliest.   In the issue of June 5, 1880, *The War Cry* reported that the Temple was so crowded that the band had to get in by using a private entrance at the back. About that time Ilkeston boasted a drum and fife band.

The honour of being the first band in London belongs to a corps that today does not exist: Whitechapel, the No. 1 Corps of The Salvation Army. In September, 1880, Captain Tom Payne, himself a cornet player, purchased two cornets and several other instruments from Halliday's, in Whitechapel Road, and another eight from a pawnshop. He sent postcards inviting eight likely young men of the corps to come to the hall to select instruments. A young convert, Hugh Whatmore, finding his card waiting upon his return from work, ran all the way to the hall to make sure of getting a cornet!

Another to receive a postcard was John Agar, son of Christian Mission pioneers, who became the first Bandmaster of the corps. Whatmore became an officer and, after many years of outstanding service, which included the command of a number of overseas territories, died in 1939 with the rank of Commissioner.

There is no record of another London band having been formed during that eventful year, but many from the provinces which have since become household names can trace their beginnings to that time. Portsmouth is among them. Captain Valentine Case, appointed to take command in October, 1880, set the fashion. An accomplished musician before coming into the Army, he, with his two daughters, started to learn brass instruments. Others joined them and a band was soon formed. Mrs. Case played the cymbals. It was not long before the Captain was reporting the band as ' blowing salvation down every street '.

The Portsmouth enthusiasts had their musical appetites whetted before the coming of the Case family. Mrs. Captain Abram Davey, wife of the previous commanding officer, made it known through the pages of *The War Cry* that she wished to obtain a cornet, and so become the first woman to play a brass instrument in the Army. It would appear that her wish was granted for in a photograph published in *The War Cry* of July 31, 1880, she is shown with a cornet in her hand.

Although many bands date their history from drum-and-fife and string-cum-wind beginnings, in the early 1880s bands, purely brass in character, came into being at an amazing rate. By 1883 there were 400 bands in the British Isles alone. Among these were South Shields, Carlisle, Stockton-on-Tees and Sheffield. Merthyr and Ebbw Vale were among the first in Wales, and Hamilton in Scotland and Belfast in Ireland were not far behind. The Christian Mission had indeed become an Army of marching musical men.

* * *

Two years after a band was formed at Whitechapel, a second was installed in the London area, although at more than one established

centre there was a motley group of instrumentalists already in action.
Regent Hall, Clapton Congress Hall and Chalk Farm were among
those formed in 1882, and those stalwarts who took part in the humble
beginnings of these now famous bands could not, in their wildest
dreams, have foreseen the part they were to play in the history of
Army music.

Regent Hall, a converted skating-rink situated a few yards from
Oxford Circus in London's fashionable West End, had a musical
opening. The event was given prominence in more than one daily
newspaper. A reporter wrote: 'The hall is well supplied with
illumination and behind the gilded gates of the entrance rows of gas
jets burn in a seductive glare, enough to make the gin palaces look to
their laurels.'

Before the meeting began there were scenes of great enthusiasm.
'Fiddles were scraping and Army songs were humming,' says another
report, and everywhere there was a sense of keen anticipation. Outside was a howling and hooting which could be heard inside the
building.

General William Booth received a wonderful welcome. Hands
and handkerchiefs were waved in ecstasy and the excitement was
'suggestive of the first Christian Pentecost'. A 'converted comic
singer'—presumably Captain James Bateman since he wrote the
chorus referred to—sang 'Under the Army flag we will fight our
way to Glory'. When the soloist pointed to the colours, the Training
Home Band (trombones, cornets, fiddles, flutes and fifes) 'burst forth
in all its power'.

With the Founder that March afternoon was a short, bewhiskered
young man whose duty it was to accompany the singing on a cornet.
It was Trumpeter Arthur Sheard. He stayed on at Regent Hall to
form the corps' first band.

When string musicians from a chapel in the Holborn district
became Salvationists at the 'Rink', an orchestra for indoor meetings
was soon in regular service. Some four months later a supply of
nickel-plated instruments was purchased from a firm of musical instrument makers in Holborn Circus. On Sunday, July 30, 1882, the 'Rink
Silver Band'—Sheard and twelve others—marched along Oxford
Street for the first time. A month later, the corps, with arms linked,
four abreast and band playing, marched through the Marble Arch to
hold the first Salvation Army meeting in Hyde Park.

Ever since, Regent Hall has been the Army's mecca—its London
shop window. It stands in the City of Westminster and can claim in
its district Buckingham Palace, Westminster Abbey, the Houses of
Parliament, Trafalgar Square and many another famous landmark.

On Sundays the band varies its open-air stand. One week it is in the narrow streets of Soho; the next in a wide thoroughfare in Mayfair. Today's march to the hall may be past Broadcasting House, home of the British Broadcasting Corporation, and on to Oxford Circus; tomorrow's through Piccadilly Circus and round the fine sweep of Regent Street. The spiritual vision built up over the years has not become dimmed.

Present with his parents at the opening of the Regent Hall was young Bert Twitchin, not then eight years of age. The family linked up with the corps, the father becoming one of the first sergeants. Trumpeter Sheard became Bert's boyhood hero and the youngster made up his mind that, given the chance, he would play a cornet.

How he reached his ambition is now history. As a cornet soloist ' H. W. T.' became world renowned. He played variation solos years before they were popular in the Army and rendered the first arrangement of this character to the International Music Board in 1926. His own compositions, ' Silver Threads ' and ' Wondrous Love ', are popular solos of this type. He toured Canada and the U.S.A. in 1927. His musical thoughts at the piano, upon which he accompanied his cornet solos, were a feature of ' Rink ' festivals for many years.

After serving for twenty-five years as Deputy Bandmaster, Herbert Twitchin became Bandmaster in 1909 and served with distinction in that capacity for thirty-seven years. He was admitted to the Order of the Founder by General Evangeline Booth upon her retirement from office in 1939, and in 1946 was awarded the M.B.E. for sixty-four years' voluntary work with Salvation Army bands. He retired a year later.

His happy Salvationism won for Bandmaster Twitchin many friends. Although he encountered what some would consider to be more than his share of life's sorrows and disappointments, his faith came shining through the darkness of doubt and despair, and smilingly he would dedicate himself to the future.

This happy spirit was not reserved for the public platform. It was in evidence in the band room during those never-to-be-forgotten monthly spiritual meetings when his ' family ' would gather around him and share fellowship and exchange experiences, thus strengthening each other for the battle of life.

In his business, too, he was the genial ' governor '. From a Smithfield Market van boy he became managing director of a large firm of provision merchants, and throughout the long years revealed during the week the same brand of Christianity he preached on Sundays.

Bandmaster Twitchin was promoted to Glory on October 21, 1954, a month after his eightieth birthday.

On the day of the funeral, at a time when London's lunch-hour rush was at its height, policemen signalled Oxford Street's stream of traffic to a standstill as, headed by the band with which he was associated for seventy-two years, Bandmaster Twitchin made his last journey. An hour before, the coffin, on which rested the Bandmaster's Bible and baton, cap and cornet, had been carried into the old hall through an avenue of men, most of them grey-haired, who had marched with their beloved leader through the West End streets.

*   *   *

With Regent Hall, Chalk Farm is among the best known of Army bands. The Salvationist visitor to England does not consider his trip to be complete unless he has heard these two bands.

The beginnings at Chalk Farm were not nearly so spectacular as those of the ' Rink '. The hall was a disused Baptist chapel set back some 100 ft. from the road and approached by a passage 10 ft. wide which passed under a house *en route*. This poorly situated, dingy old building remained the home of the Chalk Farm Corps for forty-four years and became a Bethel to countless souls.

Two Sundays after the opening of the corps, in 1881, Whitechapel Band came over to assist in the meetings. A young man, Tom Lee, was attracted to the Army that day. When a band was formed Lee became the first drummer and continued to ' beat for the Lord ' for more than fifty years.

Describing those early days, Tom Lee said:

> After the opening of the corps we got hold of an old friend whose name was Bull. He played a cornet and was acquainted with a Mr. Falkus, who had been a bandmaster in the Volunteers. It was in the house of this military man that a few of us converts started to practise. I think we numbered nine. After several weeks out we went, dressed in frock coats and bowler hats!
> Mr. Falkus usually walked on the pavement whenever we were on the march. It was close on Christmas time, I remember, and we tried some caroling. But the first effort lasted only about half an hour, for some roughs took a dislike to our music, for reasons better understood in these days than those.
> When the question of some sort of uniform was mentioned, there was a difference of opinion; but two of us went down to a military outfitters in Woolwich and for a few pounds got hold of some tunics, which smartened us up quite a bit. We had a drum-major who marched in front of the band, flourishing his wand in great style. We soon found a new leader in Bandmaster Worboys, and commenced to go about a little.

After the band had had five Bandmasters in eleven years, seventeen-year-old Alfred W. Punchard was commissioned to that position on April 3, 1894. This appointment was considered rather a risk. The timorous shook their heads. Was it wise to put young Fred Punchard, as good a boy and as promising a musician as he was, in charge of a band of twenty-three men, the majority of whom were his seniors by many years?

Within a year of A. W. P.'s appointment, the bandsmen were taking part in a Crystal Palace Day, attracting attention by their playing and by wearing white linen attachments to their caps, bearing the name of the band at the front and with a part hanging down over the back to act as a sun protector.

Before long, the band began to be known beyond the confines of its own neighbourhood. Soon it was a household name all over the world, especially on the continent of Europe.

The first campaign carried out by the band was a ten-day tour of Scotland in 1902, starting at Aberdeen and working back to Glasgow. Arrangements for the journey were completed following an invitation received from the Commanding Officer at Inverness. Although the band has toured Scotland on two occasions, Inverness is still awaiting a visit!

With the bandsmen's appetites for travel thus whetted, it is not surprising that they were off again the following summer, this time to the west of England. Penzance and Land's End were visited and the campaign finished at Bristol.

In 1909—Holland (twice) and Germany had been visited in the interval—the band campaigned in Ireland, commencing at Dublin and extending to the Giant's Causeway and Larne and including Belfast. Two years later the band's first motor campaign was undertaken, this taking place through the Midlands and Yorkshire. The men returned by way of Hull, Grimsby and the Eastern Counties. This lasted thirteen days, a period increased by a day two years later when a similar motor campaign was carried out through the west of England.

No corps band in the Salvation Army world can have travelled so extensively as Chalk Farm. But if, in future years, a band from Britain conducts a week-end campaign in Australia, it is hoped that the fortunate participants will spare a thought for the pioneers whose twenty-mile journey in a ' modern ' automobile was considered a daring adventure in the early part of the century.

* * *

Another band to remain in the public eye is Clapton Congress Hall. Privileged to take part in so many great Army events, the band led the march to Abney Park Cemetery at the funeral of William Booth in 1912.

Among those who as Bandmasters laboured so well to establish the high standard of musical efficiency which the band has striven to maintain were Caleb Burgess, Walter Prestage, John Howard, William M. Brand, Commissioner William Dalziel, Brigadier Archie Burgess, Colonel Ernest Wellman and Colonel Albert Jakeway.

The band has always included in its ranks several members of the International Staff Band. Lieut.-Colonel Bernard Adams is an old Congress Hall bandsman, having become an officer from its ranks. Others who have played in both bands include Commissioner Edgar Dibden, formerly the Chief of the Staff, Lieut.-Commissioner George Grattan and Brigadier James Sansom.

*   *   *

From the earliest endeavours the purpose of Salvation Army bands was made clear. In officers' councils in January, 1884, the General laid down what he called ' our general rule for them ':

> They are to work for the good of the corps and for the salvation of souls, and for nothing else. We are not going to stick them up on the platform, nor march them through the streets for them to perform, and to be admired. They are to go there and blow what they are told, and what the Commanding Officer thinks will be best for the good of the corps and the salvation of souls, and if they won't blow for this object, let them stop their playing.
>
> We want nobody like that amongst us. The man must blow his cornet and shut his eyes, and believe while he plays that he is blowing salvation into somebody and doing something that will be some good. Let him go on believing while he hits the drum, or blows his cornet, and he will be just as anxious about the prayer meeting—he won't want to buckle up and rush off—he will say: ' What is the use of all my beating, and blowing, if I do not see someone come to the Penitent-form? '—all his beating and blowing is to get the people first into the barracks and then to the Penitent-form.

This standard has sometimes been too high for would-be Salvation Army bandsmen. A brass band formed in the Nottingham area in December, 1880, had ' left the ranks' by April of the next year. Maybe the General's determination that the men should be converted and of good character was too much, for in the early days bandsmen who had played in prize and other secular bands found the discipline of the Army too rigid.

The fact that the fundamental discipline has never been relaxed or the standards lowered is sufficient proof of the Founder's rightness.

CHAPTER FOUR

ALONG THE QUEEN'S HIGHWAY

BY 1885 the military terminology of The Salvation Army had expanded to include 'flying squadrons', 'cavalry corps forts', 'jaunting-car crusades', 'iron horse artillery' and 'flying columns'. In that year, too, the Life Guards set forth from the National Training Barracks at Clapton to evangelize Kent.

The training of a cadet for officership in those days consisted of a three-month course of lectures and classes and a similar period of practical instruction, when the cadets were sent to 'the field' in brigades to conduct special campaigns in as many towns and villages as possible.

The men cadets who, during May and June, took part in what was known as 'The Great Kent March' were described as 'Life Guards'; each wore a white pith military helmet, a red guernsey, blue trousers and gaiters, and carried a knapsack and a waterbottle. They were under the direction of Herbert Booth, who was then in charge of training for men.

The cadets were headed by a band of twenty-five brass instrumentalists known as The Band of the Life Guards. Later it was suggested that a permanent band might be established to continue the good work.

In *The War Cry* dated March 12, 1887, there appeared a notice asking for volunteers to form a band that was to be organized for continuous service. The bandsmen would be dealt with in the same way as candidates for officership. No salary was offered and no guarantee given apart from supplying food and clothing. Within a month twenty-five men had been accepted for service. They gathered at Clapton and in the officers' dining-room met for the first time Staff-Captain Harry Appleby, who had been appointed to take charge.

A bandsman was detailed to take the names of the men and the instruments they were able to play. The questioning went something like this:

'What instrument?'
'Cornet, sir!'
'Anything else?'
'Bombardon, sir.'
'Anything else?'
'Trombone, sir'—until the Bandmaster interrupted with: 'What

a clever set of men I've got! It takes me all my time to play one instrument. I think I had better be a bandsman and someone else the Bandmaster.' And so the enthusiasts had their first lesson in humility from Appleby, who had been a military bandmaster before becoming a Salvationist.

The first band practice was in the basement of the Training Home at Clapton, in what became known as the ' Glory Hole '. So congested was the space that it was like playing in a box. The sound could not escape. The instruments had been in a riot at Northampton and were the worse for wear. After the men had played the first tune with the Bandmaster's ear at the bell of each instrument in turn, he said: ' Well, well! I thought I asked for men who could read music at sight.' At the end of the practice the bandsmen were told to get a certain amount of scale practice every day.

During April and May, the Household Troops, as the band was known, underwent extensive training. The men learned how to play. They also learned how to pray and to respond to discipline. Theirs was to be a man-size job and they would need to be fit from every aspect.

On June 1st the Household Troops Band was ready for the road. A whistle blew, the men fell in for inspection in the forecourt of Clapton Congress Hall. This over, the headgear was removed while a voice was raised in prayer, and then the gates were thrown open. A stentorian voice commanded ' By your left! ' and to the vibrating drums and the brazen throats—amid a glitter of scintillating brass and a flood of salvation sound—the bandsmen marched proudly around the corner of Linscott Road, amid prancing steeds, waving handker-chiefs and cries of ' God bless you! ', to become trail blazers.

The Household Trooper did not travel light on that first momen-tous journey. His uniform was made up of oddments from a military store, including a short, ill-fitting patrol tunic of a very dark green, a couple of brass S's fixed to the shoulder strap, and a pair of guardsman's overalls, including the usual red stripe down each leg. Over the tunic were tied a knapsack, a pair of military blankets and an overcoat. An old military helmet completed the outfit.

The tunics had belonged to Her Majesty's Rifle Brigade, and the many bloodstains gave rise to the story that they had been worn in battle. The tunics, designed to be buttoned the whole length, did not make for hygiene in that intensely hot summer of 1887 and were discarded after the first tour!

' They were replaced ', says Colonel Fred Hawkes, a Trooper of those days, ' by a proper Army-made tunic of the Norfolk jacket variety; the straps extended over the shoulder, back and front—also the belt—being trimmed with red braid. In addition, two bands stretched across the front of the jacket, upon which the words " Salvation Army" were embroidered. These uniforms were certainly much more "Army" in appearance and, as they were made to measure, the fitting was good.'

The first tour of the band lasted six weeks and included the Midlands and Black Country. The men were in Birmingham for Queen Victoria's Golden Jubilee celebrations and were marched through the poorer streets of the city. Here the decorations consisted of all sorts of rubbish, including effigies, old and dirty clothes and dead cats and rats.

Sometimes they were fortunate enough to be billeted in the homes of wealthy friends of the Army. Upon other occasions a blanket on the floor boards of a hall had to suffice.

What rejoicing there was when, upon parading at the hall before leaving for the next phase of the journey, a Trooper was able to report that he had led his host or hostess to God!

The day's work usually began at 8.30, when the band mustered at the hall. On the stroke of time—the Bandmaster was a strict disciplinarian—the whistle would blow, the drums would roll and to the strains of some ' rip snorter' march written especially for them by Staff-Captain Slater, the pioneers would sweep out of the town for the high road, where the order was given to ' Go as you please'.

' Who's for the drum?' would be the cry. There was never any difficulty in getting a volunteer relief in this connection, for until a man had lent a hand with the drum he could hardly enjoy his long walk! The first bandsman to arrive outside a town generally found the officers and a small crowd waiting. He had the longest rest; the last man arrived to the accompaniment of friendly banter from his colleagues and had no rest at all. The band would now form up and enter the town with clockwork precision to impress the inhabitants who had been advised of the arrival time.

After a morning's march the men would be ready for dinner and could always be relied upon to do justice to the meal provided. At Luton the gallery of the hall was filled with girls from a straw-hat factory, who came at twopence per head to see the Troopers eat. Evidently it was a sight worth seeing!

Then came the afternoon march and meeting and, later, the evening march and meeting. The men considered themselves happy to reach their billet—or ' kip down' on the floor boards—by eleven o'clock.

More than one night was spent in a barn, the men sleeping amid the sweet-smelling hay on rough-and-ready couches. Bugle call at five o'clock would wake them from their dreams, and a munch of crust saved from supper and a swill at a nearby stream would precede their return to the road.

Back at Clapton after one of the many adventures, the Troopers enjoyed an experience surely unsurpassed in all the events of the band's existence. After a good swinging walk from St. Albans the men braced themselves for the last mile. They thought ' Dixie Land ' an ill-advised march to cheer their flagging spirits, but the Band-master's wisdom was justified. The jumpy, jerky, little ragtime piece quickened the slackening, and this despite the fact that they had marched twenty miles since reveille.

Suddenly an undreamed-of thing happened. A door flew open on the left of the wide avenue along which they were marching and there on the top step stood their beloved General. His wife, now frail, was by his side. It was difficult for the Troopers to keep playing, especially when the General ran nimbly down the steps waving his handkerchief and breathing benedictions upon them. ' We could have marched twenty miles after that,' wrote one of the weary but heartened marchers.

After the band had been tramping the highways and byways of England for some eight months it conducted a three weeks' campaign in Ireland. The day following the arrival in Belfast the band marched to hold a meeting in the Ulster Hall. Policemen who had been taking an interest in the band since the S.S. *Princess* docked, decreed that whilst crowding the main thoroughfare the procession had obstructed a tram car and a milk cart. The Bandmaster and four bandsmen—Shaw, Nicholson, Amey and Carter—were summoned and fined a shilling or one day in prison. They chose the latter.

While they were in their cells their comrades had prison clothes made for them, which they wore for the remainder of their Irish tour.

The fame of the Household Troops Band, which in twelve months had travelled more than three thousand miles, fifteen hundred of them on foot, spread like wildfire.

Commissioner Thomas Coombs, then in charge of Army work in Canada, was anxious to raise a thousand pounds to complete the erection of a social institution. He asked that the band might be allowed to visit the great dominion to conduct an evangelical campaign, and at the same time raise sufficient money to end the project.

Before the men left London for their adventure the Chief of the Staff (Bramwell Booth) called the bandsmen to International Head-quarters where, in an upper room, he spoke to them and prayed God's blessing upon the coming great venture. With words of admonition, counsel and encouragement ringing in their ears, the pioneers set out to discover a new world.

The day before they sailed, Commissioner George Scott Railton met the men at Birkenhead. News of some discontent among them through having to travel steerage—it was usual for Salvation Army officers to travel second class—had reached him.

He said: 'I understand that some of you don't want to travel steerage to Canada. We thought you would take it as a compliment if you travelled third class. You must blame yourselves and the splendid reputation you have made for having this honour conferred upon you. You have tramped all over the kingdom most cheerfully while your other comrades have ridden from town to town. And we are proud of you for it! And we thought—really we did—that as you will be on the Atlantic during Self-Denial Week you would prefer to travel by the cheapest way and least luxurious route!'

There was no further complaint. The next day, October 4, 1888, the thirty men left Liverpool on the S.S. *Polynesian*—nicknamed 'Rolling Polly' for obvious reasons—to make Army band history across the Atlantic.

The journey of the Household Troops Band across the Atlantic took ten days. Each bandsman was issued with a tin mug and tin plate which had to be used for tea, soup and everything else. With these dangling from their belts and with straw mattresses on their backs they made their way amidships to a lower sawdust-strewn deck. They slept in hammocks in the same compartment as forty Welsh miners. Upon arrival at Montreal the Troopers were treated to a Canadian bouncing, being tossed into the air by three burly Canadians who skilfully withdrew once their victim had ascended, leaving him to descend with whatever grace he could muster.

The tour was a tremendous success, the band making a wonderful impression. What a cross-fire of interrogatives the men had to face! 'How is the General?'; 'Have you seen the Queen?'; 'Is your Bandmaster the world's best cornetist?' were but three.

Staff-Captain Appleby quickly won the hearts of the Canadian Salvationists. He was a spectacular personality whose particular flair was marching at the head of the band playing brilliant improvised cornet variations to the tune his men were playing. The Canadian *War Cry* commented, 'Staff-Captain Appleby is a slashing, full-blooded Englishman, a typical member of his profession with soldierly bearing. He has perfect command of his men, and can render a cornet solo with exquisite taste and skill. Nearly all the members of the band are fine soloists and can all sing well, too.'

The Englishmen found the Canadian winter a trial. Soon the white helmets and red tunics were discarded and instead they were supplied with warm, fleecy capes, with collars of enormous width, and beaver caps, which on occasions they could pull down over their ears.

It was not unusual for the bandsmen to be conveyed to their billets, after an evening meeting, by horse-drawn toboggans with sleigh bells ringing.

After five months in Canada—dangerous opposition was encountered in Quebec City—the Household Troops Band crossed into the United States of America, where it campaigned in the New England States. In two months the meetings brought in £750, beside clearing the expense of the return fare to England. The band journeyed back on S.S. *Aurania*—second class this time! It was sixty-four years before another band from England crossed the Atlantic.

During the band's absence in Canada and the U.S.A. a second band was formed in January, 1889. Both combinations continued to campaign separately for two years, at the end of which they were amalgamated for a visit to Holland.

On July 25, 1891, after playing in Southampton at General Booth's farewell for South Africa, Australia and India, the enlarged band proceeded to Margate, where for three months it played on the sands twice a day. There had been great opposition to the Army's opening fire in this Kent holiday resort. The advent of the band changed things considerably. A large marquee was erected and attracted many of the townspeople, a number of whom were converted.

The bandsmen camped out in a field which 'Lord' George Sanger used as a home of rest for his circus horses. At Self-Denial time it was announced that the Household Troops would be making sacrifices in common with all Salvationists. Imagine the bandsmen's embarrassment when a stream of boys from butchers, bakers and grocers, as well as hotel attendants, began arriving at the compound with baskets laden with provisions. That year the H.T.B. raised the second highest total for the Self-Denial Fund in the British Isles.

Soon the band was the most popular feature in the town. Railway companies running excursion trains to the coast advised Londoners to 'Go to Merry Margate, enjoy the health-giving air and hear the Household Troops Band'. The enterprising owner of the *Skylark* invited the band to provide music on board in exchange for the promise of a bumper collection.

The men were not sure that they had done the right thing in accepting. They did not know till afterward that a woman on board had set out on that trip with the intention of committing suicide, so entangled had become her domestic affairs. Through her contact with the Household Troops bandsmen that morning, and through listening to their music, she was led to abandon the idea of taking her life. This was revealed when the woman attended a tent meeting and knelt at the Mercy Seat. She became a uniformed Salvationist at Regent Hall.

Hundreds of others were influenced for The Salvation Army through the Household Troops Band. In Durham City Fred Hawkes was billeted at the home of Edward Astbury, who was associated with the Dean and Chapter of Durham Cathedral. Young Astbury was so impressed by the life of the Trooper that he gave up his top hat and frock coat for the woven jersey of the Army. Two years later he, with his wife, became a Salvation Army officer and eventually reached the rank of Lieut.-Colonel. One of his sons is Commissioner Ranulph Astbury. Another, Mortimer, was a member of the International Staff Band for some time.

Commissioner Charles Rich was attracted to the Army by the band during its visit to Eastbourne at the time of the riots. When the band paid a second visit a year or two later, he was one of the corps' most enthusiastic soldiers.

When, after a life of six years, the H.T.B. was disbanded in 1893, it was estimated that 126 men (including three Bandmasters) had marched in its ranks. Many were appointed in charge of corps and some became well-known officers. Among these were Colonel Hawkes, Colonel William Nicholson, Major 'Bobby' Edwards, Brigadier Tom Robertson, Major Charles Coller, Major James Gilliard (father of Commissioner Alfred J. Gilliard), Lieut.-Colonel Robert Winn and Staff-Captain Harry Green. Other Troopers included Enoch Kent, Henry Carter, William Parkhouse, Teddy Cork, George Halliday and 'Ted' Millard.

The Bandmasters, apart from Harry Appleby, were a former military conductor named Webber, who was appointed in charge of the Number Two band when the 'originals' were in North America, and Caleb Burgess, who took over the augmented band when Appleby was selected for special service in connection with the Founder's campaigns.

How would the playing of the Household Troops Band compare with that of the best Army bands today? That is a question that will never be answered. The music used was not of the calibre of modern Army classics, but we can be sure that the playing of the band was before its time. Richard Slater said: 'I am indebted to the band, not only for the pleasure and stimulation I derived from its labours, but also for the inspiration and impetus it gave me as a composer and arranger of Army music.'

Upon the occasion of the band's second reunion, held at Regent Hall in June, 1924, Slater paid further tribute:

> The band acted as a pioneer for Army bands, at least to a great extent, in the favour of the musical people, the critics, the musically trained part of society, proving that Army band music could arrest, impress and give

C

satisfaction to the musically cultured as well as gain the attention of the average man and woman.

One of the astounding things about the history of the band is that its vast success was gained on what, from the modern standpoint, was but the 'ABC' of Army band music. It is proved thereby that simplicity of means, with true efficiency of rendering, secures more than displays of mere technical ability. The band used its simple means as an outlet of expression and so was able to move the hearts of its hearers. . . .

The band has never been surpassed by any other band for fullness, purity, unity of tone and sustaining power. The band's command of the degrees of force was another of its outstanding merits. It made as much of a *pianissimo* as of a *fortissimo*.

This view was shared by Colonel Hawkes, who declared that a range of four or even five octaves, with clear tone and good tune, could be obtained by a number of Troopers. He attributed the band's sustaining power to the constant practice—this is where the H.T.B. had the advantage over today's musicians—and the youth of the men, all of whom were between twenty and twenty-five. 'The brotherhood of the H.T.B. was a tremendous force,' said the Colonel, 'and its repercussion was strikingly evident in its performances.'

One of the most sacred memories the Troopers took with them into old age was their visit to Catherine Booth, the Army Mother, at Clacton-on-Sea, shortly before her promotion to Glory. To them, as representing all other bandsmen of The Salvation Army, she said:

We had a great deal of argument regarding the first introduction of bands into the Army, and a great many fears. I had always regarded music as all belonging to God . . . but, unfortunately, God has not His rights here, and the Church has strangely lost sight of the value of music as a religious agency.

I think God has used the Army to resuscitate and awaken that agency—to create it, in fact—and while the bandsmen of The Salvation Army realize it to be as much their service to blow an instrument as it is to sing, pray or speak, and while they do so in the same spirit, I am persuaded it will become an ever-increasing power amongst us. But the moment you (or any other bandsmen) begin to glory in the excellency of the music alone, apart from the spiritual results, you will begin at that moment to lose your power.

CHAPTER FIVE

THE INTERNATIONAL STAFF BAND

ON the night the Household Troops Band was welcomed back to Clapton Congress Hall from its triumphant tour of Canada and the United States of America (April 22, 1889), the Junior Staff Band was commissioned.

Under the direction of Bandmaster Samuel Webber, who had led the Household Troops No. 2 Band, this was made up of office boys and junior clerks at the Army's international centre in Queen Victoria Street. Among them were George Mitchell, Will Haines, Harry Haines, Tommy Drage, Joshua Smith, Hugh Findlay, Henry Deverell, Fred Punchard, John Kitchenside, Samuel Hurren, Arthur Goldsmith, Clem Sturgess and George Holmes.

When, on June 26, 1889, the band took part in a great ' Prisoners for Christ's Sake' Demonstration in the Exeter Hall in the Strand, the march from International Headquarters down Ludgate Hill and along Fleet Street was broken up by the police, some of whom were not reluctant to handle the boys roughly in order to disperse the procession. Driven to the pavements, the bandsmen at last, hot, dusty and exhausted, were bundled, pushed and hustled into the Exeter Hall.

From then on the boys carried their heads like veterans. They had tasted battle, as the Household Troops had done before them. A further test came when the band was called to Whitchurch to assist in the fight against the prejudice there.

But these lads were not old before their time, even if early responsibility did tend to put old heads upon young shoulders. Once, when selling copies of *The War Cry* at Woolwich on a Saturday afternoon before a week-end campaign, the more daring of the boys abandoned their duty, placed the unsold stock beneath their capacious guernseys, went for a row on the river and were nearly drowned.

After the Junior Staff Band had been in existence for two years and the ' boys' could no longer be included in that category, the International Headquarters Staff Band was formed.

There had, however, been an unofficial headquarters' band for some years before 1891, led by an elderly man, Captain George Storey, but its appearances had been irregular and all the players past middle age. Bandmaster Storey was a Major when he died in the U.S.A. at more than eighty years of age.

In October, 1891, a Memorandum issued from the Chief of the

Staff's office brought into being the International Headquarters Staff Band, built from the nucleus of the junior combination. Staff-Captain Fred Fry was appointed to take charge a few weeks later and, in August of the following year, led a band of 'crack lips' when it accompanied the General on a campaign in Holland.

This, then, was the beginning of the premier band of The Salvation Army, which has set and maintained a standard of Salvationism, deportment and brass band efficiency.

But the band was by no means quickly established. During the first two years it underwent many changes and experienced teething troubles. The Household Troops Band was still in being and in 1891 Staff-Captain Appleby was asked to form a band at National Head-quarters (then called the Home Office), which was situated at 179 Queen Victoria Street, close to Blackfriars Station. These two factors presented problems when it came to personnel. Each band possessed outstanding players and it was not unusual for a soloist to be required for duty by all three bands. Then, again, practices were not easy to arrange. With officers and employees pledged to be prepared to work 'long and arduous hours', the band would often be depleted because of a department being required to work late.

In September, 1893, the band was reorganized. A Minute issued by the Chief of the Staff placed it upon a properly constituted basis. The Chief of the Staff has ever since appointed every new member. The Minute decreed:

> In order to supplement the work of the Army in and around London during the coming winter and henceforth, it has been decided that:
>
> 1. The band shall accept appointments for one week-end in every three and upon one evening in each week, either at corps, slum posts, shelters or in unoccupied territory.
>
> 2. There shall be a band practice on one evening in each week.
>
> 3. The Leader of the band is hereby empowered to requisition the attendance of any or every bandsmen for the above-mentioned engagements, and will supply Heads of Departments with a list of engagements as far forward as possible, so that business can be arranged accordingly.
>
> 4. No member of the band must be absent from band practice or any engagement without the permission of the Leader.
>
> 5. The officers of the band have been appointed as follows:
>   *Leader:* Adjutant Marshall
>   *Bandmaster:* Brother Lyne
>   *Treasurer:* Captain Green
>   *Secretary:* Captain Sturgess
>   W. BRAMWELL BOOTH (signed).
> September 23, 1893.

The term 'Leader' as applied to the senior officer of the Staff Band is a misnomer which has led to confusion, especially among non-Salvationists. He is neither the Bandmaster nor the principal solo cornetist, as the leader of an orchestra is the principal violinist. He is the officer responsible for the spiritual welfare, deportment and discipline of the men. Arrangements for meetings are his care and he is required to bear the brunt of the public speaking. Despite attempts to change the designation, the title has been retained since the band's official inception.

The earliest Leaders of the International Staff Band were playing members, among them Major Thomas Marshall, Commissioner Wilfred Simpson, Colonel Edwin Le Butt and Colonel Henry Haines; but, with the appointment of Colonel Charles Swinfen, in 1931, a new era began. The Colonel, immaculately clad in his frock coat, dignified and courteous, set an example in non-playing leadership which his successors worthily maintained.

Jabez Lyne, the first Bandmaster to be officially appointed, did not remain a Salvationist for long. He entered the field of local politics, served on the Walthamstow Urban District Council for many years and became an Essex County Councillor, being respected for his Christian influence in civic affairs. White-haired and fresh-complexioned, a boyish enthusiasm reflecting in his twinkling eyes as he remembered the past, he was present at the band's golden jubilee celebrations.

For a time Caleb Burgess was the Bandmaster, the Household Troops Band having by now finally broken up. Then, when the Staff Band was five years old, something happened that was to influence the band for twenty-five years and Army musical history for all time: Captain George Mitchell became the Bandmaster.

A Haggerston boy and the son of Christian Mission converts, George went to work at International Headquarters straight from school and played in the Junior Staff Band. Now, at twenty-two years of age, a veteran among many youthful veterans, ' G. M.' took charge.

The story of the Staff Band during George Mitchell's quarter of a century at the helm is a fascinating record, with the personality of the Bandmaster its central theme. He dominated everything. He was often referred to as the ' Sousa of The Salvation Army ', for he was a demonstrative conductor. In a festival he, with his long white baton, a swinging frock coat, a lock of hair continually falling over his forehead and repeatedly being pushed back, was always the centre of attraction. It is said that he would sometimes stand motionless and let the band get on with a *pianissimo* passage, and then literally leap into action with a change of force or tempo in the music.

Until 1932 the band practised in a small room on the top floor of the old International Headquarters. Here the bandsmen would sit around with the backs of their chairs hard against the walls with 'G. M.' in the middle. He was usually in a red guernsey. Practice time was precious indeed. The great man's cornet was always handy and he would not hesitate to demonstrate how he wanted a particular passage played, or to run over a difficult part with the instrument concerned.

But music was not his god. George Mitchell was a natural and forceful speaker who was at his best in an open-air ring. For a while the band Sunday night selection was 'Guide me, O Thou Great Jehovah'. The piece would finish on three mighty chords, the effect intensified by the Bandmaster's dramatic gestures. The congregation would be electrified. He would then swing round, the baton still in his hand, give out a text and begin a powerful address. He was in his element when 'fishing' or leading a prayer meeting.

His mind was not 'one-tracked'. He was the Head of a Department at International Headquarters when he was twenty-three and continued to carry heavy responsibilities throughout the period of his Bandmastership. No ordinary man could hold the appointment of Chancellor of the Exchequer or Managing Director of The Salvation Army Assurance Society and continue his Staff Band duties, as well as find time to take active part in the struggles of a small corps.

Commissioner Mitchell was a humble Salvationist. His cornet was not dedicated primarily to band use but to salvation witness. He said he had been called to be a missionary to the man in the street and to this end kept up his practising. At Haggerston he played his cornet on Sundays and week-days when he was home; when on holiday he would take his instrument to help the corps officer with a beach meeting. Even when he relinquished the baton and was appointed to Sweden, he could be seen at a Sunday afternoon open-air meeting in Stockholm—not as the Territorial Commander but, with his cornet, as a soldier of the Temple Corps.

Once, when on a visit from Sweden, Commissioner Mitchell called in to the Staff Band practice room while Bramwell Coles's meditation, 'When I survey the wondrous Cross ("Wareham")', was being rehearsed. He was persuaded to lead the band through this piece, which, although new to him, was conducted in characteristic style. At the end he laid down the baton and said: 'Gentlemen, that's the frame; don't forget the picture.' That was his last visit to the old band room.

As the year 1929 was drawing to its close, the Commissioner lay seriously ill at his home at Penge. The doctors had intimated that nothing more could be done for him. It was a Sunday night and 'G. M.', glancing at the clock in the bedroom, remembered that the march would soon be passing the bottom of the road on its way to the hall. Calling his wife and members of the family, he begged to be allowed to dress and walk to the end of the street. As the Penge Salvationists marched by a little later, the Commissioner, in full uniform with Mrs. Mitchell by his side, stood to attention, his hand at the salute in silent tribute. He went slowly homeward. A month later he received his heavenly Home-call.

When Commissioner Mitchell relinquished the Bandmastership of the International Staff Band in 1920, for two years the band ceased to function—as in the case of other Army bands, the war years had taken their toll; then, in 1923, it rose again like a giant refreshed and at Bideford, Devon, commenced a chapter of history that has run unbroken to this day.

The new Bandmaster was Major (later Colonel) George Fuller. He became a member of the International Staff Band in 1891, before he was fifteen, and for twenty-three years was Deputy Bandmaster to Commissioner Mitchell.

Forsaking the surplice, cassock and Eton collar of a choirboy at a fashionable church in his native Marylebone for the red guernsey and pill-box hat, George Fuller became a bandsman at the Great Western Hall, developing into an outstanding cornet soloist. One day the young enthusiast sought the advice of the great Appleby. Triple tonguing was at that time becoming the vogue, and George wanted the master's opinion on the craze.

' They tell me you can't triple tongue,' young Fuller mastered sufficient courage to say, repeating a rumour which was fast gaining ground. Appleby smiled, reached for his cornet, and gave an exhibition of the new art in a manner which silenced the critics.

' Now, my boy,' said Appleby, ' always concentrate on the improvement of your tone.'

George Fuller took Appleby's advice, and gained a reputation for himself as a soloist. One of his greatest successes was during the International Congress of 1904, when, in the selection, ' Memories of childhood ', he featured the solo, ' I think when I read that sweet story of old ', with a beauty of tone and depth of feeling that remained a pattern of cornet playing in the minds of those present.

As a band trainer Colonel Fuller had few equals. Becoming a Bandmaster at Marylebone at the age of eighteen, he worked at himself and learned all he could from the leading conductors of the day. It is not without significance that he was present at the first of Mr. Henry J. Wood's Promenade Concerts in the Queen's Hall. For nearly fifty years he stood in the centre of a Salvation Army band. When he was still Bandmaster at Marylebone, Deputy Bandmaster of the

Staff Band and Band Instructor at Harrow, he was approached by Cambridge Heath Band to become its instructor. Later he acted in a similar capacity to the bands of Leyton Citadel and Leyton Lea Bridge Road.

In a tribute, his son-in-law, Lieut.-Colonel Harold Read, himself a Staff Bandsman for some years, has said: ' Colonel Fuller was not a man to change easily. Most of his officership was spent with The Salvation Army Assurance Society; he was Instructor at Cambridge Heath for thirty-three years, and he lived in the same London district for thirty years. This may have accounted for his even temperament. He was good company and a ready wit. . . . He was never a preacher, unless consecrated music, skilfully handled, could be a sermon.'

This, then, was the man, frock-coated and unruffled, who conducted the I.S.B. through a period in which Army brass band technique advanced beyond recognition. It is to ' G. F.'s ' credit that he kept pace with the progression and emerged as a genius in the art of interpretation, whilst remaining immaculate and correct in his conducting. For nineteen years he consolidated the work accomplished by his eminent predecessor and on a Saturday afternoon in September, 1942, in Regent Hall, he handed his baton to another, but not before the Chief of the Staff (Commissioner Alfred G. Cunningham) had decorated him with the medal of the Order of the Founder. By the end of that year the beloved ' Cockney Colonel ' had received a Higher Award.

With the passing of Colonel Fuller ended the second chapter of I.S.B. history. He had been associated with the band for all of its fifty-one years and was the last surviving link with 1891. His going heralded the beginning of what could be called the ' modern ' era, although Salvationists of A.D. 2000 will doubtless be amused by the adjective.

The choice of Major Eric Ball to succeed Colonel Fuller was extremely popular. Although he had never been a playing member of the Staff Band, for twenty years his name had been a household one in Army music circles. A born musician, his studies added power to his genius and at an early age he reached the top as a Salvationist composer.

Although the Second World War was still on, the future of the Staff Band, under its youthful new Bandmaster, looked promising. Not for a moment seeking to lighten the tone which Colonel Fuller had cultivated, Eric Ball brought musicianly polish to the playing and a brilliance which the changing times demanded.

Colonel Bramwell Coles, the Head of the International Music Editorial Department, conducted the Staff Band for the latter part of the 1943-44 season, after which Lieut.-Colonel William Stewart was appointed Bandmaster. He had played solo cornet in the band under the baton of Commissioner Mitchell and Colonel Fuller and had farewelled from its ranks some eleven years before.

Will Stewart was a Salvationist of the old school and steeped in I.S.B. tradition. He did not forget the time when he—a Scottish boy from Stirling recently arrived to work in London—attended a salvation meeting led by the Staff Band at Islington. Commissioner Mitchell gave the address, after which Commissioner Hurren led the hard-fought prayer meeting while the remainder of the men, as was their custom, left their places to help sinners to decision. Eleven people knelt at the Mercy Seat that night.

On such scenes as this, and those at Ramsgate when the band discarded its instruments to take part in a Saturday night lantern procession, Will Stewart had been nurtured. He led the I.S.B. through a most difficult period and kept alive the true purpose of Salvation Army banding.

The present Bandmaster is Lieut.-Colonel Bernard Adams, who in 1947 succeeded Lieut.-Colonel Stewart, under whose leadership he served as Deputy Bandmaster for fifteen months.

As a boy, playing soprano cornet in Clapton Congress Hall Band, Bernard Adams was asked to substitute for Colonel Arthur Goldsmith in a Staff Band festival. This began an association which, with the exception of six years (one in the training college and five as a corps officer), has lasted to this day. For more than twelve years he was the band's cornet soloist.

With little experience of corps Bandmastership, Lieut.-Colonel Adams found himself in the most important practical musical appointment in The Salvation Army. He rose to the occasion and brought the band to the peak of its prowess. A born instrumentalist, he is a sensitive musician with fine tastes.

Included in the instrumentation of the International Staff Band in the early days were three clarinets and two circular basses. Woodwinds were not destined to form a permanent part of Army bands, but Captain Wormald, Captain Pellet and John Newnham rendered conspicuous service as clarinet players. Newnham, with twenty years' military band experience, was an old seaman of the S.S. *Bacchante* when Prince George (later King George V) was a midshipman aboard her. The Prince once stole Newnham's shaving water, for which he afterward apologized. On posters announcing Staff Band visits individual members were also advertised. For instance: ' The Fairy Queen and Prince George ', ' The Pizzicato Violinist ' (a man named Scott) and ' The Hallelujah Humorist ' (Harry Green).

Adjutant Harry Green was a character. He was a gifted pianist and had already made a name for himself with the Household Troops Band. But on early Staff Band programmes he was featured as a singer of Salvation Army ' comic songs ', for which he accompanied himself in brilliant style at the piano. Songs like ' Me join 'em? ' and ' Nothing else to do ' were considered classics of good sense, good religion and good fun. Later he was appointed to Canada, and lost his life when the *Empress of Ireland* sank in the St. Lawrence River while bringing Canadian Salvationists to London for the 1914 International Congress.

No one really filled Harry Green's place, although years afterward, when the band was reconstructed after the First World War, there emerged a charming character whose dry humour and lovable personality for many years had a place on I.S.B. programmes. He was Brigadier Archie Burgess. With his concertina as his constant companion, he would delight his audience with his masterly chord work and fine sense of music. Usually his solo was prefaced with a good story, for he was a raconteur of undoubted gift.

Colonel Reginald Bovan, who for twenty-seven years was the Staff Band drummer and one of its most able public speakers, has paid tribute to Brigadier Burgess: ' His old-world courtesy and intense sincerity are sweeter to the memory than all the superb wizardry of his chord work. There were finer harmonies in him than he ever produced on the concertina. . . . Audiences expected him to tell funny stories, but he was much more than a humorist: he was a lover of souls.'

A member of the original band—and the Junior Staff Band before it—was Henry E. Haines. For thirty years he was the Band Secretary and for nine years added to that responsibility the duties of Leader. It was due in a large degree to his dynamic persistence that the band once more took to the streets after the long break caused by the First World War. Overcoming the problems of reorganization in a determined fashion, ' H. E. H.' raised practically a new band. But George Fuller and he were there to see it through and, with a ' By the right, quick march! ' the Leader set the pace through the narrow streets of Bideford to open a glorious chapter of I.S.B. history.

The tall, soldierly bearing of Colonel Haines matched his personality, for at heart he was a soldier. A strict disciplinarian, his word was law. If the coach was due to leave at eight o'clock on Monday morning to return to London after a week-end campaign, it left at that hour. He loved the I.S.B. and did not spare himself to serve the men who played in its ranks.

It was at the request of Colonel Haines that the Staff Band played ' The stilling of the storm ' during its diamond jubilee celebrations at the Clapton Congress Hall in October, 1951. He had been in the band when, forty years before, this Bible picture had been played for the first time in that hall. On that occasion the composer, Lieut.-Colonel Richard Slater, had commented: ' This is the most difficult thing ever attempted in the history of Army bands; it is quite hazardous! '

Henry Haines was again at the Congress Hall when the band granted his request. He sprang to attention to acknowledge the applause of the crowd when his name was called. Soon afterward his daughter quietly mounted the platform to lead the old soldier off. His sightless eyes had not seen the I.S.B.

A London audience did not see him again, but a few months later the Staff Band, on its way to an evening engagement at Tunbridge Wells, called at a retired officers' residence to play to its old Leader. The Colonel put on his Staff Band cap and overcoat to conduct ' Deep Harmony'. Seven months later, in September, 1952, the band played its last tribute as the earthly remains of ' H. E. H.' were carried into the Ilford hall. His beloved I.S.B. cap was on the coffin.

When Colonel Haines relinquished the Band Secretaryship this responsibility fell upon Colonel Ernest Wellman, who already held the appointment of Deputy Bandmaster. The Colonel was a well-known Staff Band personality for forty years, for twenty of which he was the ' end man ' euphoniumist.

Each of the Colonel's brothers—William, Harold and Gordon—also played in the Staff Band, but not all at the same time. Another family—the Halseys—hold a similar record, for the four sons of Major Charles Halsey, the Army's first cadet for officership—Albert, Edgar, Wilfred and George—were all members of the I.S.B. at the same time.

General Frederick Coutts was a member of the Staff Band for a period during the Second World War, appearing on the programmes in pianoforte items, and two former members, Commissioners Charles Baugh and Edgar Dibden, and a former Leader, Commissioner Norman Duggins, have each served as Chief of the Staff.

How fortunate the band has been in its corner men! George Fuller set the standard for cornet playing nearly seventy years ago. Among those who followed him were: Fred Buckman, Will Carroll, James Sansom, Will Stewart, Edgar Dibden, Walter (' Dick ') Ward, Tom Giles, Bernard Adams and Frank Lyndon. Nor must Arthur Goldsmith be overlooked in this connection. Prince of soprano cornetists, he was a member of the band for twenty-eight years.

There have been favourites on every instrument, but among other outstanding players were Harry Bell and Laurie Ward on trombone; Leopold Murch and Arthur Best on euphonium; the Jakeway brothers

(Albert and Victor) and Fred Sherwood on bass, and Bert Greenwood and Albert Samuels on bass trombone.

When, many years ago, Staff-Captain John Tuley left the band to serve as a missionary in India, he became the first of a long line of Staff Bandsmen to lay down their instruments and set aside the crimson and white tunics to live—and sometimes die—among a needy people.

When, in 1898, the band was presented with its first colours Captain (later Colonel) Alfred Hamilton was appointed Flag Officer. In later years the Colonel reflected: ' I had length of leg and enthusiasm but no musical ability whatsoever.' Besides his first duty with the flag in every march, the Captain organized the sale of song sheets and the taking up of collections in the open air. Particularly did this last-named responsibility apply to the mammoth beach meetings at seaside resorts. The first Flag Officer held his appointment for six years.

The long-distance campaigning of the International Staff Band is described in more detail elsewhere, as are important events in which it participated, but there is one experience that merits special mention here.

In April, 1953, Dr. Ralph Vaughan Williams, O.M., presided over a festival given by the band at Dorking. Addressing himself to ' these musicians who play so finely ', Dr. Vaughan Williams expressed pleasure at the ' sincere, healthy music ' they played and added: ' I have heard many bands, but never a band with so fine a sense of style—a real classical style.'

This encounter resulted in the great composer's expressing a desire to write something for the band. The outcome was ' Prelude on three Welsh hymn tunes '.

CHAPTER SIX

ASSOCIATED HEADQUARTERS BANDS

Home Office

THE debt Salvationist-musicians owe to Herbert Booth is incalculable. The gifted third son of William and Catherine Booth was a natural musician with a sensitive response to some of the finest aspects of harmony. Perhaps more than anyone else in the Army of his day, he could foresee the great possibilities of that music which is dubbed ' peculiarly Army '.

When in charge of the men cadets at the Clapton Training Garrison, Herbert Booth organized the Life Guards campaigns through the towns and villages of England. The formation of the Household Troops Band was also his inspiration, as was the Singing, Speaking and Praying Brigade, of which he was the leader.

Later, when ' Mr. Herbert ', as he was affectionately known, became Commandant for Britain, an appointment comparable with that of British Commissioner today, it was not long before he announced the formation of a Home Office Band. The Household Troops Band had recently returned from campaigning in Holland with Commandant Herbert Booth, and the Bandmaster, Staff-Captain Appleby, was appointed to take charge of the new headquarters band.

That was in 1891, a year which also marked the official recognition of the International Staff Band, and to celebrate the inauguration of the first associated headquarters band a united festival by the two groups was held at Clapton Congress Hall later the same year.

The Home Office Band was in existence only eighteen months, but it played its part in week-end campaigning and furthering the cause of dedicated music, encouraging the bandsmen at the centres visited and helping to consolidate the Christian experience and musical interest of the Home Office bandsmen themselves. Among these were several who eventually became members of the Staff Band and others who earned names for themselves as corps Bandmasters.

When the International Staff Band visited Cardiff in 1932, Sir David Morgan, a wealthy industrialist who supported the chairman, made it known that he had played in the Home Office Band. He was the son of early-day Army officers stationed in Wales, and had for some time been employed at the old ' 179 ' headquarters.

Another bandsman was William M. Brand, a one-time officer and later Bandmaster at Tottenham Citadel and Clapton Congress Hall.

Sixty years after the event, he recalled a Christmas caroling experience. Appleby, with about a dozen of the men, travelled from St. Paul's Station to Kent House, where Commandant and Mrs. Booth lived. Outside the house they provided the familiar seasonable melodies and were invited in to partake of refreshments. Compliments of the seasons exchanged, the group set off on the return journey, only to find that a thick fog had descended while they were in the house. They eventually boarded a train which at a snail's pace reached London very much overdue. This was not the chief worry of the men. It was a Friday and Christmas Eve in the bargain, and they had not received their salaries before leaving headquarters. Christmas Eve with no money! All ended well, however, for when they arrived at ' 179 ' a gas glow in a ground floor window signified that a friendly cashier had awaited their return.

Trade Headquarters

IN April, 1895, it was decided to form a Trade Headquarters Band from the officers and employees working at the important branch of activity then situated at Clerkenwell Road. The Bandmaster was Ensign Fred Hawkes, who in a very short time brought the band to a state of efficiency said to be in advance of the times. The instruments were made on the premises and included a soprano cornet and double B-flat bass, certainly an innovation for Army bands of those days. Several bandsmen had helped to make the instruments they played.

The staff of ' Trade ' was proud of its own band—which must have made the International Staff Band look to its laurels—and showed its interest by collecting a weekly subscription for the band's funds. This generous gesture made it possible for a new set of uniforms to be obtained quite early in the band's history.

While week-end ' specialing ' formed a great part of the band's activity, its duties were exceptionally varied. For instance, it was used with great effect to advertise the bargain sales at the Trade Head-quarters. Upon one occasion the band was transported through a district of London by a horse-drawn wagon upon which had been constructed a monster tea-cup and saucer. The cup, 8 ft. high, was sufficient to hold twelve bandsmen. Those with large instruments occupied the saucer.

For the whole day the band paraded in this novel fashion, to the delight of thousands of onlookers. But the bandsmen were not so exuberant. Perhaps they may be forgiven for not regarding their mobile festival as ' triumphant ' as the tea they advertised. The horse was not inspired by the music and proceeded at *largo* pace, the men finding the greatest difficulty in balancing, their playing receiving a series of unexpected joltings. Only once did the horse show sign of excessive animation. In descending a hill it was coerced into an involuntary trot which accelerated as the weight it drew hurried it on toward a low railway arch. Just in time the bandsmen saw the danger and quickly interrupted their selection to disappear inside the cup.

The Trade Headquarters Band shared with the Staff Band the main musical support at the Army's first exhibition at the Agricultural Hall, Islington, in 1896. At intervals during the week the bands featured programmes of the latest music and concluded each day with an epilogue. For the last day it was decided that both bands should participate in the finale. The I.S.B. played two sombre hymn tunes. Sensing the mood of the great crowd, Adjutant Hawkes decided to play his own brilliant arrangement of the 'Italian March', not then published, and 'Rule Britannia'. The crowd went wild with excitement. This was something new.

But this evidence of progressive thought was not appreciated by all the listeners. When the cheering was at its height, William Booth appeared. He had been resting in an ante-room, and the stirring music and subsequent sounds of enthusiastic acceptance had not met with his approval. That was the end of the Trade Headquarters Band.

S.P. and S.

THIRTY-TWO years were to pass before another band was formed at Trade Headquarters, which by this time had removed to premises in Judd Street, King's Cross, via Fortess Road, Kentish Town, and the establishment had become Salvationist Publishing and Supplies, Ltd.

At the express wish of General Bramwell Booth, the S.P. and S. Band was formed by Commissioner Richard Wilson, the Secretary for Trade, in 1928, to demonstrate the effectiveness of a small number of players and to emphasize the usefulness of the Second (now Triumph) Series Band Journal. Captain Eric Ball became the Bandmaster and the band, originally consisting of eighteen members, set a new standard for small bands.

The first week-end appearance of the band was at Winton, Bournemouth, in October, 1928. General Frederick Coutts, who as the Commanding Officer had invited the band, remembers the impact made by this small group of players upon the Salvationists of the south coast. A year later the band conducted a campaign in the Channel Islands. By now firmly established, it was taking part in national musical events and, from 1931, sharing with the Staff Band the responsibility of preparing and presenting new manuscripts to the International Music Board. The band received its death-knell when, with the outbreak of the Second World War, the majority of its players were called up for military service.

Eric Ball remained Bandmaster throughout the twelve years of its existence.

The first Deputy Bandmaster was Major Robert McBeth, and Major (later Colonel) Charles Cox also served in that capacity. Lieut.-Colonel James Valentine was the band's Leader for some time and the two Secretaries during its life-time were Gurney Doe and Lieut.-Colonel William Cozens.

Men's Social Work Headquarters

FOUR years before the S.P. and S. Band came into being a band was formed at the headquarters of the Men's Social Work, then situated at 22 Whitechapel Road, a building which was the Army's Headquarters before a move was made to Queen Victoria Street. The chief function of the band was to assist in evangelical meetings held in institutions in the London area. Week-end campaigns were also conducted, among the earliest being one at Harrow where a seeker for salvation knelt at the upturned drum in an open-air meeting.

The first Bandmaster was Adjutant (later Commissioner) Charles Durman, and others associated with the band in its beginnings were Major (later Commissioner) Ranulph Astbury, Captain (later Lieut.-Commissioner) George R. Bell and Captain (later Lieut.-Colonel) Ernest Rance.

When Commissioner Durman was transferred to National Headquarters as the Secretary for Bands and Songster Brigades, in 1931, Colonel Arthur Goldsmith, at that time Financial Secretary for the Men's Social Work in Great Britain and Ireland, became the conductor. This commenced a period of remarkable advance in the efficiency of the band. The Colonel's long experience was placed unstintingly at the disposal of the men, who grew to respect his musical knowledge, Army background and many gifts.

Colonel Goldsmith remained as the band's conductor until 1934 and, two years later, returned to lead the band until his retirement in the early months of the Second World War. Like its famous counterpart, the S.P. and S. Band, the M.S.W. Headquarters Band was a wartime casualty.

A much-blessed ministry of the band was carried out in H.M. prisons, from Parkhurst, on the Isle of Wight, to Durham, in the north.

Another record standing to the credit of the Men's Social Work Headquarters Band is that of being the first Army band in the world to fly to an appointment. In December, 1933, the band flew from

Portsmouth to Ryde (Isle of Wight). This is not a great distance compared with modern flights—the journey took no longer than ten minutes—but this was before the days of air transport planes. The bandsmen travelled in two- and three-seater planes which were called upon to make several crossings before the thirty men were all landed safely at Ryde.

This band also took part in an unusual event which can have few, if any, parallels. On New Year's Eve, 1937, it travelled by coach from London to Newcastle upon Tyne to participate in the new year festivals. It was arranged for a watch-night festival to be given at Royston, Yorkshire, en route.

Leaving the Middlesex Street Headquarters in the mid-afternoon, the coach should have been in Yorkshire in good time for the festival, timed to start at 11 p.m. The planners had not reckoned with fog, with the result that the band arrived at Royston barely in time to welcome the new year. The hall was filled and the band went through with its advertised programme, the crowd staying until after 1.30 a.m.

Six hours later the bandsmen were at the hall, after a few hours' snatched sleep, ready to continue the journey north. On the return trip, two days later, the band again stopped at Royston to provide an afternoon festival to coal miners who had just come off the morning shift.

Several renowned soloists were one-time members of the band, among them Lieut.-Colonel Charles Skinner, who played soprano cornet until he entered the training college, the brothers Douglas and Arthur Rolls, trombonists, both of whom became Staff Bandsmen, Courtney Bosanko, euphonium, and Tom Jordan, Holden Beaumont and Bramwell Allington, cornet. The death of Holden Beaumont at the age of thirty robbed the Army of a gifted soloist and the Regent Hall Corps of a popular and promising Songster Leader.

Lieut.-Colonel Rance, who had served as Deputy Bandmaster, was Bandmaster for some time, and another member throughout most of its history was Alfred Vickery, another well-known song-writer. Commissioner Kaare Westergaard was once the drummer. A great champion of the band was Colonel Gerald Freeman, who during his appointment as Chief Secretary led many campaigns with the band. A Salvationist of the old school with a ' Colonel Blimp ' appearance, the Colonel was full of original ideas. One such was centred around a set of new tunics, similar to the I.S.B. pattern, presented to the band in 1935.

For the men merely to appear in their new regalia was not good enough for their Chief Secretary. He was inspired to include a ' transformation scene ' as an item in a festival held in the Victoria Homes,

D

Whitechapel. His plan was for the band to begin to play a march wearing the old tunics. The curtains would then close and the march would continue while the men took it in turns to exchange their old uniforms for the new, which lay neatly folded in cardboard boxes by the side of the chairs.

It was a brilliant idea. The scene backstage had to be witnessed to be believed. Waving, shirt-sleeved arms did everything but slay the remaining bandsmen who continued to deal faithfully with the intricacies of the ' Wearside ' march. And then, resplendent in the new tunics, one by one the bandsmen took up their instruments to let their comrades go through the drill.

At long last the transformation was complete and the curtains opened to reveal the band with the new look. The beaming audience applauded vociferously. The bandsmen sought to look as nonchalant as if this were an every-day happening. Colonel Freeman was obviously proud of his inspiration. It was not until after the festival that it was learned that a large mirror at the side of the platform had reflected all that had happened behind the curtains—for the benefit of the audience!

Bands of the S.A.A.S. Ltd.

THE Chief Office of The Salvation Army Assurance Society Ltd. was a hive of musical industry in the years between the two world wars. In 1928 a band of fifty players was formed with Fred Buckman, a former cornet soloist of the International Staff Band, as Instructor. Included in its personnel were several youthful employees who later became members of the International Staff Band, among them Bernard Adams, Geoffrey Dalziel, Arthur Hook and Cyril Brisley.

This band marched in the Lord Mayor's Show on November 9, 1928, when the Army participated in this popular parade for the first time. The Lord Mayor was Sir Kynaston Studd, one of the famous cricketing brothers, who revealed a lively and practical interest in Army affairs during his term of office, including the presentation of new instruments to Regent Hall Band.

The Chief Office Band did not last for long but another section functioning at that time, the Assurance Headquarters Boys' Band, remained, under the direction of Bandmaster Henry Nott. ' Boys' ' was eventually dropped from the title.

One of the first leaders was Colonel Joshua Smith, a foundation member of the International Staff Band, and when he became the Staff Secretary at International Headquarters, Major (later Brigadier) Joseph Owen succeeded him. In 1939 the band was honoured by inclusion in the annual Associated Headquarters Festival at the Clapton Congress

Hall. Up till then the event had been confined to the Staff Band, the S.P and S. and M.S.W. Bands and the Assurance Songsters.

While three headquarters bands ceased to exist when the exigencies of the Second World War made their continuance impossible, there was one which owed its advent to those days.

When large-scale bombing threatened London, it was decided to transfer the Chief Office of The Salvation Army Assurance Society to a large residence, ' Rosehill ', formerly a convent, at Caversham, near Reading. Offices were built in the grounds and the staff was accommodated on the premises and in the neighbouring districts. Among the employees were several bandsmen who missed their normal corps activity and, finding themselves with plenty of spare time, suggested that an attempt be made to form a band. This would provide the men with a musical outlet and help them to keep their lips in.

Commissioner Charles Baugh, then Managing Director, gave permission for the venture, and with a number of remaining instruments from the disbanded Assurance Band, and several loaned from the Reading corps, the dream rapidly became a reality. That was in February, 1940. Major Walter J. Ward, a Staff Bandsman for some years and Bandmaster at Cambridge Heath at the outbreak of war, became the Bandmaster, and ' Rosehill ' was an obvious choice for the name.

Within six months of its formation the band had attracted the notice of the British Broadcasting Corporation. An audition was successfully passed and the band established a record by broadcasting within such a short time of its inception.

As in the case of all bands in Britain conscription seriously affected the personnel, but its high standard of musicianship was maintained. Festivals given in many parts of war-time Britain included visits to military centres and prisoner-of-war camps. During those years the band shared with the I.S.B. the task of playing manuscript music to the International Music Board.

A unique fellowship sprang up among the men, who turned the national emergency to good account. The requirements of war were not forgotten. No fewer than twelve members of the band were attached to the Reading Rescue Service and several others enlisted in other local civil defence units.

In April, 1942, Eric Ball succeeded Walter Ward as Conductor, but his term of service with the band was short-lived, for he was appointed Bandmaster of the Staff Band a few months later. Colonel Albert Jakeway then became conductor and continued in that capacity until June, 1951, when the band, like others before it, passed into Salvation Army musical history.

The first official Leader of 'Rosehill' Band was Lieut.-Colonel Fred Stoker, who was followed in turn by Colonel Harry Coote and Lieut.-Colonel Albert Gardner. Among other officials were Staff Bandsman Cyril Brisley, who was Deputy Bandmaster for seven years and conducted lunch-time practices in an old barn until the staff returned to its new London premises in Tottenham Court Road after the war.

Few bands could have had so much basic talent at their inception. Many of the players had served with leading Army bands and had a firm grasp of brass band technique. Even with war-time restrictions, the band remained star-studded, and successfully introduced new soloists of the calibre of Derek Smith, later cornet soloist of the New York Staff Band, and Will Jenkins, horn soloist in the I.S.B.

It will be seen from this record that, with the exception of the International Staff Band, the bands of the various Associated Headquarters in London have been but temporary affairs, but each contributed something vital to the Army's musical make-up—from the Home Office Band of 1891, which sometimes varied its mid-day rehearsal by practising marching and counter-marching along the wide thoroughfare of Queen Victoria Street, the one and only Appleby providing flourishing improvisations on his cornet as he headed the march, to the 'war-time inspiration' which was 'Rosehill' Band. This, the most recent London headquarters band to rise—and fall— was disbanded exactly sixty years after the other was formed.

CHAPTER SEVEN

STARS OF THE STATES

THE earliest settlers in the New World, being Puritans and Quakers, would not permit the use of musical instruments. It was left to the German and Swedish colonists to plant the seed of music on the American Continent. Other immigrants from Europe brought their music with them. The first band in New York City consisted of four sturdy citizens from Holland who played the trumpet, flute, violin and drum. This was in the 1630s. A few years later seven younger, better-looking men made up a rival band. They played louder and became popular.

By the early days of the nineteenth century the German bands which played on the streets—they were called gutter bands—were augmented and, in fact, almost completely superseded by the small-town bands. The features of these groups were noise and gay uniforms. The smarter the band looked the better it must play; and the band-master seemed to concentrate on his hat in those days. Plumes were popular, as was the tall hat with a gay rosette of ribbon or flowers. The bandmaster usually wore epaulets so trimmed that they looked like glistening jewels, and sported a beard or, at least, a well-waxed moustache. As America's population increased almost every village and town introduced its own band.

The spectacular military band was well established in the United States of America when Commissioner George Scott Railton and seven Salvationist lasses arrived in New York, in 1880, to begin Army work. Some eighty years before, the now famous U.S. Marine Band had been formed from a nucleus of the drum major, fife major and thirty-two drums and fifes which had constituted the very first Marine Band two years earlier. The U.S.A. Navy Band was also in existence.

A few months after Railton and his assistants claimed America for The Salvation Army something happened in U.S.A. musical history which was to have widespread influence throughout the American continent and, indeed, throughout the world. A twenty-six-year-old musician of distinctive appearance—black bearded, wearing gold-rimmed spectacles and immaculately dressed—was summoned to Washington to become bandmaster of the Marine Band.

The young man was John Philip Sousa. He set to work upon the group of well-trained but disorganized musicians and built the Marine Band into the finest marching band in all America.

For Sousa this appointment was in the nature of a home-coming.
He had been born under the shadow of the Capitol. At thirteen he
had enlisted in the Marine Band as a music apprentice. Soon he
became an expert cornetist and began to compose music. When the
band began to lose its glamour for the boy, through the influence of
the Assistant Secretary of State, who had taken a personal interest in
him, he was released from the service and, returning to his first love,
the violin, he played in several leading orchestras of his day.

It was while Sousa was living in Philadelphia that Railton moved
his headquarters from New York to that city. Within ten weeks of
the Salvationists' arrival in the U.S.A. ten corps had been opened and
some 200 meetings were being held weekly.

The young man who later was to become the world's ' march
king ', a title coined by a London newspaper man, never forgot the
sight of those Army pioneers in Philadelphia.

William Booth and John Philip Sousa met upon several occasions.
The musician often recounted an occasion when the Founder told
him that the way the Army dealt with the ' down and out ' could be
expressed in three S's—soup, soap and salvation, in that order.

In 1930, writing in an American musical journal, Sousa said:
' Music, even in its most primitive forms, seems to have an influence
upon some portion of mankind. The Salvation Army, for instance,
has depended upon banjos, accordions, guitars, tambourines—anything
that was musical—to spread the gospel. From this have grown many
fine bands. I was recently honoured by having a request from that
great woman, Evangeline Booth, to write a Salvation Army march.
Of course, I gladly complied. . . .

' How close to God beautiful music brings us, does it not? If you
want to know one of the very good reasons why the world needs
bands, just ask one of the Salvation Army warriors who for years have
marched, carrying the message of the Cross, through the back alleys of
life. Let him tell of the armies of men who have been turned toward
a better life by first hearing the sounds of a Salvation Army band. The
next time you hear a Salvation Army band, no matter how humble,
take off your hat.'

The march which Evangeline Booth requested Sousa to write in
connection with the Army's golden jubilee celebrations in New York
was conducted by him. A massed band of 300 players took part and
at the conclusion of the item the great crowd of some 10,000 stood to
its feet to give the distinguished visitor round after round of applause.
He was seventy-six years of age.

The march was called ' The Salvation Army ' and included the
Founder's song, 'O boundless salvation!' When Lieut.-Commissioner

William H. Barrett, then Training Principal in New York, gave the composer the words and music of this song, he was asked to sing a verse so that Sousa might get the Army slant on it. When the Commissioner came to the refrain:

> The whole world redeeming, so rich and so free,
> Now flowing for all men, come, roll over me!

he was asked to repeat it. He did so with Sousa joining in with his tenor voice.

' After Sousa had studied the words for a few minutes,' reported Lieut.-Commissioner Barrett, ' he looked up and said: " Your Founder was a mighty man of God and was certainly inspired when he wrote that hymn. It is a classic and will live on "; then he asked if Salvationists still sang " We'll roll the old chariot along " and added: " Don't let those old songs go to the scrap-heap. Keep them alive. They are typically Salvation Army." '

Although there was much musical background to the Army's beginnings in the U.S.A., its brass bands did not come into being easily or rapidly. Some months after Railton's ' invasion ', a group of instrumentalists here and there was used to assist with the meetings, but it was not until 1887 that the first official band was formed in New York to provide instrumental and vocal service at larger meetings and to campaign in the vicinity of the city as musical evangelists. The band's first engagement was on June 18th of that year at a meeting held in the Brooklyn Lyceum.

Because the National Headquarters for the U.S.A. was in New York, the new organization was named the National Staff Band. (It became the Territorial Staff Band in 1920.) Its first appearance on Broadway was spectacular. A newspaper report said the bandsmen ' rode on bicycles in tandem style—one to pedal and one to blow! Their National Commander headed the procession riding in a side-car. They carried banners calling themselves " Speaking, Singing, Praying and Blowing Troubadours of God ". They wore neat uniforms with white trimmings and a double knotted white cord across their chests. All seemed to be intelligent! '

Although no mention was made in this report of the white helmets that formed an attractive part of the original uniform of the National Staff Band, the New York *War Cry,* September 3, 1887, announced that the ' old-fashioned white helmet which has been surveyed and condemned has been replaced by a better and more substantial black helmet '.

In 1904 the band attended the International Congress in London dressed as cowboys. Four years later it accompanied General William Booth on his last tour through the U.S.A. and in 1914 again visited

London for the International Congress. Forty-six years were to pass before the band again played on English soil. Its campaign of June, 1960, will be described in a later chapter.

The New York Staff Band—by which title it is best known—has campaigned in Canada, played at the White House, Washington, for five Presidents, has been heard in New York at the Metropolitan Opera House, Carnegie Hall, Madison Square Gardens and at the World's Fair, and in great halls, universities and cathedrals in all parts of the U.S.A. It accompanied General Evangeline Booth, then the National Commander, on her great motorcade across America in 1930.

The band today is maintaining the excellent standard of musical efficiency and Christian influence for which it is noted. Radio and television performances are regular appointments, gramophone recordings have become numerous, especially in the new field of long-playing productions, and the normal programme of evangelism is proceeded with in New York and neighbouring cities.

The first Bandmaster of the New York Staff Band was William Bridgen, he being succeeded in turn by Adjutant Charles Straubel, Staff-Captain Edward Trumbull, Lieut.-Colonel Charles Anderson, Envoy Robert D. Griffith, Colonel George Darby, Adjutant J. Stanley Sheppard, Brigadier William Broughton, Major George Grainger, Lieut.-Colonel William Bearchell, Colonel William Slater and Brigadier Richard Holz. Captain Vernon Post was appointed in August, 1963.

Many members of the band rose to high rank, among them Commissioner John J. Allan, for seven years the Army's Chief of the Staff, Commissioner Donald McMillan, Commissioner Edward J. Parker, Commissioner William C. Arnold, Commissioner Claude Bates, Commissioner Alex Damon and Lieut.-Commissioner William H. Barrett. Commissioner Allan was the band's cornet soloist and Leader for some years. Commissioner Holland French is a former Leader and Colonel Charles Bearchell was Band Secretary for a long period. Other former Executive Officers include Colonel Paul Kaiser, who succeeded Colonel William Maltby in 1965.

Colonel Kaiser's father, also named Paul, was a lonely German lad living in London's West End in the early days of this century, when he was attracted by the playing of Regent Hall Band. This led to his attending meetings and becoming converted. He became a soldier of the German Corps then in operation off the Tottenham Court Road and later was commissioned as an officer. During Captain (later Major) Kaiser's command of the West Croydon Corps his son, Paul, was born. The Kaiser family emigrated to the U.S.A.

where the father and mother continued to give God-honouring service. The son entered training, in New York, in 1929.

*　　*　　*

One of the earliest corps bands in America was that at Buffalo 1. This, made up largely of converted drunkards, held weekly practices in the attic of an old church in which the corps conducted meetings. As there was no Salvationist capable of taking the oversight of the band a professional instructor was engaged, each bandsman being required to contribute ten cents a week to pay him for his trouble.

In addition to giving scale practice and teaching tunes from the Tutor and Band Journal Nos. 1–30, he arranged pieces to play on the march. These were based on popular melodies of the day and explain why more than one bandsman in the U.S.A. made his début playing the second cornet part of 'The man who broke the bank at Monte Carlo'.

The subsequent enforcing of regulations and strict adherence to the law of copyright put paid to such escapades. (There seems to have been no restrictions placed on the Army bands in America for some time.) In 1904 the New York Staff Band used all secular arrangements at the International Congress gatherings. When the Founder listened to the band playing what would now be termed an air varié on the old English tune, 'Long, long ago', he was obviously displeased. He demanded to know from the National Commander, Commissioner Frederick de Lautour Booth-Tucker, what it was all about. The explanation that it was 'Cleansing for me' seemed to suffice.

One of the smartest of early Salvation Army bands in America was the New England Guards Band, which was attached to the Provincial Headquarters in Boston, Mass. Resplendent in braided tunics with fancy belts, Prussian-like spiked helmets with metal chin-straps, highly polished leather gaiters and boots, the men thought they were more than a match even for the British Grenadier Guards.

The Bandmaster, a man named Delaney, had been a cornetist with Sousa's band and had a most remarkable range. He could play all the notes from high C to the G above clearly and quite fully, and then on up to an additional high C. His uniform was distinguished by an extra adornment of gold braid.

All went well until William Booth saw the array during a visit to Boston in 1898. 'What are you?' he asked. The Bandmaster introduced himself and was promptly instructed to remove his gold braid. 'Only the General wears gold braid,' he was told. Delaney put back his gold braid when the General returned to England!

Another Staff Band in the United States is that attached to the Headquarters of the Central Territory in Chicago. This, the second Staff Band to be formed west of the Atlantic, was started by nine officers and employees of the Territorial Headquarters in a small room one lunch hour in 1907. The man behind the plan was Major (later Colonel) John Fynn, who became the first Leader. The Bandmaster was the youthful Captain William Broughton, who relinquished the baton three years later to Captain R. C. Blurton; he returned as the conductor in 1913 for a further period of three years.

Those with long memories affirm that this was one of the most brilliant phases of the band's long history and included participation in the 1914 International Congress in London.

A former member relates: ' The trip to London on the great ocean liner, S.S. *Olympic*, was a never-to-be-forgotten experience.' The 700 Salvationists on board included four bands which gave daily programmes. Ex-President Theodore Roosevelt was a passenger and the 'thrill of being photographed with " Teddy " ' is remembered vividly.

Other Bandmasters of the Chicago Staff Band have been Captain Arthur Fynn, Lieut.-Colonel Hubert Burtenshaw, who was also the band's drummer for many years, Harry Otway, William Stevenson, Raymond Ogg, Bernard Smith, John Stewart, Brigadier Howard Chesham, Colonel Douglas Norris, Brigadier Carl Lindström, for a long time the band's outstanding trombone soloist, Major Victor Danielson and Brigadier Cyril Everitt.

In October, 1950, the band visited the city of Waterloo. A few days before the event the local radio announcer interrupted a broadcast programme to say: ' Word has been received that several " flying saucers " may be expected over the town at 5 p.m. on Friday, October 20th!'

At a minute to five on the eventful night, townsfolk looked toward the sky as the hum of approaching aircraft was heard. Suddenly, thousands of discs floated toward the earth. The people clamoured to catch them. They were made of cardboard, 7 in. in diameter, and announced in bold letters the visit of the Central Territorial Staff Band for a festival in the Hippodrome on the following evening.

In giving permission for this 'visitation from a neighbouring planet', which attracted two thousand people to the festival, the Mayor of Waterloo said, ' You can fly as low as you wish; just don't knock the top off the city hall.' Commissioner Norman Marshall is a former member of the Chicago Staff Band.

Among the many fine bands in the Central Territory must be mentioned those at Flint and Detroit. Although there was a corps at

Flint as early as 1893, it was not until thirteen years afterward that the first band was organized. This was made possible by the transfer of a noted motor company from Jackson, Michigan, and the arrival of four Salvationist bandsmen from Canada. The first Bandmaster was Orval Shoemaker, one of the original four, the others being William Beacraft, and John and George McDougall.

Although there were oddments of instrumentalists assisting in meetings at Detroit from soon after the corps opened in the late 1880s, a band as such did not come into being until the early 1900s. This advent was encouraged by the opening of the Ford Motor Works in the city. Employment was available for hundreds of men and attracted many Salvationists to Detroit.

Among those who served as Bandmaster were Staff-Captain Reuben Keeler, a well-known song-writer who led the band for several years, and Richard Herivel, his Deputy Bandmaster and successor.

* * *

When the Western Territory was inaugurated in 1920, it was not long before yet another U.S.A. Staff Band came into being at the new Headquarters in San Francisco. The Bandmaster was Captain (later Lieut.-Colonel, O.F.) Ernest Higgins, a son of General and Mrs. Edward J. Higgins, and the band was in existence for some years.

Among the best bands in the Western Territory are Oakland Citadel, Los Angeles Congress Hall, Hollywood Tabernacle and San Francisco Citadel. Brigadier William Broughton, who was so actively engaged with music in the Eastern and Central Territories in his younger days, served as Music Director for the Western Territory until his retirement in 1948.

* * *

Although Salvation Army bands are not too numerous in the Southern Territory, there was at one time a Staff Band attached to the Headquarters in Atlanta. The Bandmaster was Adjutant (later Lieut.-Colonel) Albert Baldwin, and the band, even if it did not last long, made many friends for the Army in the Deep South through its regular broadcast programme.

CHAPTER EIGHT

IN THE LAND OF THE MAPLE

WANTED

Bandsmen who are good instrumentalists, to volunteer for service in a Permanent Brass Band for the Household Troops. We are anxious to raise a good Permanent Brass Band (similar to that led by Staff-Captain Appleby) to travel through the towns and villages of the Dominion, and for duty in special demonstrations. Also to conduct, under an experienced staff officer, weekly and fortnightly special campaigns, for the salvation of souls. No pay will be given. Any thoroughly converted bandsman who would like to devote himself altogether to the salvation of souls, should apply at once to the Commissioner. Let every applicant say what instrument he can play, and if he can provide a uniform or twelve dollars to get one.

SUCH was the clarion call that sounded throughout Canada in the spring of 1889. The recent visit of the Household Troops Band from England had made a great impact upon Salvationists of the Dominion. An awareness of the power of brass band music to attract the sinner and convict of sin had been created and there was a widespread desire to maintain the interest and consolidate the spiritual work of the Troopers.

The call of Commissioner Thomas B. Coombs was timely and met with ready response; from numerous applications a group of men of sterling Salvationism and musical competency was selected within weeks.

Under the leadership of Staff-Captain McHardy, and with Captain Leonard as Bandmaster, the band left Toronto for Niagara on Tuesday, August 13, 1889, to begin its first campaign. The leader prayed that ' as the boat left a track on the water, so might the band leave behind it from town to town the fiery track of the Holy Spirit '.

As the Fry family band and the Household Troopers had fired the imagination of would-be musicians in England, so did this Canadian Permanent Brass Band play its part in sowing musical seed in many corps throughout the great Dominion.

Instrumental music had been in use in Salvation Army meetings before that date. On the front page of the first edition of the Canadian *War Cry* (November 1, 1884) there was a report of the territory's second anniversary celebrations: 'About ten o'clock the various contingents from different parts of the Dominion began to arrive at the depot and marched with bands playing and colours waving.' Hamilton and Toronto were two of the bands and a large timbrel band also took part.

Earlier than this, concertinas, paper-covered combs, flutes, drums, violins and tambourines were introduced, the Welsh Minstrel (Staff-Captain Griffiths) and Professor Wiggins proving themselves a musical attraction. In his history of The Salvation Army in Canada, Colonel Arnold Brown records that the Welsh Minstrel not only charmed the ear, but provided a somewhat startling sight with his quaint uniform of personal design, including gaiters, red stockings and fur headgear.

In April, 1886, a band of fifty instrumentalists took part in the opening of the Toronto Temple by Ballington Booth, the second son of William and Catherine Booth. A year later the Montreal Band— known as the 'Montreal Marvels'—assisted the Territorial Commander at the first anniversary of the Army's work in the Province of Quebec.

Opposition encountered there was more cruel than the Canadian Salvationists had expected. In the autumn of 1886 the Founder, on his first visit to the Dominion, had dedicated pioneers of what became known as the French Work. It was not long before mob violence made its presence felt. A home-made bomb was thrown into the meeting-place while the Salvationists were on their knees in prayer. A telegram to Headquarters told its own tale: 'Attempt to blow up the French barracks during the meeting last night. Great explosion: windows smashed, but nobody injured. Devil raging.'

Those who attended the first anniversary in Quebec City, therefore, were well aware of the strong feeling against the Salvationists. After the Montreal bandsmen had led an afternoon meeting all the participants lined up for a grand march. For the sake of general safety it was decided to keep to a main street route.

All went well until the procession was about to pass the Basilica. Then, without warning, the mob which had been hiding behind the cathedral fence attacked the marching Salvationists with stones and clubs. In the ugly scene that followed twenty-one Salvationists were seriously injured, an officer was stabbed in the head with a knife and the eye of the Quebec drummer was gouged out on his cheek.

Thus receiving their baptism of fire in the heat of battle, the bands of Canada made consistent and rapid progress and soon spread from the east coast across to Vancouver.

Large-scale emigration from Europe in the early days of the century saw the arrival in Canada of many experienced Bandmasters and capable musicians, and such Salvationists have played their part in helping to build and maintain the many fine sections still to be found. Among those bands with a long record of splendid service are Dovercourt, Earlscourt, Montreal Citadel, Toronto Temple, Peterborough, Vancouver Temple, Winnipeg Citadel, Windsor, Brantford,

Hamilton Citadel, London Citadel, Calgary, Edmonton and Regina.

Montreal Citadel Band, formed in 1887, has a number of Canadian 'firsts' to its credit. In 1932, two years after Norman Audoire—a former bandsman at Cambridge Heath and Carlisle Citadel and Bandmaster at Earlscourt, Toronto—became Bandmaster at Montreal, the band became the first to broadcast over the Dominion-wide hook-up; in 1939 a campaign in New York made Montreal Citadel the first band from Canada to visit that city, and in 1949, with a flight to an engagement in Nova Scotia, air travel history was made. Former Bandmasters at Montreal Citadel include W. G. Lambert, who had been Songster Leader at Highgate, London, before settling in Canada, and William Goodier, who later served as Corps Sergeant-Major.

Formed in 1906, Dovercourt Band remains one of the most efficiently organized bands in Canada. Alfred Pearce, a Devonian, trained and conducted the band for many years and other leaders have been Colonel Bramwell Coles and William J. Habkirk, who was at the helm from immediately after the Second World War until he relinquished the baton through ill health in 1963.

In 1936 Earlscourt Band made national headlines when it accompanied Commissioner William R. Dalziel (then Colonel and Chief Secretary) for a week-end campaign to North Bay, Ontario, a city some two hundred and fifty miles from Toronto. During the visit arrangements were made for the bandsmen to play to the famous Dionne Quins, whose birth two years before had created something of a sensation.

Callander, the village in which the Government had provided a hospital for the upbringing of the quins, was some nine miles distant. Although Dr. Allan Dafoe, who had brought the children into the world, had given permission for the visit, some anxiety prevailed as to how the quins would react to hearing brass band music for the first time.

Quietly the band played 'Gentle Jesus, meek and mild', and then awaited permission to continue. A wave of the hand from a nurse assured the men that all was well and then the little girls ran to the fence which marked the hospital boundary to gaze at the bandsmen and their instruments, clapping their hands with delight. After the brief programme the quins were introduced, the nurse checking each name to make sure which was Annette, Yvonne, Cecile, Emily and Marie.

Canada must be the largest territory in The Salvation Army world so far as distances are concerned. As provinces across the great Dominion bear their own characteristics and thrive on a distinctive culture, so the people reveal varied backgrounds and temperaments. But the brand of Salvationism is basically the same, even if expressed in a number of different ways.

It is natural for the bands to vary in efficiency and peculiarities. In sophisticated Ontario there is a British approach to this brand of service. The carefree but hearty expression of evangelism to be found in Newfoundland is reflected in the happy banding there. Corner Brook Citadel, Corner Brook East and Grand Falls are the most efficient sections.

Nineteen sixty-one was a memorable year for the bands of Newfoundland. In the summer Corner Brook East and Grand Falls met for a week's music camp conducted by the Bandmaster of the International Staff Band, Lieut.-Colonel Bernard Adams; and a few weeks later the former section conducted a week-end campaign at Glace Bay, Nova Scotia, the first band from Newfoundland ever to visit the mainland of Canada.

More than 3,000 miles away, on the west coast, quite a different setting is experienced in northern British Columbia. Here a faithful work is carried out among the Alaskan Indians and the corps at Canyon City can boast of a band of twelve players, six of whom are members of the Azak family. One of the brothers, Henry, is the Bandmaster.

Long before the Army opened fire amongst the Indians of the Nass and Skeena rivers, instrumental music was known and loved by the Christians residing in that area. Father Duncan, the pioneer missionary of the Church Missionary Society, arrived in Northern British Columbia from England in 1856. He won many converts for Christ among the pagan Indians and noticed their love for music when he established the first Christian village.

A few years later Father Duncan engaged a bandmaster to teach the men to play instruments. As a result every village along the rivers, regardless of church affiliation, has a silver band.

For many years the Canyon City Indians waited in vain for a missionary teacher. Finally one of their number, Chief Henry Azak, was converted in an Army meeting and started meetings in his own home. He was determined to build a hall and then invite the Salvation Army authorities to take over the work. This tireless leader transported all the lumber up the treacherous river in his own fishing boat. To prove their break with the old customs, the Indians used their richly carved cedar totem poles as foundation posts for the Army hall.

This was the third building for the worship of God they had erected. One of the former had been destroyed by fire and the other levelled by a high wind.   The Army hall was opened, free of debt, when the first officer, Captain Alice Kenny, arrived in 1931.

Major Ethel Brierly, a former editor of the Canadian *Young Soldier*, served among these faithful Salvationists for some time. She says: ' I shall always remember with gratitude their consideration when I was the officer, teacher and nurse. As I was the only white person the band played " No, never alone " in my honour each Sunday! '

From the first of June until September the village of Canyon City is deserted. The people are employed in the canneries at the mouth of the rivers. Fishing for salmon is arduous work and all hands must be on deck.

During the winter months the men spend their time in repairing their boats and in band practices. Transportation is by water only, for there are no roads in the area. In the winter they travel by dog team. Money to provide instruments and music is secured by selling wood to the government school, which is under the care of a qualified Salvationist teacher.

When Colonel Arnold Brown visited Canyon City he was so impressed by the efficient band he found in action that he felt moved to present Bandmaster Azak with the baton that Lieut.-Colonel Bernard Adams had used to conduct the International Staff Band at Buckingham Palace in 1951. Colonel Brown, who had accompanied the band on that occasion, had been given the baton as a souvenir.

Canada's most noted band in the mid-west is undoubtedly that of Winnipeg Citadel. Under the direction of Bandmaster Henry Merritt it made a name for itself throughout the Army world for its sterling Salvationism and able musical interpretation. The good work continues and the band is still making history.

In the summer of 1961 Winnipeg Citadel Band spent a long weekend at Fort Churchill, on the Hudson Bay, where deeply appreciated service was rendered to military personnel stationed in that isolated area. No other Canadian band had been so far north and the bandsmen relished the experience.

Families of Eskimos were among the Friday evening audience. Next day the band journeyed to the town of Churchill, passing a new Eskimo village along the banks of the River Churchill, which was still plugged with ice even in June. A white seal came up from the bay, sending a village hunter hurrying for his kayak.

On the Sunday afternoon the bandsmen left for home by air with the temperature in the low thirties. When they landed the temperature was well into the nineties. Such are the weather contrasts to be encountered on the vast North American continent.

The Merritt family is unique in Canadian musical history. Colonel

James Merritt is remembered for such compositions as ' The Canadian ', ' A Christmas reverie ' and ' Lift up the banner '; Bandmaster Henry Merritt served with distinction at Winnipeg Citadel for many years until his promotion to Glory in 1946; Deputy Bandmaster Percy Merritt, of Winnipeg Citadel and Dovercourt, is the writer of several band pieces, including the marches named after the two Canadian corps mentioned above; William was Bandmaster at Dovercourt for some time, following Colonel Coles in that appointment, and Benjamin was a Senior-Captain and a member of the Chicago Staff Band at the time of his passing in 1958.

Since 1955 musical affairs in Canada have been the responsibility of Major Kenneth Rawlins, first as Territorial Secretary for Bands and Songster Brigades and, from 1959, as Music Secretary. He is the first to hold such an appointment in Canada, and pays tribute to the splendid service of Deputy Bandmaster Percy Merritt, of Dovercourt, who undertook the part-time duties of Territorial Band and Songster Brigade Inspector from 1948 to 1955.

The Deputy Bandmaster gave unstintingly of his time and talent in training and encouraging smaller bands in the territory, travelling great distances to fulfil his commitments.

* * *

As in other territories, there were musical groups formed at the Toronto Headquarters from the early days of the Army's history. It is said that an officers' staff band was in existence at the time the Canadian Household Troops Band was inaugurated in 1889.

In 1907 Commissioner Thomas Coombs, who had returned to Canada three years before to begin his second period as Territorial Commander, advertised in The War Cry for thirty young men to form a Territorial Staff Band. In July of that year The Bandsman and Songster reported: ' The Canadian Staff Band has come to stay.'

The first Bandmaster was Major Morris and among the band's first engagements was the provision of music at tent gatherings in Toronto and the leading of meetings in Peterborough. Another early campaign was conducted in Quebec, where the police chief met the band at the station and headed the march to the hall. This was the first Salvation Army procession through the city since that ill-fated night twenty-four years before when a number of Salvationists were seriously injured by mob attack.

For seven years the Canadian Territorial Staff Band rendered yeoman service and built up an ever-mounting reputation for good playing. Excitement increased as the International Congress in London loomed nearer.

E

On Thursday, May 28, 1914, the *Empress of Ireland* left Quebec and slipped out into the St. Lawrence estuary, bound for Liverpool. On board were 167 Salvationists, including Commissioner and Mrs. David Rees, the Territorial Leaders, and the Staff Band. As the distance between the shore and the liner widened the band played ' God be with you till we meet again '.

That night the Salvationists were the centre of attraction among the thousand passengers. Ensign ' Olie ' Mardall presided at an impromptu programme and Adjutant Harry Green, a Staff Bandsman, gave some of his brilliant pianoforte items. At about two o'clock the next morning the *Empress of Ireland* collided with the S.S. *Storstad*, a Norwegian collier, in fog.

The *Empress* sank in fourteen minutes, with Commissioner and Mrs. Rees and, with the exception of a few men, the Canadian Staff Band, including Adjutant Ted Hanagan, the Bandmaster, who had wielded the baton at Croydon Citadel before emigrating to Canada. Among the survivors were Ernest Pugmire, George Wilson, George Attwell, Rufus Spooner, Alfred Keith, James Johnson, Willie Measures, Kenneth MacIntyre, Ernest Green and Bert Greenaway.

On Saturday, June 6th, 7,500 people attended the funeral service of the first fifteen victims whose bodies had been recovered. This was held in the Toronto Arena where, behind the platform, sat the massed bands of Toronto and bands from Guelph, Oshawa, Hamilton and Chatham. 'Abide with me' was played as the mourners, survivors and headquarters staff slowly entered the Arena. Thirty-seven empty seats behind the platform told their sad story.

A month later the first party of Canadian Salvationists returning from the Congress in the *Calgarian* passed near the spot where the *Empress of Ireland* had sunk. The speed of the liner was slackened and the Peterborough Band played ' Nearer, my God, to Thee ', the passengers and crew joining the Salvationists in singing the hymn.

Each year, on the Sunday nearest May 29th, the survivors of the disaster meet in a corner of the lovely Mount Pleasant Cemetery in Toronto to remember their fellow travellers of that eventful night.

There has never been another Canadian Staff Band. When the Territory was divided in 1915 and headquarters set up in Winnipeg (West) and Toronto (East) an attempt was made to form an Eastern Territorial Staff Band under the leadership of Brigadier Fred Beer, a former Bandmaster at Southend Citadel and Wood Green and a member of the old Trade Headquarters and International Staff Bands, but the venture was short-lived.

Perhaps that is how it should be. Canadians have not forgotten the *Empress of Ireland* disaster.

Bermuda

WHEN thinking of Canada one must not forget the beautiful islands of Bermuda, so pleasantly set amid the rolling waters of the mighty Atlantic. Army work began here in 1896 and since 1933 has been under the command of Canada.

With such a British background it is not surprising that brass banding was early established and today most of the six corps have a band. The largest, that at Hamilton, can be depended upon to give a good account of itself and always to look its smartest.

CHAPTER NINE

SOUTH OF PANAMA AND THE CARIBBEAN

South America

THE first musical instruments used in the Army's ministry in South America were the violin and cornet. The work in Buenos Aires, Argentina, was commenced by Colonel and Mrs. Henry Thurman and two Captains, William Bonnett and Fred Calvert, on January 1, 1890. A few months later two more officers arrived to augment the pioneers: Staff-Captain (later Lieut.-Commissioner) Stanley Ewens and ' Scribe' (later Commissioner) Alfred Benwell.

Ewens was the son of the first editor of *The War Cry* and Benwell, who had been a member of the Junior Staff Band, hailed from Shoeburyness, Essex, and brought his cornet in his modest baggage. The use of Ewens's violin and Benwell's cornet to accompany the singing did much to disguise the fact that the songs were being sung in English in a Spanish-speaking country!

The cornetist did his best to interest some young converts in playing brass instruments, but they quickly tired and nothing permanent resulted. Benwell was later appointed to Tala, where he was sentenced to two months' imprisonment for playing his cornet and preaching the gospel in the open air.

It was not in Buenos Aires that a brass band was used for the first time in Salvation Army meetings in South America, but in Santa Fé, a corps in the interior. Later, in Paysandu, in the north of Uruguay, an entire family was converted and formed a band. The corps lost its musical forces when the family transferred to Pergamino, Argentina. Here a string band was formed and maintained by the family for some fifteen years. Although the guitar is the most popular instrument in South America, stringed instruments have not been used a great deal in Salvation Army service.

Brass bands did not make an instant appeal. In 1896 a band of seven players was formed to provide music for the special meetings convened to celebrate the sixth anniversary of the Army's beginning in Argentina. For some years after this bands were confined to groups organized to assist in special celebrations.

The first uniformed permanent band was formed in 1911 by Brigadier (later Lieut.-Commissioner) Reinert Gundersen. This octet of instrumentalists was known as the Territorial Staff Band and included Robert Steven, who became an officer from Manchester,

England, and served for forty years in the South American republics, retiring as a Lieut.-Commissioner. This band, to which more members were added with the passing of the years, set a standard for brass band activity for a long period.

An early Bandmaster was Captain (later Brigadier) John C. Martin (his son, the present Brigadier John Martin, later served in this capacity), and another Englishman to lead the band for a time was Brigadier Edward J. Bax. Lieut.-Colonel Dan Richards, a member of a well-known Army family, and Lieut.-Colonel Joseph Stone both played in the Staff Band for some time, while other bandsmen were bearers of such noted names as William and Bramwell Booth (sons of Brigadier Henry Booth, but no relation to the Founder's family), Allemand, Palací and Lungren.

Throughout the years a number of officers have given impetus to the musical affairs of the territory and have trained young musicians. Colonel Victor Rich, a former member of the International Staff Band, was particularly outstanding as a musical leader and was Bandmaster of Buenos Aires Central Band during the period of his service in South America.

Today there are relatively few bands in corps away from the capital city, but Rosario, Montevideo, Tucumán, Salto and Bahia Blanca have small bands which render effective service.

In this field of activity, where the work has never been easy, Territorial Headquarters has been called upon to help substantially with the purchase of instruments. The first silver-plated instruments were brought from England in 1915. Some are still in use. Subsequent leaders, including General George Carpenter and Commissioner Marcel Allemand, also gave much appreciated encouragement to the bands, while the territory was fortunate to have for some time as its Chief Secretary such an enthusiast as Colonel Thomas Dennis, who served as a member of the International Staff Band for two periods.

Musical activity in the other South America territories (Brazil and South America West) is confined to isolated groups of instrumentalists which, if limited in their selection of music, give splendid service to form a link in the chain of consecrated music which girdles the world.

Some thirty years ago there was a Territorial Staff Band in Rio de Janeiro (Brazil). Under the bandmastership of Captain Hjalmar Eliasen, now a Colonel and Territorial Commander in Buenos Aires, and later Colonel William G. Effer, this band brought a new interest to Salvationists of Brazil, but such groups must in the nature of things be few and widely scattered.

As lone instrumentalists have been used to extend the Kingdom of God in other countries, so in Brazil. In 1932 The Salvation Army 'opened fire' in the small industrial town of Joinville. A German-born Captain and his wife were given the privilege of pioneering in this new area and when they arrived, although the town boasted a population of some 10,000, they found there was little sympathy with their work.

The Captain had a cornet, and that proved a good thing. Years before, he had been a member of the German Staff Band and had developed tastes for high-quality music. When he arrived in Brazil, however, he was soon to learn that most of his music-making would have to be by solo efforts. But this did not matter. If his cornet playing could help the Kingdom of God, then he must do all in his power to use his music to that end.

So it was that on that day in 1932 Captain and Mrs. Bruno Behrendt stood on the corner of a street, the Captain, through the dulcet tones of his brass instrument, seeking to attract the passers-by. It worked. People stopped to listen. Some accepted the invitation to attend indoor meetings.

Among the first to show interest in the cornetist was an eleven-year-old boy who, seeing and hearing the Captain, ran home as fast as his legs could carry him to proclaim breathlessly to a wide-eyed parent: 'Father, come quickly, I have seen the Angel Gabriel; the end of the world is here.'

'It cannot be,' was the impatient reply. 'But can't you hear music?' asked the boy.

The father was a notorious drunkard. When he was in liquor his wife and family went in fear of their lives, often hiding until he was in bed and asleep. Upon one occasion he had taken an axe and threatened to murder them.

The boy's plea was persistent; rather unsteadily the man followed his excited son along the street to see 'the Angel Gabriel'. Although he immediately realized that the boy's powers of identification had been sadly at fault, there was much in what he saw and heard to captivate him. He stood transfixed. Not only did the playing arrest his attention, but when the music ceased and the Captain spoke to the increasing crowd, he heard a message of divine love which was entirely new to him.

The Captain noticed the father and son and at the conclusion of the open-air meeting had some conversation with them. He later visited their home and eventually persuaded the family to attend meetings in the hall. One glad day the father surrendered his life to God at the Mercy Seat. He claimed deliverance from the chains of drink which had enslaved him for so long, and after a while was sworn in as a Salvation Army soldier.

Brother Tavares became the drummer and very soon instruments were secured for other converts. 'There is nothing like keeping converts busy,' thought the Captain.

Inspired by such biographies as *The Angel Adjutant,* the drummer grew in grace and the understanding of spiritual life and shed a splendid influence in the neighbourhood and among the people with whom he worked. To them the change in his life was a miracle. He remained the drummer until his promotion to Glory in 1942.

Young Valdemiro, the boy, grew up to become an Army bandsman and for some time served as an officer. There is still a good corps at Joinville and a few years ago the Captain, now a Colonel and Territorial Commander in São Paulo, returned to preside at the laying of the foundation stone of a social centre attached to the corps.

'The Angel Gabriel' was delighted to find children and grandchildren of those early-day converts playing in the band.

Central America and West Indies

ALTHOUGH brass banding in the Central America and West Indies Territory is limited to small groups functioning in isolation on the various islands in the sun, the faithful enthusiasts who maintain their witness by means of musical expression must have a place in this record of service.

Because of the difficulty of obtaining instruments—the high cost of purchasing has proved prohibitive to the Salvationists of this territory —the musical sections have remained small, but some bands have been in existence for a long time. As the territorial centre, Kingston, Jamaica, has always enjoyed the valued assistance of officers well qualified to undertake the responsibility of forming and teaching a band.

In recent years Mrs. Major Joseph Craig, now stationed with her husband in Canada, devoted much skill and energy to teaching boys at the Army home to play brass instruments. It would be more correct to say ' a brass instrument ', for with only a trumpet available the keen youngsters took it in turns to be put through their paces.

It was a wonderful day for the home when a consignment of renovated instruments arrived from England. These had been in use by the cadets band in London for forty years, and with the conclusion of the ambitious instrument scheme at Denmark Hill, the ' old warriors ' were donated to various mission fields, a large percentage finding their way to Kingston.

Major Winifred Garner is another officer who has worked hard to maintain brass band interest in Jamaica. It is typical of the Major that when she was awarded a cash prize for a successful entry in a *Musician*

Christmas competition, she requested that the money might be spent in securing a set of Unity Series music for her band in Kingston.

*   *   *

Most bands of any size are united groups which function in the divisional centres, those in Barbados and Trinidad being typical. The divisional band in British Guiana is possibly the most efficient in the territory. This has been in continuous service for the past thirty-five years and was formed by Brigadier Ellis Hackett when he was the Divisional Commander. The players are drawn from the eight city corps and regularly supply the music for the weekly holiness meeting. They also accompany the Divisional Commander on campaign. For a number of years this band played once a month in the Botanic Gardens and also gave a monthly half-hour broadcast programme. The band is still very active, especially at Christmas time, when hospitals and institutions are visited. Christmas playing is the band's main source of income and from it an attempt is made each year to purchase a new instrument.

A musical pioneer in the West Indies was Lieut.-Colonel Alfred Narraway who, with Mrs. Narraway, arrived there in 1908. Soon afterward the Colonel, who had been an able violinist since his boyhood, organized a brass band whose activities at many centres created great interest and were the means of leading numerous people into the Kingdom of God.

*   *   *

There are a number of hard-working corps bands as well. In 1930 an enterprising young British officer formed a band at St. John's, Antigua. He was Captain John Stobart, who as a Colonel and the Territorial Commander for Ceylon was promoted to Glory in 1960. The faith of the Captain was fully justified and today a small but healthy section still functions as an effective group of musical evangelists.

Corps in which bands are also in existence include Panama, Port Limon (Costa Rica) and Savanna-la-Mar (Jamaica).

Salvationists of the Bahamas are proud of their Nassau Central Band, which takes its service more seriously than some larger sections.

A would-be bandsman attends a learners' class and at the end of the course a written examination is given. He is required to have a knowledge of music theory, including expression marks and metronome indications, and to be able to repeat from memory the bandsmen's regulations. An application form is then completed and the recruit is permitted to attend band practices and to share an old, dilapidated instrument with its present player. This is not a very hygienic method, but constitutes the only chance for the future bandsman to have a 'blow'.

The next step is for the learner to undergo an audition, in which he is asked to play scales and tunes containing up to four flats and sharps. If successful he is commissioned—still with no instrument—and becomes a reserve. Thus a high standard of efficiency is reached in theory, but the young enthusiast is not able to put his knowledge to practical use because there is no instrument for him to play.

*   *   *

The opening of The Salvation Army's work in Puerto Rico in February, 1962, was heralded with a blaze of musical glory provided by members of the New York Staff Band.

This island, administered by the U.S.A., is under the command of the Eastern Territory for Salvation Army purposes, and Commissioner Holland French, at that time the Territorial Commander, officially unfurled the Army flag in the capital, San Juan, to the accompaniment of trumpets.

CHAPTER TEN

IN THE ANTIPODES

Australia

THE young officer cut an imposing figure as, with his wife, he disembarked from the *Aconcagua* at Adelaide amid the heat of a midsummer day in February, 1881. He wore a red tunic, navy blue trousers and a spiked white helmet with a brass chain under his chin. His wife wore a dress of the princess robe style and a small bonnet. Included in their luggage were twelve similar uniforms (six of each) and a pocket cornet.

Captain and Mrs. Thomas Sutherland were the first Salvation Army officers to set foot in Australia. But there was an Army waiting for them on the shimmering sand dunes. Sixty-eight soldiers had already enlisted under the flag since Edward Saunders and John Gore, both converted in Christian Mission meetings in England, had first held gatherings in the Labour League Hall in Adelaide.

It was in response to repeated appeals from these pioneers that William Booth appointed Captain and Mrs. Sutherland to take charge of the work so faithfully begun in Adelaide. The Captain, who, because of his enthusiasm, was nicknamed ' Glory Tom ', commenced a band shortly after his arrival and by the end of that year Adelaide I Band had eleven players. The instrumentation was two clarinets, three cornets, a tenor horn, euphonium, two baritones, a bombardon and a drum. One of the clarinet players was James Hooker, an ironfounder and engineer who built the first Army hall in the city. He later became Bandmaster. This was the first Salvation Army band to be formed south of the Equator.

Another early-day Bandmaster at Adelaide was Bert Fry, a member of the pioneer Salisbury family.

It was Captain Sutherland who, with a blast from his cornet, also began Army work in Sydney, New South Wales. Posters in the city and suburbs announced, ' On Saturday evening, December 2, 1882, The Salvation Army will begin an attack on Sydney at Paddy's Market, with heavy field guns and light artillery, with sharpshooters bringing up the rear.'

The group consisted of Captain and Mrs. Sutherland, Captain Alexander Canty and Sister Mary Ann Cox. A trumpet call from the Captain's cornet attracted the attention of the hilarious crowd gathered at the market, and the first meeting was commenced with ' We're a band that shall conquer the foe '. Both men played instruments; the women sang and beat tambourines.

Converts were soon won—eleven hundred in two weeks at one time—and the first band in New South Wales was formed. This consisted of the two men officers (cornet and euphonium) and Brothers Mudiman, Thorn and Beckwith (baritone, bass and drum). A Bandmaster named Lewis was appointed.

With such a humble beginning the famous Sydney Congress Hall Band has gone from strength to strength, attaining an important place in the music life of the state. Bandmaster Sam Winley, an officer of a Government department, conducted the band for some years and Territorial Band Inspector Harold Scotney was Bandmaster for a period. The name of Territorial Bandmaster Harold Morgan has also been associated with this section for many years.

When John Gore became an officer and took command of corps, his son, Will, a gifted musician, became responsible for forming and developing bands at centres at which his parents were stationed. He had learned to play a cornet when Captain and Mrs. Sutherland had come to live in the Gore home upon their arrival from England. He had also studied music in his spare time and received tuition from an old bandmaster of the British Army. At fourteen years of age the boy found himself Bandmaster at Port Pirie, where there was a band of sixteen players.

The next corps to which Captain Gore was appointed was Port Augusta, where a band was in the process of being formed. The previous officer had secured a set of instruments, called a meeting of his proposed bandsmen and, as they entered the hall, presented each man with an instrument, irrespective of ability. ' We will have a practice and I will be the Bandmaster,' he announced. They were playing in the streets the next Sunday, producing a noise described as ' like a saw mill '. Upon the arrival of the new officers, young Gore took over, started the men on scales, which had hitherto been thought unnecessary, and cancelled the band's outdoor activities until it could give a good account of itself. On a Sunday morning two months later the band ventured forth very much reformed! A local newspaper observed: ' The Army has got a new tune.'

When Will Gore was sixteen he began work at the South Australia Headquarters in Adelaide, his task being the formation of a Staff Band. Among its members were William Peart, later a Commissioner and the first Australian officer to serve outside his homeland, John Dean and Herbert Lindsay, both of whom rose to the rank of Colonel. In 1887 the Adelaide Staff Band attended the first inter-colonial Congress in Melbourne.

From Adelaide and Sydney the Salvation Army brass band movement spread across Australia. Limited at first to the isolated musician who had sufficient interest and patience to teach a handful of raw recruits, enthusiasm knew no bounds when travelling bands began to tour in Australia and New Zealand.

Between 1890 and 1909 many such groups were formed. No doubt the first of these received the encouragement of the Territorial Commander, Commissioner Thomas B. Coombs, who had recently arrived from Canada. During the six years of its continuous existence, the No. 1 Australian Guards Band travelled some 7,233 miles throughout the Antipodes and saw 2,000 seekers kneeling at the Mercy Seat. A second band was formed some time later and, after a while, the two groups combined.

The inhabitants of many of the towns and villages had never heard a brass band before. Like their famous British counterparts, the Household Troopers, the bandsmen were often required to sleep in a hay loft above a barn in which a programme had been given. When the band visited Kadina, South Australia, the Bandmaster, with the corps officer, was fined £2 5s. for infringing the bye-laws. The Bandmaster, refusing to pay, was sent to prison, where he was serenaded by his men.

Another travelling musical force to function about this time was the Federal Band, formed by Commandant Herbert Booth, who succeeded Thomas Coombs. Following the band's marching through the streets of Walhalla, Victoria, Adjutant (later Lieut.-Colonel) James Dutton was prosecuted and convicted. This was later quashed by Mr. Justice a'Becket in the Victoria Supreme Court, the council having to meet the costs.

With such vast distances to be travelled, the personal oversight of Army bandsmen in Australia has always presented something of a problem, but Harold Scotney rendered valuable service in this direction. Transferred from Wellington Citadel, New Zealand, in 1934, this Yorkshire-born composer of note became Bandmaster at Sydney Congress Hall and was appointed Band Inspector for the Eastern Territory, a position he held until retirement.

Much interest was created by the Austral Women's Band, which travelled some 16,000 miles during 1905-6. There were twenty-one instrumentalists and the ' Bandmaster ' was Captain Ruby Baker, who had been ' Corps Bandmistress ' at Calac, Victoria.

Corps bands in Australia now rank with the Army's best, those of Brisbane Temple, Petersham, Norwood Citadel and Hawthorn Citadel being among those that have made great strides in recent years.

The best-known band in Australia is undoubtedly the Melbourne Territorial Staff Band, which was formed in 1890. It was early in the leadership of Commissioner Thomas Coombs that a decree was made forming a ' Headquarters Brass Band '. There were nine players at first, officers and employees of the old Exhibition Street Headquarters, and the function of the group was to take part in the Commissioner's meetings and other important events, such as the opening of new halls.

The first Bandmaster was Staff Officer Jeremiah Eunson. He had played in the Founder's meetings in England, and had linked up with the Army in Melbourne when that city was ' invaded ' by Major and Mrs. James Barker. He taught many converts to play and helped to form many of the first bands in Victoria. He did, in fact, hold the commission of Staff Bandmaster before there was a Staff Band and usually took charge of any instrumental groups of officers formed for special occasions.

Bandmaster Eunson wrote the parts out by hand, working in an upstairs room at headquarters. He kept his cornet on a table, taking it up every now and again to try over the part he had just completed.

Within a year of the foundation of the band the Bandmaster left Melbourne to join one of the newly formed Guards Bands.

There were other conductors before Captain ' Ebbie ' Jackson took up the baton in 1896. The Captain had been Bandmaster of one of the Guards Bands and, with his appointment and that of two other Captains, Rook and Hamilton, to headquarters, prospects for the future were decidedly bright. In that year Herbert Booth became Territorial Commander and the band began to occupy a place of greater importance in the spectacular demonstrations in the Melbourne Exhibition Building and other numerous events organized by the Commandant. A full-page congress announcement of those days said: ' The Territorial Headquarters Staff Band will add to all public meetings the dash and fire of their well-known musical efforts.'

At that time the unmarried bandsmen lived together in a house in East Melbourne rented by the Army. It was not long before week-end campaigning became a regular feature of the band's activity. Some of these expeditions to the suburban corps involved a ten- or twelve-mile walk. When Lord Brassey, then Governor of Victoria, presided at the opening of a Salvation Army rescue home in West Brunswick, The War Cry described the band as ' blazing away in fine style '.

Something of a crisis occurred at one corps one Sunday morning when a few of the bandsmen arrived on bicycles, newly invented machines. Alarmed at such a happening, some local Salvationists returned to their homes without attending the meeting. This prejudice was soon overcome, however, and the band became a cycle brigade.

The more adventurous members purchased motor-cycles when these more speedy machines came on the market.

In 1897 Captain Aenas McGregor began his thirty-seven-year-long association with the Staff Band. He was a picturesque character who became responsible for the marching of the band and gave himself the position and title of ' Drum Major '.

The position of Staff Band Leader was created in 1903, the first to hold that appointment being Major (later Commissioner) John McMillan, who became the Army's fifth Chief of the Staff. The Deputy Leader was Major (later General) George Carpenter. Other well-known officers who spent their early days as members of the Melbourne Staff Band include Commissioner Benjamin Orames, Commissioner John S. Bladin, Lieut.-Commissioner Herbert C. Colledge and Lieut.-Commissioner Robert S. Harewood.

Lieut.-Colonel Reuben Edwards, a former member of the old Adelaide Staff Band, was Leader for some eight years, while others who have served in that capacity are Colonel Ambrose Henry, Colonel Percival Dale (four occasions), Lieut.-Commissioner Robert Harewood, Lieut.-Colonel Cyril Brimblecombe and Lieut.-Colonel Allen Sharp.

For some years from 1905 the band was conducted by Staff-Captain (later Major) William H. Gore, he being succeeded by Brigadier William Rook, who had been Deputy Bandmaster for sixteen years. When the Brigadier retired from band activity in 1929 he had served with the Staff Band for thirty-one years.

Soon after the First World War the band enjoyed a period of outstanding musical excellence with the appointment as conductor of Captain Robert H. McNally. Officially the Deputy Bandmaster, the Captain brought the band to a high standard, a special feature of its programmes being his series of ' Great Masters ' arrangements.

The band suffered a setback when a new territory was formed in 1920 with headquarters in Sydney: eight of the bandsmen were transferred from Melbourne. For twelve months Staff Bandsman Herbert Dutton, who had gained a reputation for his horn and cornet playing, was the conductor, and then George H. Dickens became the Bandmaster, a position he held for six years. During that period the Staff Bandmaster was in charge of the Music Department at Territorial Headquarters.

Bandmaster Norman McLeod, O.F., succeeded George Dickens in 1936 and served in that appointment for twenty-seven years. He first became a Staff Bandsmen in 1917 and was also Band Secretary from 1927 to 1936. Bandmaster Charles Scott was appointed in 1963.

With the resumption of normal activity following the Second

World War, interstate campaigns again became a feature of Staff Band life. In 1946 permission was granted by the International Music Board in London for the band to play certain compositions awaiting publication and featured up till then only by the International Staff Band. This was a greatly appreciated privilege and the first movement of Schubert's 'Unfinished Symphony' was the first piece to be so introduced.

Apart from regular visits to small corps in the vicinity of the city, the band on several occasions has conducted services in churches. Prior to one such visit the younger folk in the church had presented an ultimatum that dancing be introduced into the social life of the community. Following the band's Sunday visit, the deputation informed the minister and others that the young people had been so impressed by the evident happiness and sincerity of the Salvationists and the forthright message that they had decided to abandon the idea. A present-day Salvation Army officer was one of the young people who attended that day.

In sending a message to the Melbourne Staff Band upon the occasion of its diamond jubilee in 1950, the Chief of the Staff at that time, Commissioner John J. Allan, said: 'I know of nothing in the Army that can be of more value in bringing blessing, arousing enthusiasm and building public opinion quickly than the consecrated efforts of a Staff Band.'

That the lives of numerous men and women have been changed through the ministry of the Territorial Staff Band in Melbourne is sufficient testimony to the truth of these observations.

* * *

A Music Department was formed in Melbourne in 1907 with Staff-Captain William Gore in charge. The Australian Band Journal was launched at this time, the Staff-Captain being responsible for the production of a single sheet of music every fortnight. He did the arranging and editing himself, and the stamping of the originals with steel discs from which the zinc plates were etched for printing. In addition, Gore was manager of the Musical Instruments Department at the Trade Headquarters, Bandmaster of the Territorial Staff Band, Instructor of the Cadets Band and sole adviser on all Army music matters in Australia and New Zealand.

A Bands Department was inaugurated in the Eastern Territory in 1946. Two years before, Commissioner William R. Dalziel, then in command of the Southern Territory, set up a Territorial Music Board under the chairmanship of Colonel James A. Hawkins, who had been a member of the International Staff Band and had served as Bandmaster at Tottenham Citadel.

When volunteers were being urged to join the Armed Forces in the Second World War a number of Salvationist-musicians enlisted at the City of Melbourne Drill Hall on July 15, 1940, six members of the Staff Band among them. In a body they went to training camp shortly afterward, their Christian conduct and high principles earning the respect and admiration of all with whom they served. The idea had been inspired by Bandmaster Arthur Gullidge, of Brunswick, who was quickly promoted to Sergeant and appointed bandmaster of the battalion band. His Salvationist comrades comprised the band.

The fifteen hundred men of the 2/22nd Battalion of the Australian Forces, with its band, sailed for New Britain, where they became garrisoned at Rabaul. In 1942 the men and the local volunteers were overcome by their enemies. Nearly all those who did not fall in the first attack were taken prisoner. Band Sergeant Austin Creed managed to escape into the dense jungle, but was overtaken by illness and died in the mountains. Two former Staff Bandsmen were separated from the main party by their stretcher-bearer duties and were killed. In June of that year the remainder sailed for Japan on the *Montevideo Maur*, which was torpedoed off Luzon and lost, apparently without a survivor. Brunswick Salvation Army hall, situated in the suburbs of Melbourne, was a rallying centre week by week for wives, mothers, sweethearts and children for three and a half years until they received news of the tragedy.

A tablet in the citadel at Brunswick bears the names of Sergeant W. A. Gullidge, Divisional Bandmaster; Sergeant R. A. Watson, Librarian; Private H. D. Harvey, Divisional Songster Leader; Private A. B. Creed, Band Sergeant; Private R. J. Watkins, Bandsman; Private J. Stebbings, Bandsman.

The Melbourne Staff Band Room contains another list: Staff Bandsmen R. H. Cook, K. R. Drew, T. W. G. Haines, H. J. Pannell, S. R. Parker and F. M. Thomas. Others in the company were Bandsmen B. Collinson, R. Cairns, A. Fry, S. French, F. Medding, B. Morgan, F. Meyer, J. Robinson, N. Smith and N. McPherson.

Arthur Gullidge composed many band pieces. His marches, the first of which was the 'Melbourne Temple', possess an originality easy to identify. Such titles as 'Victorious' and 'Unconquered' are singularly expressive and the selection, 'Divine Communion', has been a well-loved piece for many years.

★   ★   ★

No record of musical life in Australia would be complete without reference to the many timbrel bands which efficiently function in many parts of the continent. Rhythm and out-and-out Salvationism go together in these groups and they well illustrate the 'ancient and modern' in Salvation Army life and activity. The graceful 'strike' has been worked out to a fine art, and there is no more attractive sight in a Salvation Army festival than a group of well-trained timbrelists.

Australia has featured this form of expression from the earliest days. Its example has been followed in many other parts of the Army world. Since the visit of the Australian delegation to the International Youth Congress in 1950, a revival of timbrel groups has been evident in the land of the Army's birth and on the continent of Europe.

Timbrelists from 'down under' were popular participants in the Centenary Celebrations in London.

New Zealand

WITH a population of two and a half millions, New Zealand does well to possess sixty Salvation Army bands. True, not many of them are large, but when the size of the country is remembered—this must result in scattered communities—the percentage is comparatively high.

Two young men, one twenty and the other a year younger, began Salvation Army operations in the 'land of the long white cloud'. They were Captain George Pollard and Lieutenant Edward Wright. The Captain played the concertina and his colleague the cornet, and with

Captain George Pollard and Lieutenant Edward Wright, pioneers in New Zealand

these instruments, on April 1, 1883, they stood on the steps of the fountain in the centre of the city of Dunedin to announce in song: 'We're bound for the land of the pure and the holy'. When the Salvationists of New Zealand held their first Congress only nine

F

months later, four or five fully equipped bands took part in the celebrations.

As may be expected, the first corps band was formed at Dunedin Fortress. New Zealand has always been 'band-minded' and among the first converts in that city were several men who had received previous instruction. Led by a brilliant cornetist, named Tucker, this band quickly settled down and soon was able to give a good account of itself. The present band worthily maintains the tradition.

Invergill followed Dunedin's example, and Dunedin South, Oamaru, Timaru, Christchurch, Wellington Citadel and Auckland Congress Hall were not long behind. At the end of four years, these, and others like Atahuhu, New Plymouth, Napier, Petone, Ashburton and Waimate, were well established and rendering splendid service.

The New Zealand Territory was fortunate in its early-day band trainers. Bandmaster 'Ebbie' Jackson, of Oamaru, was one of these. He edited the New Zealand Band Journal for a time and is remembered by veteran Salvationists in that land for his arrangement of 'Master, the tempest is raging' in connection with a service of song entitled 'The wreck of the Wairarapa', which was popular some sixty years ago.

'Wingy' Hodson was another. He was Bandmaster at Auckland and so nicknamed because he had only one hand. A steel hook was worn in place of the other. When Hodson was captain of the Skeleton Army in Auckland, the hook was useful for tearing uniform from the backs of the Salvationists!

He also edited the New Zealand Band Journal for a period and, although self-taught, was a capable band arranger and composer. Bandmaster C. Fowler, of Christchurch, completes a trio of musicians who did much to lay a sure foundation of Army bands in New Zealand.

In 1890 a Territorial Staff Band of ten players was in existence. The 'stars' of this group were the brothers 'Ebbie' and George Jackson, who between them arranged most of the music played. The first-named later became Bandmaster of the Melbourne Staff Band.

Another feature of early-day musical service was the introduction of a lasses' band of twenty members which drew large crowds. The Bandmaster was Captain T. Robinson, and the band was attached to the Christchurch Corps. Later a lassies' band was formed at Wellington Citadel.

The bands of New Zealand are still marching—and how they can march! Wellington Citadel, Wellington South, Newton, Auckland Congress Hall, Christchurch Citadel, Palmerston North, Dunedin Citadel, Timaru, Napier, and the rest, with flags unfurled, still set the pulse of 'God's Own Country' beating in ever-quickening rhythm.

No history of Salvation Army banding in New Zealand could be complete without tribute being paid to the long and outstanding service of Brigadier Henry C. Coffin, composer and conductor for nearly sixty years. The Brigadier was appointed Territorial Secretary for Bands in 1935, when a Music Board was also formed, and continued to serve the musicians of that territory until his retirement. Even then, the work of instructing and inspiring went on, the never-tiring enthusiast travelling extensively throughout New Zealand and in both Australian territories in the interest of Army music.

CHAPTER ELEVEN

ACROSS THE CHANNEL

France

THERE was no helpful music to support the ' invasion ' of France by Salvation Army forces. It was hand-to-hand fighting from the day the attack was launched and Catherine Booth, eldest daughter of the Founder and Army Mother and later named the *Maréchale*, with her courageous assistants, Florence Soper (later Mrs. Bramwell Booth) and Adelaide Cox, was compelled to maintain the bridgehead without even a cornet.

One reason for this was that no open-air meetings were permitted. Some other method of reaching the people had to be found. An answer lay in the production and sale on the streets, under police licence, of *En Avant* (' Forward! '), the French equivalent of *The War Cry*. Thousands of citizens bought copies.

Another point of contact was established when a band of five women cadets began visiting cabarets, distributing papers, singing salvation songs and inviting the patrons to Army meetings. The word ' band ' obviously referred to a company or group and had no instrumental connotation.

But when the first procession of Salvationists through the streets of France took place on Bastille Day, July 14, 1882, it was reported that ' a glorious company of our happy soldiers marched, with music at their head ' in the neighbourhood of Vincennes.

The French are cultured people. Classical music is in their tradition and they do not take kindly to brass bands, the music of which is considered low-brow. This may be why this medium of expression has not been more extensively incorporated into Salvation Army activity. Stringed instruments have always been more popular.

But visits of efficient Army bands from other territories have always met with enthusiastic approval from Salvationist audiences and the general public.

Although many and varied efforts to organize bands and to train bandsmen have not yielded much success, there has, at intervals, been a resurgence of interest. When Brigadier (later Lieut-Colonel) Arthur Best, a former euphonium player in the International Staff Band, took up a financial appointment on the Paris Territorial Headquarters shortly before the outbreak of the Second World War, he formed a brass quartet to prove what could be done with four efficient instrumentalists. The group consisted of Adjutant (later Lieut.-Commissioner)

Francis Evans and Captain (later Lieut.-Colonel) Willy Crausaz, and Adjutant Bardet, a former soloist of the Swiss Officers' Band attached to the Territorial Headquarters in Bern.

After a few weeks the party conducted a highly successful tour in northern France and in the spring of 1939 it campaigned in Alsace-Lorraine. This proved a memorable event for the four officers. War clouds were already hanging low over that inherent trouble area and the musical evangelists valued the opportunity of proclaiming the message of hope in a variety of ways.

The tour began at Nancy, where professors and teachers of the Conservatoire of Music, invited to attend by the corps officer, expressed surprise at the volume and tone achieved. At another centre the quartet was supported by the local military band, which played three times to give the visitors a rest.

In 1958 the official records revealed that there were ten bandsmen in the whole of France, most of them members of the group functioning at the Paris Central Corps. When General and Mrs. Wilfred Kitching led Congress gatherings in the capital in the autumn of that year they were supported by a band of thirty! The nucleus was augmented by officer-musicians of the territory and a few visitors.

' The band's " big moment " ', wrote a *Musician* reporter, ' came at the very commencement of the Congress programme. . . . On Saturday morning the Army's leader was ceremoniously received by the Lord Mayor of Paris and presented with the distinctive award of " Friend of Paris ". The bandsmen were present, having marched the General to the magnificent town hall in the heart of the city.'

With all their traditional non-brass background, Salvationists in France, realizing the attraction of even a few instrumentalists, are flexible and resourceful in their methods. When, in May, 1962, General Kitching visited Lyons to open a new people's hostel, the night public meeting was a venture of faith. How could the people of the district be persuaded to attend the first meeting in the new hall? On sudden inspiration open-air meetings were planned and five instrumentalists formed into a ' modest but valiant band '. This unusual impact on the neighbourhood resulted in many people making close contact with the Army for the first time, and in crowds attending the meeting, row after row of chairs being required to accommodate the newcomers.

Belgium

THE Salvationists of Belgium, whilst having few of their own, have a genuine affection for brass bands. The visit of a section from another territory is an occasion.

When Chelmsford Band spent Easter, 1949, in Belgium, it was the
first British band to visit the country since Chalk Farm Band called
at Brussels during its continental tour of 1927. That is why the
Salvationists of this small territory were still talking about the Chelmsford visit when it was announced in June, 1962, that Shaw Band from
Lancashire was to campaign in their country.

In speaking of his bands, the Belgian Salvationist is quick to
mention Quaregnon and Brussels Central. The latter combination,
whilst conscious that it is not up to the standard it enjoyed when
British servicemen stationed in the city lent ready assistance to its
Festival Series presentations, maintains consistent form and is grateful
for the valued help of Territorial Headquarters officers.

This corps is also proud of its guitar brigade, and through the years
this distinctive expression has been effectively utilized in Salvation
Army meetings. The piano-accordion, too, has proved a useful
addition in recent years and, as it is not difficult to tune brass instruments of low pitch to this handy ' portable organ ', it is often enlisted
to augment the band.

Until 1922 Quaregnon Corps had merely the nucleus of a band,
the constitution of which was decidedly odd, and it was obvious that
the enthusiasm of some of its members was not matched by musical
ability. This is the opinion of soldiers of that corps, looking back on
those days following the end of the First World War.

Then Bandmaster Albert Delwarte was appointed and given the
task of making the group into a musical section, formed of disciplined
Salvationists prepared to accept the regulations applicable to such a
combination.

The band was officially recognized from that time, and for twenty-
seven years under the same leader it rendered valued service in the
mining community and made considerable musical progress. In 1949
Bandmaster Delwarte handed the baton to his son, David. This move
was popular with the young people of the corps. They eagerly rallied
around the youthful Bandmaster who, like most of them, had been
associated with the flourishing scout troop.

An accomplished musician, Bandmaster David Delwarte began by
teaching his men, many of them little more than boys, the rudiments of
music, fundamentals of brass banding and loyalty to first things. For
months the band limited itself to the Band Tune Book with a view
to reaching the highest possible standard in everything that was
played.

Inspired by the leader's zest for work and desire for musical
efficiency, the bandsmen responded wholeheartedly, and eventually
easy marches and selections were added to the repertoire. With

assiduous practice the band gained the considerable efficiency which it has today and which is being widely appreciated.

The band's most noted product was Henri Becquet, who became an officer from the corps, pioneered Salvation Army work in the Congo and, as a Commissioner and International Secretary for Europe at International Headquarters, was promoted to Glory in March, 1962. The Commissioner's earthly remains were taken home to Quaregnon for burial.

The story of Belgian music-making would not be complete without reference to Bandmaster Jules Vanderkam, composer of 'The Wanderer' and 'My Fortress', both Festival Series classics of their day. The Bandmaster will have his rightful place in another chapter, but his faithful service at the Jumet Corps cannot be overlooked.

When a brass band ceased to exist, the Bandmaster, in 1940, formed an orchestra, with himself at the piano, to take part in Sunday meetings. He continued this service until his promotion to Glory in 1958, at the age of eighty-five.

The Netherlands

THE work in Holland began with a touch of music, supplied by Lieutenant Gerrit Govaars on his violin. That was in the first meeting held in Amsterdam. When the first territorial leader farewelled two years later *The War Cry* reported: ' An improvised orchestra consisting of two violins, one viola, one cello and a *cornet-à-pistons* accompanied the singing of the congregation.'

Until 1891 no mention was made of bands in the Army's press, but in that year a report stated: ' The first band of Amsterdam 1 (Mother Corps) has been of great help in the meetings.' It is likely that the visit of the Household Troops Band served as an impetus.

Hague Congress Hall had a band in 1892 and made a great impression at the annual field day in the presence of General William Booth. Rotterdam Congress Hall also soon formed a band, and so it was in several other towns, where smaller or bigger combinations were pressed into service primarily to accompany the singing in the meetings. At this time open-air meetings and marches were strictly forbidden by the authorities and granted only by special permission.

Utrecht 1 Band, formed in 1908 with eight instruments which once belonged to Chalk Farm Band, overcame the no-marching ban in an effective manner when visiting the Hague in its early days. A tram car was hired from which the band played and attracted people to the meetings. That campaign resulted in seventeen seekers at the Mercy Seat.

Steady progress was made throughout the territory, and in 1901 there was a total of 146 bandsmen on the official register. The first visit of the International Staff Band, in 1903, further encouraged the music-makers and set a new standard for twentieth-century banding.

A great move forward was commenced in 1910 when the Territorial Commander, Commissioner William Ridsdel, introduced a National Staff Band, with Ensign (later Lieut.-Colonel) J. P. Rawie as Bandmaster. This was a travelling combination. The bandsmen received five shillings a week, out of which they bought their uniform, which was similar in design to that of the International Staff Band. The seventeen men travelled for sixteen months and visited every corps in the territory. Up till then only simple music had been used, but with the advent of the Staff Band the band journal published in London was used for the first time.

When the Dutch Staff Band ceased to function, five of its number became officers, among them Colonel Douglas Ridsdel and Brigadier François Bulterman, the Deputy Bandmaster, who died in a railway accident in 1936.

In 1948 Schiedam Band celebrated its fiftieth anniversary and claimed to be the first Dutch band to do so. Bandmaster K. de Jong was in charge for forty-three years. Other musical leaders with a long record of service are Jan van Dalen, of Rotterdam and the Hague, and Marinus Knippenberg, of Rotterdam Congress Hall. Bandsmen of the Netherlands are also indebted to overseas officers who served for some time in their territory and gave considerable musical help, among them Colonel Andrew Jones and Lieut.-Colonel Harry Taylor.

When Commissioner Bouwe Vlas was the Territorial Commander, he set up, in 1930, a music section with Major Gerrit Claeijs as the Secretary. Lieut.-Colonel Taylor rendered valuable help in preparing the Dutch Band Book, which is still in constant use. After the Second World War Senior-Captain (later Major) Douglas Rolls, a former member of the International Staff, Men's Social Work and 'Rosehill' Bands, was appointed Territorial Secretary for Bands and for some years he travelled the territory seeking to bring encouragement and musical progress to the instrumentalists who had suffered considerable set-backs through the war years.

During the command of Commissioner Charles Durman a National Band was formed in 1948. The men were drawn from the South and Central Divisions and travelled to Amsterdam for the weekly practice, which lasted usually for nearly four hours. It was necessary for each prospective bandsman to be backed by his Divisional Commander and to pass an examination in playing, the theory of music and Salvation Army doctrines before he was accepted.

This band, under its able conductor, toured extensively on the continent of Europe, visited Britain, and reached the peak of its career with a campaign in the U.S.A. and Canada. It was disbanded soon afterward.

In 1961 a third musical group was formed with Captain William Palstra as the Bandmaster. Originally known as the Territorial Head-quarters Ensemble, a year later this was renamed the Amsterdam Staff Band, and visited London in 1965 for the Centenary celebrations.

The first bandsmen's congress in the Netherlands was conducted by Commissioner Samuel Hurren, in 1922. Every year this popular annual event attracts to Amsterdam more than six hundred bandsmen from all parts of the territory for a series of festivals and councils. Practically every band takes active part, either unitedly or as solo participants, in the Saturday festivals held in the Concertgebouw.

CHAPTER TWELVE

MID-EUROPEAN MELODY

Germany

THE idea of using brass bands in their meetings did not appear strange to the Salvationists of Germany. Marching instrumentalists were part of the nation's heritage and in the days of the seventeenth century German street bands were to be found in other continental cities and in England.

From the earliest days of this century there has been an affinity between the bandsmen of Germany and Britain, heightened, no doubt, by the visit of the International Staff Band in the years immediately preceding the First World War.

There was also a German Staff Band at that time, and there are many who remember this smartly, if unconventionally, attired group taking part in the International Congress, in London, in 1914. The names of Percy and Sidney Treite are inseparably linked with the band of those days.

The German Staff Band was formed in 1910 and existed until the outbreak of the First World War. Its only Bandmaster was Colonel Percy Treite. In 1912, Commissioner Wm. McAlonan, the Territorial Commander, reorganized the band, appointing Brigadier (later Lieut.-Commissioner) William J. Haines as the Leader and confirming Brigadier Treite's commission as Bandmaster. The Deputy Bandmaster was Adjutant Samuel Richards and Staff-Captain Max Gruner, later to become the Chief Secretary, was appointed Secretary. Other bandsmen were Lieutenant Carvosso Gauntlett and Adjutant Otto Döring. Forty years later they were Territorial Commander and Chief Secretary together in Germany.

Following the Armistice of 1918 the bands of Germany made a valiant effort to recapture their former strength and glory and for years the rebuilding went on.

Again, by the end of the Second World War, the musical forces had been reduced to the state of beginning again, and their reconstruction is one of the miracles of Army musical history. But the work is hard and tedious. The cessation of youth work under the Hitler régime and the ban on open-air activities; the closing of the training college in 1932; the loss of promising leaders and capable instrumentalists in air raids and on battlefields decimated notable bands which had functioned for years.

At Berlin-Friedenau Corps in 1932 Lieut.-Colonel Frederick Biggs, then a Captain, started a band—himself, his Lieutenant and a helper. One after the other some scouts joined the group and later Brigadier Heinrich Tebbe. The following year Bandmaster Herbert Gruner was appointed. Zeal and perseverance made the group of great service in open-air activity and in connection with visits to prisons.

When the Second World War broke out, several bandsmen were called up. Some of these, with Bandmaster Gruner, were killed during the fighting. In 1946, Major Wilhelm Kiesel, then the corps officer and now a Colonel and Germany's Chief Secretary, re-established the band. At the Major's farewell Brother Zeh took over and when he was reaccepted as an officer he was succeeded by Bandsman Richard Roestel, a former member of the German Staff Band. He had served as Band Instructor for some time and had much to do with the teaching of new players. In 1952 the band undertook a tour in Western Germany.

Like so many German bands, in 1946 that at Berlin-Schöneberg made a new start with nine bandsmen who had come safely through the war. A year later Brother Goll, who had been the Bandmaster before the war, handed the baton to Bandmaster Fritz Neureuter.

This enthusiastic group, averaging sixteen players, makes a speciality of visiting corps that have no bands and helping on special occasions like weddings, funerals and outings.

Bandmaster Neureuter was among those who escaped from what was termed the 'hell of Stalingrad' in 1942. In April, 1943, he was in Berlin on leave and called at Territorial Headquarters after finding that his house in the suburbs had been destroyed. There the news was broken to him that his wife and child, together with a thirteen-year-old niece, had been killed in an air raid. It was not easy for the Bandmaster to overcome this great sorrow. After six weeks' leave he rejoined the Forces and was later taken prisoner. He says:

> A few days before the end of the war I had a chance to kneel before God in a field, far away from anyone else. I asked Him to cleanse me completely. After this prayer I felt new strength and the desire again to take my place as a Salvationist. Upon being released I made my difficult way to Berlin. What a sight was the city! Having secured a bed for the night I headed for headquarters the next morning and was happy to meet a number of Salvationists with whom I served before the war. I longed to play again to the glory of God, and a few bandsmen, with myself, were happy indeed when we could play in the first meeting.

> We looked a poor sight. Partly we were still wearing our old military uniform. We had no polish to clean our shoes and make them shine, no soap, no razor blades, and nothing with which to mend our clothes.

Later Bandmaster Neureuter married again, and he is giving valiant service for God and the Army in Berlin. He is also in charge of the Divisional Band, started just after the war under the inspiration of the Territorial Commander of those days, Lieut.-Commissioner Johann Büsing. Major Kiesel was the first Bandmaster, the present leader taking over in 1947. The Bandmaster's wife is in charge of the Berlin String Band.

Since the beginning of the century there has been a band in Bielefeld. During the war all the instruments were destroyed, but in 1947 youthful Wilfried Naujoks undertook the responsibility of securing new instruments and teaching people to play. In February, 1962, the nine-strong band celebrated the fifteenth anniversary of that reformation. Most of the bandsmen remember learning to play by drubbing on the table with their fingers, no instruments being available.

At Hamburg, immediately after the war, the remaining bandsmen began to meet for practices under the leadership of Bandmaster (now Major) Walter Flade. Many young men were taught to play and the bandsmen were soon proclaiming the gospel in the streets and on the market-squares. When the Bandmaster became an officer, Brother P. Pudrikins, who had led the Latvian Staff Band at one time, took over, later becoming the Bandmaster at Bielefeld. A similar story could be repeated at Bremen, Lübeck and many other centres. With no more than a dozen instrumentalists at these corps the high ideals of Army bandsmanship are being upheld and rewarding service rendered.

With Hanover Band the theme has a slight variation. Before the war there were seven or eight instrumentalists at this corps. After the war it was a different story. With the establishment of the Red Shield Club, Salvationist servicemen from many parts of the world were able to augment the local aggregate. Brigadier Frank Ellingham, in charge of the club for some years, gave generous help.

Thus enthused, former Army bandsmen, living in towns where there was no longer a corps but still within easy reach, joined the band. Later the children and grandchildren of the bandsmen learned to play and took their places, and soon a group of some twenty could be counted on whenever the band was on duty.

The Bandmaster was Karl Kumm, who had been in charge of the band at Breslau, Silesia, from 1924 to 1933. He had been both the Leipzig Divisional Bandmaster and a member of the German Staff Band. Whilst visiting Hamburg with his band in the treacherous winter of 1961, he caught a cold which, aided by the severe weather conditions of the Christmastide, led to his promotion to Glory in February, 1962.

Czechoslovakia

WHEN, in 1913, the German Staff Band crossed Germany's south-eastern frontier, it became the first Salvation Army band to play in what later became known as Czechoslovakia. Six years afterward, following that country's recognition as an independent republic, Salvation Army operations began in Prague and in December, 1919, it was decided to form a band in the capital.

Not one Salvationist in the city had any experience of brass band activity. Musicians in the town prophesied that it would be two years before an Army band could perform in public. They were wrong. Three months later, in March, 1920, eleven hundred people crowded one of the city's largest halls and applauded vigorously every item rendered by the Prague I Band at its first public appearance.

The activity of the band had commenced with fifteen learners, including six women. Two of these were the daughters of Brigadier Holm, the General Secretary. Adjutant (later Lieut.-Commissioner) S. Carvosso Gauntlett was the Bandmaster.

The drum presented something of a problem. Skins were so scarce in Czechoslovakia at that time that the price of a drum was almost prohibitive. After diligent searching, a second-hand instrument was purchased at reasonable cost, and it was a proud Bandmaster who carried the drum through the streets of the capital to head-quarters where, with tender hands, he renovated it and made it fit for use.

It was not easy to find a man to carry the drum. It was customary in processions for the drum to be drawn along on a little cart by a donkey. The drummer marched behind to administer the necessary beats. The idea of a drummer carrying his instrument was new, but at last a willing man was found.

Those early meetings were disturbed by groups of students and street hooligans who misunderstood the Army's intentions. Upon one occasion the attack was particularly severe, the drummer coming in for more than his share of kicks. The men eventually reached their hall and, although still suffering the effects of the onslaught, held a prayer meeting, which was led by the Territorial Commander, Commissioner Karl Larsson. This was followed by a band practice, the first tune, by coincidence, being ' No retreating, hell defeating '. About this time a corps string band was formed under the leadership of Mrs. Adjutant Gauntlett.

In November, 1920, the Territorial Staff Band made its first appearance. Under its Bandmaster, Adjutant Gauntlett, it had been practising for two months. Among the pieces played upon that historic occasion were a march ' Armáda Spásy ' (The Salvation Army in Czech), by Bandmaster George Marshall, and a selection of national songs arranged by the then Captain Wilfred Kitching. Both pieces had been especially written for the event. A critic's comments in the newspaper the next morning read: ' The band's playing was like the sound of a large iron ball ponderously rolling down a lengthy flight of stairs.' Perhaps it was not as bad as that!

When a number of students became converted at Brno it was decided to form a band at that corps. Captain Leslie Taylor-Hunt was deputed to take some instruments from Prague to Brno. His precious cargo presented no difficulty during the actual train journey, but when the passengers were requested to change trains at a large railway junction the Captain's anxiety began.

Without any help at all forthcoming—officials and passengers alike looked askance at the Salvation Army uniform—he had to transfer the instruments from one train to the other, all the time fearing that either would depart leaving some instruments in both and the remainder in course of carting. He need not have feared, however, for the second part of the journey was commenced only after what seemed an age. At Brno the students were at the station to meet the train and lovingly inspected the instruments they hoped to play without undue delay.

When neighbours objected to the boys' practising in the hall, another venue had to be found. One morning at six o'clock Taylor-Hunt was awakened by tappings at the hall window—his bed was a form in the building. It was the learners, who requested that they should continue their practising in the country lanes outside the town. And so an alternative was discovered. Each evening, too, the boys and their leader would adopt the same methods before returning to dispose of copies of *Prapor Spásy* (Banner of Salvation) in the cafés and on the crowded dazzling thoroughfares.

The first appearance of the band in the streets of Brno coincided with the arrival of Colonel Alfred Braine to distribute food to the needy. The Colonel had been a member of the International Staff Band and welcomed the opportunity of being associated with this new venture, playing E♭ bass.

Five years later, when Colonel Arthur Goldsmith visited Czecho-slovakia on international audit duties, he played with Prague 1 Band of fourteen players under the leadership of the corps officer, Ensign (later Colonel) Albert Jakeway, who was later to become world-renowned as a composer and fourth head of the International Music Editorial Department. The Prague 2 Band was led by Adjutant (later Lieut.-Colonel) James Nicklin. Another instrumentalist serving in the territory at that time was Captain (later Commissioner) Norman Duggins. These three English officers, with those already mentioned, did much to encourage the infant musical forces. Captain Duggins also formed and led officers' bands in Hungary and Yugoslavia. As Chief of the Staff, he was promoted to Glory in March, 1961.

After the ,Second World War, The Salvation Army in Czechoslovakia rose from the chaos. In 1946 Colonel Thomas E. Dennis went to Prague to conduct congress gatherings, the first since 1937. A special congress band was formed for the occasion and played ' No, never run away ' as its first number. The march, ' Czechoslovakia ', was also featured. This, composed by the Belgian musician, Bandmaster Jules Vanderkam, had been played during the war years as ' We still live ', the original title being banned.

Lieut.-Colonel Herbert Climpson, the Officer Commanding, and Senior-Captain (later Major) Harold Davies, both former members of the International Staff Band, sought to bring inspiration and encouragement to the handful of faithful Salvationists who so loyally stood by the Army flag in those dark days following the end of the war. The Army's work was suppressed in June, 1950.

Switzerland

THE flag of The Salvation Army was unfurled in Switzerland in the face of bitter opposition. Severe persecution and mass imprisonment were meted out to the brave pioneers, and it was not surprising that when musical groups were formed they, too, became caught up in this tidal wave of hatred.

Liestal Corps was opened in 1888 and a band was formed soon afterward. The first Bandmaster was Alfred Baumgartner. Although marching was permitted, the civic authorities would not allow officers to play in the bands or the bands to play in the indoor meetings.

The persecution measures were directed toward the officers, some of whom were arrested for permitting their meetings to go on later than nine o'clock, and others for breaking the non-playing regulations.

It will be seen that the illogical legislation allowed for the bandsmen to play out of doors as much as they liked. When officers were sentenced to prison for periods ranging from ten days to three weeks, the bandsmen played to them, to the great joy of the inmates, Salvationists and others.

In those days the Liestal Band, twelve to sixteen strong, was one of the best. When it played at the wedding of an Army leader in Zürich in 1896, a local newspaper described the band as being ' in zeal a little above, in performance a little below the Constance (Germany) Regimental Band ', which was considered excellent.

The corps at Herisau was opened in 1887. A few years later attempts were made to start a band. When, in 1895, an officer with some musical ability was appointed he was greatly surprised to find six bandsmen all playing by ear and not knowing a single note of music. They played only in the key of C.

The officer had the greatest difficulty in explaining that other keys existed and could be used, and that a knowledge of music would be useful. They felt certain that bands using music could not play better than they did. The corps officer was adamant, and they finally realized the advantage of learning music.

This band has been in existence ever since and, even if sometimes reduced to a handful, has bravely continued in the face of many difficulties. The first Bandmaster played a double bass in the band until well into his middle eighties.

Slowly music was collected. Every band, at first, did the best it could from the limited sources available. Here and there original songs were written and the music was transcribed for musical groups. Commissioner William McAlonan, when Territorial Commander, introduced the British band books, one for hymn tunes and two for marches.

When a young officer, Captain Gottfried Gertsch, was appointed to Zürich 2, he found an efficient, if small, orchestra in operation, with a music teacher as its instructor. Songs from *The War Cry* were generally used, which had the added advantage of boosting the sales of that periodical. Often there was no music for such songs. Captain Gertsch decided to harmonize the melodies for brass instruments. This was done on the Friday, learned in practice the next day and played out on Sunday. To accomplish the difficult task the Captain took a series of studies on harmony.

In 1908 this enterprising musician, by then an Adjutant, was appointed to start a Music Department at the Territorial Headquarters in Bern. His first task was to visit the seventy bands in Switzerland to tune the instruments. A year later the Adjutant spent a month in the Music Editorial Department in London, after which he returned to prepare for publication the Swiss tunes not included in the Band Tune Book.

Lieut.-Colonel Gertsch, who has been called the ' Slater of Switzerland ', at the age of eighty-five attended events in Bern during the visit of the International Staff Band in 1954. He remembered earlier campaigns of the band and what it had done to encourage the musical sections of Switzerland. The Colonel was promoted to Glory in February, 1960.

This Swiss pioneer was succeeded in charge of the Music Department by Lieut.-Colonel Emil Nigg. During the period of his responsibility he combined the Band Tune Book, published in England, and the Swiss Tune Book. This met a greater need than ever before. He also issued a song book with music.

Courses for Bandmasters were arranged on a divisional level, so that men could meet for week-ends and be instructed in conducting and the theory of music. Examinations were held and a course was introduced which bandsmen were expected to complete before being appointed Bandmasters. This arrangement was necessary and useful, and the standard of the bands improved. Instructional material was obtained from England and translated into German.

The first band congress was held in Zürich in 1908, since when, at intervals, the musicians of the territory have met to share instruction and fellowship and to take part in united festivals.

But what of today? A visit to an Ascension Day gathering in Zürich answers that question, for in the mammoth procession which marches through the city streets may be seen and heard some excellent representative bands.

Without doubt one of the best playing bands is that of Basle 1, which was formed in 1889. This was led for many years by Bandmaster Paul Schiffman, who, playing his cornet at the head of the march in real Appleby and Twitchin style, was a familiar figure in that frontier city.

Another band demanding attention is Zürich Central, which, like that at Basle, has campaigned in other continental territories and in England. In 1928 the two corps then in operation in the city were combined and the present band was formed.

In French Switzerland, too, there are worthy musical forces. The Jura Mountains Divisional Band is unique. It came into being through the inspiration of Bandmaster Leon Gagnebin, of La Chaux-de-Fonds. Anxious to do something for the many small bands in the mountain regions of the Neuchâtel Division, he planned to group all the bands into one as a divisional band.

This collective band was to officiate once or twice a year at special festivals or at Ascensiontide annual congress meetings. His aim was to stimulate the small bands, which often had very limited possibilities, and to revive the contact between the men which had been broken for some time.

In August, 1945, on the occasion of a divisional rally, the Bandmaster submitted his plan to the Divisional Commander, who was quite agreeable to the proposal. The Bandmasters, and later the bandsmen, were informed of the project and this was received with enthusiasm, especially by the younger comrades.

In the September of that year, the divisional band, numbering forty-five, made its first public appearance.

G

Much progress has since been registered. There are demands by many corps for the band's contribution and it has paid visits to France.

But, as would be expected, Swiss musicians are by no means confined to brass instruments. The guitar brigades are a feature, and to hear the cadets of the training college blend their voices in clear harmonies whilst accompanying themselves on their stringed instruments is a joyful experience.

The Field Secretary, Lieut.-Colonel Herbert Silfverberg, is at present in charge of musical affairs in Switzerland, having succeeded Colonel Walter Zahnd, who, too, has rendered appreciated service over a number of years in the interests of musicians of the territory.

CHAPTER THIRTEEN

SKIRTING THE SKAGERRAK

Norway

THE young officer looked at the man across the table and coveted him for The Salvation Army. Then he prayed: 'Lord, make Østby unhappy. Make him so unhappy that in humility he will come to Thy Cross and find what the world cannot bestow—peace and salvation.' Østby was converted eight days later.

Klaus Østby was a brilliant musician, a military bandsman at that time. He had been a pupil of Edvard Grieg, the great Norwegian composer, and something of the master's finesse had descended upon him. 'What a power he could be for Salvation Army music!' thought the pioneer officer in Oslo. That is why Østby had been invited to coffee. That led to his conversion.

The young musician was quickly sworn-in as a soldier of the Oslo I Corps and began the work which made his name an honoured one throughout the Army world. He made a lasting impression upon Army music in Scandinavia.

It is fitting that this survey of Salvation Army music-making in northern Europe should begin with a brief sketch of one who has been called 'The Father of Salvation Army Music in Scandinavia'.

Army work began in Norway on January 22, 1888. The first hall was in the Grønland district of Oslo and the centre subsequently became known as the Oslo I Corps. It was natural that the first Salvation Army band in the territory should be formed there.

With the rapid growth of the Army arose the need for new centres to be opened in other parts of the city. Oslo II and III Corps came into being and a number of soldiers from Oslo I were transferred to the new openings, among them a few bandsmen. The band at Oslo I was formed in December, 1888, and that at Oslo III a month later. Both these sections have been in existence ever since and are among Norway's best-known bands. The last named, together with Bergen I, has for many years been noted for its musical excellence, and with numerous tours beyond the limits of Norway has made many friends in other territories.

The first bandsman in Norway was Henry Tandberg, who received his commission in 1888. He became an officer a year later and was promoted to Glory, as a retired Colonel, in 1959. This pioneer musician maintained his interest in the bandsmen of the territory and made a considerable contribution to the song-writing history of Norway.

Another musical pioneer was Lieut.-Colonel Ole Utgaard, promoted to Glory in 1954. In his early days he was known as 'The Trumpeter of The Salvation Army' in his native land. He was a member of the first Territorial Staff Band in Norway and was also Music Inspector for some time. His son was Bandmaster at Oslo III before taking up an appointment in Africa.

*   *   *

In September, 1890, a Music Department was formed at Territorial Headquarters with Klaus Østby in charge. His task was to train and encourage the ever-developing forces and this he continued to do until 1904, when he was transferred to Sweden to become Head of the Music Department in that territory, an appointment he held until his retirement in 1930.

Lieut.-Colonel Østby was promoted to Glory from a retired officers' residence in Sweden on April 27, 1945, and his body was brought home to Oslo for burial. In 1959 the then Territorial Commander for Norway, Commissioner Emanuel Sundin, unveiled a memorial stone over Østby's grave, raised by the bandsmen of Scandinavia. His Majesty King Haakon of Norway honoured Østby in his lifetime by awarding him the King's Medal of Merit for his work for Christian music.

When Klaus Østby was appointed to Sweden Staff-Captain Kristoffersen, one of two singing brothers who sang at the International Congress in 1904, took charge of the Music Department, which did not continue for long. After a lapse of some years the department was re-formed in 1949 with Major (later Lieut.-Colonel) Haakon Dahlstrøm as its director. When he sailed, in 1951, to take up an appointment on the Gold Coast (now Ghana), Major Odd Telefsen succeeded him. Upon his return from Africa some time afterward Lieut.-Colonel Dahlstrøm again assumed control of musical affairs until the beginning of a further term of service in Africa.

One of Østby's first duties when appointed to the Music Department in 1890 was to form a Staff Band, for which he was required to compose and arrange music. The Norwegian Staff Band was a travelling unit. The men were 'signed on' for twelve months, at the end of which period they were given the option of renewing their membership or resigning. Their journeyings took them to distant parts of the widely scattered territory and they would return to Oslo each year in time for annual Congress gatherings.

*   *   *

It is probably due to the conditions of service and the lengthy periods away from the centre that there have been several staff bands during Norway's musical history. It would appear that each band was allowed to be well and truly buried before a successor was brought into being.

In 1909, some years after the passing of the band of which Lieut.-Colonel Østby was the Bandmaster, a second Staff Band was formed under the conductorship of Captain (later Commissioner) Tobias Ögrim. There were fourteen players, and in the same year the band was honoured by being permitted to play to King Haakon. A third band was introduced in 1922 with Captain (later Lieut.-Colonel) Samuel Toft as Bandmaster. Other former Staff Bandmasters include Brigadier Martin Fagerli, Lieut.-Colonel Dahlstrøm and Captain Odd Utgaard. There has not been a territorial Staff Band since 1935.

The present Territorial Commander for Norway, Commissioner Kaare Westergaard, is a former member of the Staff Band, he having travelled with this group for a year as a boy of sixteen. Three of his brothers were also members.

*   *   *

Among other outstanding names in Norwegian Salvation Army musical history is that of Bandmaster Mads Hansen, of Hønefoss, who created something of a record among Scandinavian Salvationists when he relinquished the baton after serving in that capacity for fifty-six years.

There is no brass band cult in Norway. Many had not heard such music until becoming Salvationists. In spite of this the thirty-five bands in the country, averaging some ten players apiece, are made up of keen musicians and seek to maintain a good standard of efficiency. Because of geographical peculiarities, it is difficult for the bandsmen to gather for massed events in the capital city. Some journeys would take three days and nights by boat. To travel from Oslo to the most distant point, Kirkenes, takes practically the same time as a journey to the United States of America.

Despite these difficulties it has been known for the bandsmen to gather at Oslo and Bergen to benefit from the instruction and appreciated interest of some international musical personality.

The music played by Norwegian bandsmen is mainly from the brass band journals issued from London and from the Swedish Band Journal, which is arranged for a few instruments.

In common with other Scandinavian territories, string bands are a feature, the players, singing whilst manipulating the instruments, becoming songster brigades with a difference. In recent years the piano-accordion has become a rival of the guitar, but the stringed instrument is still the first choice.

Iceland

ONE of the most cosmopolitan Army bands in Scandinavia at one time was that which functioned in Iceland when the island constituted a division of the British Territory. In 1929 a Scottish visitor was impressed by the value of Army work there but felt that the addition of a brass band would enhance the effectiveness of the witness. As the result of his forwarding a cheque for £100 for instruments, a band was formed at Reykjavik, with the Divisional Secretary, Captain (later Colonel) Frederick Holland, as Bandmaster. British, Danish, Faroese and Icelandic Salvationists were among the bandsmen.

Ensign (later Lieut.-Colonel) Reginald Dumpleton, who heard the band in its early stages, reported: ' I was accompanying Commissioner Richard Wilson, who conducted Congress meetings. After tossing about on the stormy seas of the North Atlantic, we steamed into Reykjavik harbour at midnight. The band was on the quayside and the melody which came over the waters was " Old soldiers never die ".'

Denmark

'IN the front was the band, consisting of one single cornet and a violin, followed by the officers and hundreds of friends and comrades who took part in the singing.' So reported the *Krigsråbet* (the Danish *War Cry*) on a march carried out by the Salvationists of Denmark during an outing from Copenhagen to Køge in 1889.

The first reference to Army music in Denmark, however, had appeared in the same periodical a year before when Captain Fahlesom, himself a musician of note, wrote: ' Last Sunday we had a grand march out to the Grusgraven. The ranks numbered 235 and there was lilting music and song, both on the march there and back, as well as in the meeting itself.'

Toward the end of 1890 an English officer, Captain Stagg, a gifted musician, arrived in Copenhagen. His responsibilities included the training of a brass band. There were only four bandsmen to train, but in response to a personal appeal from the then Territorial Commander three more volunteered, and by April, 1891, the seven men had progressed with their musical studies sufficiently well to leave for their first tour of Denmark.

That started something. ' Why cannot every corps have its own band?' asked the Territorial Commander. Several centres took up the challenge. A new interest in music was aroused and here and there attempts were made to form groups of instrumentalists.

When Captain Stagg farewelled for Australia the following summer, Lieutenant Peter E. Andersen, who had been a member of the band from its inception, was promoted to the rank of Captain and appointed Bandmaster.

Among those who have influenced Salvation Army music in Denmark, Staff-Captain Andersen, as he became, must be given first place, for he was the pioneer in that territory. Under his leadership the Danish Territorial Staff Band journeyed throughout the land and became well known for its splendid music. Later, when he became blind, he taught himself to read and to transmit music and other signs by Braille, and as a divisional band instructor was able to continue with his teaching for a number of years.

The first Staff Band ceased to exist in 1895. Nearly thirty years later its successor was formed with Captain Sigvald Jensen as Bandmaster. Lieut.-Commissioner Reinert Gundersen was the Territorial Commander at the time and it was largely due to his interest that the band was re-formed. He had been Leader of the Staff Band in Buenos Aires.

This new band of fourteen players lasted for some years, travelled extensively within the territory and, under the leadership of Captain Harold Jensen, visited England in 1932. There was also a headquarters band for some time, with Brigadier (later Colonel) Oscar Bandsberg as Bandmaster.

* * *

As with other Scandinavian countries Denmark has no tradition of brass band activity, but valiant attempts have been made over the years to keep the spark of enthusiasm alight. Copenhagen Temple Band has over seventy years of unbroken service to its credit.

The name of Bandmaster Henry Kragh Jensen has been associated with this section for many years, but his interests have not been confined to this one band. He also serves as Territorial Bandmaster, thus having the oversight of the music of the territory, and as director of the annual music camp he has done much to inspire the bandsmen of tomorrow. In 1962 Bandmaster Kragh Jensen was admitted to the Order of the Founder.

The Salvationists of Copenhagen are also proud of Gartnergade Band which, led by Bandmaster Henning Schou Larsen, attains a high standard of efficiency.

It is natural that in many corps where there is no brass band the string band should enjoy great popularity. Composed largely of guitars, but sometimes accompanied by violins and, of course, piano, the string band is mostly used for supporting and leading the congregational singing.

CHAPTER FOURTEEN

BOTH SIDES OF THE BALTIC

Sweden

THE first Salvation Army meeting in Sweden was held in a Stockholm theatre on December 28, 1882. A report stated: ' Suddenly there was rising noise in the hall and everybody's eyes were directed to the stage, on which three women and two men appeared, dressed in unusual and strange uniform. They formed a group around the yellow, red and blue flag, which was carried by the leader of the group, Major Hanna Ouchterlony, and then fell on their knees in silent prayer.

' The congregation witnessed the opening in perfect silence and with high-pitched expectation. After a few minutes the praying Salvationists rose to their feet and commenced their first battle in the service of The Salvation Army in Sweden.

' " We're bound for the land of the pure and the holy " was the first song. When the chorus, " Will you go? ", was reached, one could see that many of the listeners no longer looked upon the Salvationists as strangers, but had realized the sincerity of these people. The eyes of many were filled with tears. This was the old religion in a new and unusual style, but at the same time proclaimed with no uncertain sound and with intensity of power.'

The sole accompaniment on that historic occasion was provided on a guitar by Lieutenant Jenny Swenson, appointed to assist Major Ouchterlony in pioneering the work.

Four years before, twenty-two-year-old Bramwell Booth, ordered by his doctor to take a rest from his arduous responsibilities in London, was invited to spend some months in the home of Mr. and Mrs. Billups, outside Varnamo. The Billups, from Cardiff, had become great friends of William and Catherine Booth and their family, and when, in 1876, it was decided to build a railway that would pass through the Swedish town, Mr. Billups, an engineer, had been given the contract.

In the household of his hosts Bramwell Booth conducted family prayers, to which neighbours and friends were invited. These gatherings grew into revival and holiness meetings, and when the home became inadequate the waiting-room of the unfinished railway station was used.

Attending the meetings, and impressed especially by the holiness preaching of the English visitor, was Miss Ouchterlony, the forty-year-old proprietor of a local bookshop. A gifted woman, in whose ancestry was French and Scottish blood, she had been educated in Helsingfors (Finland) and Stockholm, where she had moved in high school circles and was well known for her excellent dancing. Upon conversion she commenced a Sunday-school in her home, and invited colporteurs and other lay preachers to speak at cottage meetings held there.

Hanna Ouchterlony had been a professing Christian for three years when she first met Bramwell Booth and heard of the Movement his father had founded. Upon his return to London, the young Chief of the Staff corresponded with Miss Ouchterlony with regard to starting Salvation Army work in Sweden, and in January, 1881, she was invited to be a guest in the Booths' home.

During the five months she spent in London, Hanna was deeply stirred by all she saw and heard, and returned to Sweden wearing an Army brooch. Soon afterward, at the summer home of Christian friends, she met Jenny Swenson, an attractive girl, an accomplished musician with a beautiful singing voice—but with no religious persuasion.

The elder woman's attempts to interest the girl in her own new discovery, The Salvation Army, were futile, until one day Hanna Ouchterlony, in a meeting in which she herself spoke on the work of the Holy Spirit, had the joy of leading Jenny to Christ.

The pioneer's first objective had been won. With the conversion of this most acceptable singer and guitarist she felt sure that great things could be accomplished for the Kingdom of God. The two spent many hours singing the new Army songs, translated into Swedish by Fredrik Engelke, a schoolmaster and song writer. Hanna continued to fire her convert with enthusiasm for the Army's work, as she had seen it in England. Early in 1882, their holiday over, the friends left for their respective homes.

In May of that year Hanna Ouchterlony was invited to attend the opening of the Clapton Congress Hall and the National Training Barracks, as the future International Training Home was called. She intended to stay for two weeks but remained for seven months. At the end of June, Jenny Swenson, in Göteborg, received a telegram: 'Have spoken to Emma Booth about you. Come.'

Without hesitation Jenny left for England and, with her Spanish guitar, arrived in London, the first Swedish cadet to be trained for officership. Jenny's musical gifts were utilized to the full. Her guitar often accompanied Emma Booth's vocal solos and she herself sang many of those early-day thrilling songs, for the first time. Herbert Booth had just returned from helping pioneer the work in France and his latest compositions, many written originally in the French language, were passed on to the young Swedish 'nightingale' even before they were published.

A great venture of faith at that time was to have the first Swedish Army song book printed, the contents being translated from the English. The work had not yet begun in that country! The book contained forty-four songs and twelve choruses.

At a great public meeting held in London's Exeter Hall on November 28, 1882, Major Ouchterlony and Lieutenant Swenson, with three other officers, were commissioned to 'open fire' in Sweden. Their luggage included a bagful of Swedish song books. Throughout the voyage Jenny Swenson guarded her precious guitar, which today has an honoured place at the Territorial Headquarters in Stockholm.

The guitar was, therefore, the pioneer instrument in Army warfare in Sweden and, in the skilful hands of twenty-two-year-old Lieutenant Swenson, set a pattern for service that has been maintained with a high standard of efficiency throughout the years. Jenny Swenson can rightly be acclaimed as 'the mother of Army music in Sweden'.

Following the first momentous Salvation Army meeting in Stockholm, the people of the city became strongly opposed to the Salvationists. All suitable halls were closed to them and they had no other choice but to hold meetings in the backyards of the poorer areas. An old brewery cart served as a platform, and mounted on this unsteady vehicle Major Ouchterlony led her brave handful of followers into battle.

Lieutenant Swenson played the guitar, and when her fingers became stiff with the severe cold, the song continued with hand clapping and a march round, in which the bystanders took part. But people liked the songs and the happy brand of religion. Many of them knelt at wooden boxes to seek salvation. Converts were won, soldiers were recruited, and the work prospered.

It was natural that the second-in-command should become responsible for the development of musical affairs in the territory. String bands and brass ensembles were soon formed at various corps, and the converts were encouraged to try their hand at song-writing and composition.

Among those who set to work writing material in the Scandinavian idiom were Hanna Andersson, Gustaf Blom, Emanuel Hellberg, Johan Ögrim, August Storm, Johan August Tavaststjerna, Sven Nilson, Karl Larsson, Theodor Janson, Ellen Blomkvist-Bergh, Annie Hartelius and John Appelberg.

Brass bands, as such, did not come immediately, and little is known of the local development during the formative years. In 1888 there were eighty bandsmen reported on the statistical returns, but this figure could have referred to string band members, seeing that, two years later, Commissioner Hugh Whatmore, then a Major, claimed to be the ' only Salvation Army bandsman in Sweden '.

In that same year (1888) a Music Department was formed to promote the interests of brass and string bands. One of its main functions was to supply songs and musical arrangements, thus putting the Army authorities in a position to control the use of the music employed. The first head of the department was Major Otto Lundahl, a military musician, skilful cornetist and able violinist. A Territorial Staff Band was also inaugurated, with the Major as Bandmaster, and this toured the country to inspire the local music-makers.

Major Lundahl entered upon his duties with dedicated enthusiasm. In 1889 there were ninety-three bandsmen in Sweden. Ten years later 558 bandsmen were playing in eighty bands. This success was in no small measure due to the labours of the territory's first music head.

When, because of indifferent health, Major Lundahl was pensioned in 1904, Major (later Lieut.-Colonel) Klaus Østby was transferred from Norway to take his place. He controlled musical affairs in Sweden for twenty-six years and, upon his retirement, was succeeded by Major Gustaf Wallteng, whose untimely death in 1935 robbed the Army of a gifted and promising officer. Brigadier Kristian M. Fristrup, a Danish-born internationally known composer who had served in the U.S.A. for some years, was then appointed and operated in that capacity for seven years.

In 1942 Lieut.-Colonel Paul Anefelt took charge of the Music Department and built solidly on the sound foundations laid by his famous predecessors. Particularly did the string bands make considerable progress in his tenure of office.

*   *   *

Although Swedish composers have not been numerous, the quality of their work has always commanded interest and respect. Lieut.-Colonel Østby set an excellent standard and has worthy successors in such writers as Gunnar Blomberg, Erik Frödin, Elias Hedin, Folke Andersson, Bertil Andersson and Gustav Kjellgren.

Sweden's most illustrious musical son, without a doubt, was Erik Leidzén. Although this noted composer left his native land for the U.S.A. in 1915, the Swedish Salvationists always claimed him as their own and are rightly proud of his accomplishments.

In 1955 Erik Leidzén returned to Sweden for the first time in twenty-one years. As the guest conductor with Tranås Band, he appeared at the annual congress events led by General and Mrs.

Wilfred Kitching and was fervently welcomed home. He had already spent every afternoon and evening for two weeks with Tranås Band— that time being taken up with intensive rehearsal, lectures and visits to hospitals and prisons—and in Stockholm he led the band in the non-stop events.

The traditional congress Saturday-midnight festival in the concert hall of the Royal Music Academy was a never-to-be-forgotten occasion. As he addressed the audience, Erik was in reminiscent mood. For in that city he had been born—some months after his officer-father's promotion to Glory. In that same academy he had studied music and in the gallery he had sat for many an hour to hear the orchestra, a full score open in his hand as he followed the music.

*   *   *

The story of Tranås Band is one of the most captivating in Salvation Army musical history. The town is a small trading community situated in the south of central Sweden. Although for many years there has been a corps there and a group of instrumentalists to assist with the meetings, banding was not taken seriously until the visit of Chalk Farm Band in 1930. Bandmaster Gunnar Borg says: ' Band-master Punchard and his men showed us what an Army band could look like and the kind of sound it could make.' Thus fired with a new vision of possibilities, the youthful leader began to train his band along British lines, teaching his men slowly but surely the rudiments of brass band technique.

This went on through the years, even during the Second World War, when Sweden had little contact with the rest of the Army in Europe. When Colonel Bramwell Coles, then Head of the Inter-national Music Editorial Department, visited Sweden in the interests of the musicians of that territory in 1946 he heard Tranås Band for the first time. Returning to England, he was loud in its praise and his high recommendation resulted in this little-known band visiting the British Territory the following Easter.

The band has travelled extensively on the continent of Europe, in the U.S.A. and in Canada since that day, and has remained for nearly twenty years the outstanding band of Sweden, representing the brass bands of the territory at the Centenary Celebrations in London.

Tranås is not the territory's only well-known band, however; many others have a long record of faithful and efficient service, among them Stockholm Temple, Stockholm 2, 3, 6 and 7, Malmö, Jönköping Göteborg 1, 2 and 5, and Huskvarna.

With all the developments of technique evidenced by brass bands in Sweden in recent years—the appointment of young musical students to lead corps sections has had a lot to do with this move forward—the established string bands are not being overlooked. They still have their place. The rhythmic songs with the guitar background maintain their effectiveness and nowhere is this evidenced more than in the prayer meetings, in which a group of vocalists, with their stringed instruments, gather around the Mercy Seat to help a soul into the Kingdom. These smartly dressed, musically sensitive, intensely devoted Salvationists are worthy successors of Jenny Swenson. The Norrköping String Band also visited London for the Centenary Celebrations.

Finland

THERE is a Finnish word, *sisu*, for which, it is said, there is no English equivalent. One could translate it as meaning ' courage ', ' grit ', ' perseverance ', or ' determined will ' and still not have alighted on the true interpretation. But a visitor does not need to be in Finland very long to experience a deep understanding of this national characteristic, revealed in the people and particularly in the Salvationists.

In Finland every sixteenth man of military age is an invalid, every seventeenth married woman a widow and every twenty-fourth child a war orphan. Such figures will reveal the acute manpower shortage of Finnish Salvationists and something of the struggle the Army has had throughout its history to maintain an effective witness.

While singing was a necessary part of the beginning in this northern territory—the work was commenced by Hedvig von Haartman in 1889—it was some time before brass instruments were introduced. The first band was established at Helsinki 4 Corps in 1892 and a year later Helsinki Temple followed the example.

There was at that time a wave of enthusiasm concerning this mode of evangelical expression. In August, 1896, the Finnish *War Cry* declared: ' As time goes by we shall have a band at every large corps in Finland.' A year later there were ten bands in action.

That early-day optimism was, however, only partly realized. Unlike in Sweden and Norway, it has always been comparatively difficult to gain men soldiers in Finland. Because of this there has been a lack of suitable leaders. The wars, too, have taken their toll of what few men Salvationists there were.

In addition to the early corps bands, a headquarters combination was formed in 1899. Fifteen years later a Staff Band was established, but did not last very long. In 1933 another headquarters instrumental group was formed and this, a year later, was augmented and named the Territorial Staff Band. The Bandmaster was Captain Carstens Clausen, a Danish officer.

From time to time bands from other countries have visited Finland

and in 1934 Chalk Farm Band became the first British section to campaign there. Twenty-six years later Croydon Citadel Band toured the territory, travelling farther north than any other British band and extending its journeyings to within twenty miles of the Russian border. Edinburgh Gorgie visited the country in 1963. Each occasion created considerable interest and inspired the local comrades.

Over the years Finnish bands have visited neighbouring territories. Helsinki 4 Band has the unique record of being the only Salvation Army band to play in Russia. This was in 1917, when Army work was operating successfully from Petrograd, now Leningrad.

Instruments used in Finland have generally been of the continental type with cylinder valves. The Helsinki Temple Band, which has been the leading section for many years, has been using the British type of instrument since 1935.

There are some sixty bandsmen in Finland. These are mostly scattered in small groups over the territory, with larger companies here and there. At Rauma the band was re-formed after the war and soon boasted of eighteen players. Because no one was able to lead them they sought the help of a retired musician in the town. He attended the practices, was inspired by the men—and the meetings— sought Christ and became a Salvationist. Later, as Bandmaster Fabian Nyman, he was respected for the excellent service he gave until his promotion to Glory in 1955.

Finland has been fortunate to possess officers with sufficient musical ability to lend much-appreciated help in leading or playing in the bands. Lieut.-Colonel Per-Erik Wahlström instructed and conducted the Helsinki Temple Band when he was the Divisional Commander in that city. His younger brother, Brigadier Jarl, has also worked hard on behalf of the musicians of his country. During his period as Territorial Young People's Secretary he also had charge of the musical affairs of the territory and was a source of inspiration to the bandsmen.

Although the guitar is not really the national instrument, it is widely used in Christian denominations and has the advantage of not being unduly difficult to learn. Every corps has its string band, the members accompanying their own singing with guitars and perhaps a violin or two and a piano-accordion.

A Territorial Commander of Finland once reminded his people at congress time that they were not 'parade-ground but battle-front soldiers'. Something of that sturdy quality—'sisu' if you like—is evident in the faithful minority comprising Salvationist music-makers on the 'outer rim' of Army activity in Europe.

CHAPTER FIFTEEN

AFRICAN VARIETY

South Africa

ELEVEN days before Christmas, 1882, Captain Francis Simmonds and Captain Rose Clapham were married by William Booth at Clapton Congress Hall, of which corps the bridegroom was in charge. Shortly afterward the couple sailed to pioneer Army work in South Africa, arriving at Cape Town on Saturday, February 24, 1883. With them was Lieutenant Alice Teager.

After a Sunday's meetings in a drill hall, the Salvationists rented an old store in Loop Street. When the building was being altered to suit their needs they raised the question of what length the Penitent-form should be. Mrs. Simmonds urged that it should be made the entire width of the platform. The first seekers were the four workmen who had placed it in position. The next evening, Sunday, 112 seekers knelt there! What faith! And what reward!

Although no specific evidence is to hand, it is apparent that musical support was given to those first momentous meetings, for it is recorded that the 'respectable roughs' who attended the first gatherings persisted in singing songs of their own choosing while the Salvationists persevered with their own 'revival hymns'.

The brass bands of the South Africa Territory have never been numerous. They have depended to a large extent upon overseas Salvationists who, because of employment or appointment as Army officers, have resided in the vicinity. In places like Cape Town, Johannesburg, Salt River, Port Elizabeth, Kroonstad and Kenilworth bands have attained renown. Johannesburg City, under the skilled training of Bandmaster Frank Rawbone, acquired world-wide reputation. The Bandmaster, who had charge of Chalk Farm Band before taking up a business appointment in South Africa in 1952, brought this section to a high standard of efficiency and, in 1954, it became the first Salvation Army band to broadcast in South Africa.

The first band in the territory was that of Cape Town 1.

Another band with a fascinating history is that of Salt River. The corps was opened in 1905 when a new railway works in the area had caused this suburb of Cape Town to expand and become noticed.

Concerning the opening, the editor of the South African *War Cry* of that era, Colonel Robert Sandall, reported: 'The Cape Town 1 Band very kindly came along to give the newly constituted corps a good send-off and created quite a sensation as it marched and played through the streets.'

Three months later, in August, 1905, *The War Cry* report read:

> The performance of the Salt River Band was unique. Some fourteen lads, who had formerly formed a football club and had lately, with their leader, sought salvation, were lined up in a body on the platform with faces a mixture of suppressed merriment and a little, very little, shyness. ' One-two-three-four ', off they go. There was, at first, considerable wheezing and puffing, but soon the tune was clearly distinguishable, and we had ' Onward, Christian soldiers' with bass runs, after-beats and all complete, produced from tissue-paper and combs. We hope one day to see this talent lined up behind some tip-top brass instruments of Our Own Make, and then things will hum.

It was four years before the editor's hopes were realized but, once formed, the band continued to function continuously throughout the following years.

Lieut.-Colonel Bernard McCarthy, of International Headquarters, who served as Editor-in-Chief in South Africa for five years, wrote for *The Musician*, in September, 1955: ' The present-day band of some nineteen players is under the leadership of Bandmaster Jack Siebrits, who comes from a Salvationist family long honoured in Army history in South Africa. His grandfather, the late Envoy Siebrits, was a great tower of strength to the corps at Paarl, in one of the loveliest of the Cape towns. The Bandmaster's father was Lieut.-Colonel Bartholomew J. Siebrits, known to many officers and comrades in the British Territory—and indeed, in other lands, for he was an international auditor for a number of years.'

The Colonel was in fact an earlier Bandmaster at Salt River and during his period of leadership a complete set of silver-plated instruments was procured. Pretoria Band does not forget that when Senior-Major Allister Smith was the Bandmaster a new set of instruments was obtained at that corps.

Although it is not easy to maintain the musical activity in South Africa today, the European bands are doing their best to encourage their African comrades in their music-making and assisting them in conveying the gospel where it is needed.

A visit by Cape Town Citadel Band to Langa Native Township, some ten miles outside the city, is typical of this ministry. The bandsmen travelled in cars, for it would have been almost impossible to reach the location any other way. An open-air meeting, led by an African officer, was in progress when the men arrived and the interested crowd quickly thickened when the instrumentalists took up their positions on the grass verge with their comrades. A trumpet was providing accompaniment to the singing, but this rapidly went

The Musical Department
in 1883
Richard Slater, Fred Fry
and Henry Hill

Consett Band

The Fry family
of
Salisbury

Captain and Mrs. Case

and daughters, Portsmouth, 1880

The first photograph of the International Staff Band

' under cover ' when the more efficient band from Cape Town put in an appearance!

When the Divisional Commander started his short address he suffered a rude interruption. Speeding around the corner, with radio antenna swinging in a wide arc, the green van of the mobile police screeched against the kerb-edge. As it pulled to a halt just beyond the open-air stand, the majority of the congregation hurled themselves across to see what was going on. It was a police raid on gamblers. There was a chase and the car eventually made its triumphant departure with a prisoner or two. Stolidly the congregation returned. A woman sought salvation at the drum-head.

When William Booth visited South Africa in 1908, Kroonstad Band was chosen to accompany him on his campaign in the Orange Free State and Natal. While the Founder was inspecting the social farm at Durban, the band, having secured the services of a photographer, formed up on the front steps, thus blocking the exit. The band opened up to allow William Booth to pass, but a chair was in readiness beside Bandmaster John Harley, and the Founder was persuaded to sit for a few minutes while the photographer, who was also ready, took the photo. It is claimed that this was the only time General William Booth posed for a photograph with a band.

The incident of the photograph has been recalled by the Bandmaster of those days, who later became the Corps Sergeant-Major. He also remembered that before the Founder went on board ship at Durban, he took leave of the bandsmen, thanking them for their services and promising them a photograph of himself. In due course the photograph arrived, on which, in the General's own bold handwriting, was written: ' Play your music to the glory of God, the encouragement of your comrades and the salvation of the world—William Booth.' The photograph has an honoured place in the band-room at Kroonstad as a memento of that happy occasion.

There are a few national bands in South Africa. The Johannesburg African Central Band numbers more than thirty players. Being near Territorial Headquarters, this group often receives help from overseas officers stationed there. Other notable African bands include those of Sydney Road and Somtsea Road in Durban, and that of the Pietermaritzburg African Corps.

A great champion of African bands is Brigadier Ephraim Zulu, a blood relation of Cetewayo and Dingaan, the Zululand rulers whose names made news during the middle nineteenth century. He says: ' During my years of officership I have seen the African bands grow from the mere " blasting " stage to real musicianship. This reflects great credit on the corps officers concerned who, in many cases, have been both trainers and bandmasters, especially in the smaller corps.'

St. Helena

A NOTED naval base in South Africa in the 1880s was Simonstown. A corps there was opened by Mrs. Major Simmonds, who, with her husband, had commenced Army operations in the territory. A few weeks after, when she had moved on to undertake another pioneering activity, a British battleship, H.M.S. *Opal*, put into the bay. Among the sailors who came ashore and attended the meetings was Mrs. Simmond's younger brother. He, with fourteen of his shipmates, knelt at the Mercy Seat. A day or two later they sailed for St. Helena, lonely island of historical significance.

They arrived on May 5, 1884, and on their first night held an open-air meeting in Salvation Army style. An interested friend opened his home for cottage meetings and before the ship continued its journey, five days later, fifty-nine souls had been won. Eight months after, when a Salvationist soldier landed there with his regiment, meetings were being held all over the island, with many of the converts sworn-in as fighting Salvationists. Officers were appointed a year later.

The earliest editions of *The Bandsman and Songster* (1907 and 1908) reported musical activities on St. Helena, reference being made to Bandmaster Miller whose enthusiasm and magnetic personality were qualities that helped to maintain a band in the face of many difficulties.

In 1960 a British Director of Education, after a visit to the island, reported that he found ' a thriving Salvation Army band', and went on to comment that this group and other instrumental aggregations ' suffer badly from the ancient patched instruments they are forced, by economic circumstances, to use '.

' After listening to the astonishing quality of tone produced by the Salvation Army band,' he said, ' I examined some of the instruments and marvelled that notes could be produced on them at all, leave alone a rich, warm tone. Battered and worn, valve tops missing, a trombone almost home-built, instruments fit mainly for the scrap heap—yet they produced true harmony when played by their devoted owners.'

This report underlines one of the great problems of Salvation Army missionary music-making.

Nigeria

IN the April 14, 1923, issue of *The Bandsman, Local Officer and Songster* a report was published of West Africa's first band—at Lagos. Army work had commenced there three years before and Captain da Costa,

' the youngest of the West African officers ', had taken the initiative in introducing the playing of brass instruments.

That banding in these parts has had rather a chequered career is not surprising when one realizes that native music-making has followed another pattern. There is no doubt, however, that the brass band idiom has appealed to Salvationists in West Africa and a resurgence has taken place from time to time.

The last such was in 1950 when two British bandsmen working in Lagos—Bandsman Harry Batten, of Exeter Temple, and Deputy-Bandmaster Alfred Lock, of East Dulwich, London—with infinite patience and much hard work succeeded in forming a well-balanced combination.

Harry Batten was appointed Bandmaster and built up a band of enthusiastic Africans, augmented from time to time by British service-men and other western Salvationists employed in the locality. He became greatly loved by his comrades and well respected by his business associates. At the time of his death as the result of a motor accident in 1962 he held the appointment of chief pharmacist to the West Regional Government of Nigeria. The Bandmaster was due to retire from his employment in six months' time and had planned to remain in the country to serve the people to whom he had endeared himself.

Ghana

A GREAT champion of the brass band cause in West Africa was Lieut.-Colonel William Fleming. The Colonel became well known as a British red shield officer in the Middle East during the Second World War and played a leading part in forming bands at various clubs in that area. Later he became Training Principal and Divisional Commander in Lagos and continued his enthusiastic work for the young African musicians.

With emergence of self-government in West Africa and the dividing of Salvation Army work, Lieut.-Colonel Fleming became the first Officer Commanding for Ghana. His many friends in the British Territory responded to his appeals and instruments and uniforms were generously donated. Begoro Band delights to march long distances resplendent in tunics that once belonged to Chalk Farm, and this despite the tiring excessive heat!

In this town, which in addition to a good corps can also boast of an Army primary school, middle school, clinic, five-bed maternity ward and an ambulance attached to the clinic, there is an efficient timbrel brigade.

The first music camp in West Africa was held at Asamankese,

Ghana, in 1960. Eight bandsmen travelled 150 miles to be present and, although they had no instruments at their corps, returned determined to save money to buy some. At the close of the camp two students set merrily off to walk twenty miles through the bush to their homes.

Following the success of this venture Ghana's first bandsmen's councils were held in 1962.

The largest band in Ghana is that at Accra, which assisted General Frederick Coutts in a Sunday morning radio service during his African tour of 1964.

Congo

APPOINTED by General Edward J. Higgins to pioneer Army work in the Congo, Adjutant and Mrs. Henri Becquet, Belgian officers, sailed up the River Congo in September, 1934, to begin operations in Léopoldville. At the first open-air meeting Mrs. Becquet sang a song which her husband accompanied on the violin. In the first indoor meeting the organ, concertina, violin and guitar were used.

The hundreds of Africans present were greatly interested; never before had they seen such a variety of instruments used in a religious gathering. Many of them were heathen and were accustomed to hearing the wild tamtam of drums accompanying native dances.

As the work progressed with phenomenal rapidity each corps and outpost secured its own drum, a significant conversion from the secular to the sacred! Flute bands began to appear, chiefly in the bush. These instruments were either made out of branches of pawpaw trees or fashioned from a hollow bamboo.

The drums were made of antelope skin and wood and were required to be warmed up by the fire before meetings started. The drumstick was an ordinary stick on which was fixed a lump of natural gum or rubber.

With instruments provided by International Headquarters, a brass band was formed in Léopoldville in 1938 and soon numbered twelve. The difficult work of training the bandsmen was first tackled by Captain Frédéric Beney, who later became the first officer to be stationed in the thriving new centre of Brazzaville, Equatorial Africa. The Captain's promotion to Glory at a young age was a sad loss to the Army and the African people.

Following his visit to the Congo in 1955 General Wilfred Kitching made a personal appeal for instruments, as a result of which a new set was donated by the Australian territories.

From being Band Sergeant at Regent Hall, in the heart of London, to serving as Bandmaster at Léopoldville, in the heart of Africa, meant a radical change for Captain Ray Munn, but he reports: ' It is a most interesting and stimulating experience to find the same keenness for brass banding and a like desire to give one's best for the cause of Christ.'

During the Independence celebrations in 1960 Léopoldville Central Band received many invitations to assist at the various civic functions and was on duty five days non-stop. The newly formed guitar brigade of the corps was also much in evidence at the celebrations. One mayor declared: ' Your band is excellent but the guitar brigade is *sensationelle!* '

In 1962 Léopoldville Central Band, when engaged on campaign, was involved in a serious road accident which cost the life of one bandsman, none escaping without injury. Less than a week later Brazzaville Band crossed the river to play in Léopoldville for the visit of the International Secretary, Commissioner Theodore Holbrook. It was a moving moment when those of the Léopoldville bandsmen who were present at the meeting in spite of their injuries, were able to play instruments loaned by the men from Brazzaville.

General Wilfred Kitching, conducting bandmasters' councils in London, told the delegates about the Congo tragedy and the considered complete write-off of several instruments.

Before the day was over more than £300 had been promised and finally the total raised in response to the appeal reached £500. Much of this money was used to pay for the repair and reconditioning of the battered instruments at the Army's factory at St. Albans.

The band made history in June, 1965, when, attending the Centenary Celebrations in London, it became the first African Salvation Army band to visit Europe. On its way a short campaign was conducted in Belgium and the Netherlands, a programme being presented at Quaregnon, the birthplace of Commissioner Becquet.

In 1959 a second band was formed in the Congo Territory, at Stanleyville, complete with six drums and fourteen brass instruments.

Equatorial Africa

THE Army's work in Equatorial Africa—then the French Congo—began in March, 1937, when Adjutant and Mrs. Becquet, with a number of officers, a flag and a band, crossed the Congo River to hold a meeting in Brazzaville. In 1953 French Equatorial Africa became a separate command and seven years later the first band in Brazzaville, under the direction of the then Officer Commanding, Colonel Marcel Beney, was inaugurated with Major Louis Besson, a Swiss officer, as Bandmaster.

Soon after the formation of the section the Bandmaster met a six-foot crocodile whilst returning home from band practice. With

the aid of a local Salvationist and a boathook he killed the dangerous
creature whose skin was hung outside his quarters to dry in the sun.
Tropical Africa indeed!

While Brazzaville Band was supporting Lieut.-Commissioner
Francis Evans in an open-air meeting at Poto-Poto on a Sunday
afternoon during the official celebrations of the Declaration of
Independence in 1960, the President of the Republic, Abbé Fulbert
Youlou, drove through the streets of the city with the French
Plenipotentiary. As the President's car drew abreast of the Salva-
tionists the band struck up ' Saints of God, lift up your voices '.

The President halted the car, alighted and stood with the band.
When the song ended he congratulated the Officer Commanding and
the Bandmaster before continuing his drive.

Central Africa

IT took Major and Mrs. John Pascoe and their pioneer party six and a
half months to make the 1,000-mile journey from Kimberley to Fort
Salisbury, in Mashonaland (now Rhodesia). Sent out by Commissioner Thomas Estill, then Territorial Commander for South Africa,
they left at midnight on Tuesday, May 5, 1891, and in a wagon named
' Enterprise ', drawn by eighteen oxen, arrived on November 18th.
Mr. Cecil Rhodes met the Salvationists and assured them that a farm
and two building sites in the town he planned to build would be placed
at their disposal.

In the party were five men officers who had brought brass instruments with them. A correspondent of the *Cape Argus* said of
the pioneers: ' Their behaviour and presence here since their arrival
would not be discreditable to the Archbishops of Canterbury and
York, with a couple of deans and archdeacons thrown in. . . . Last
Saturday their band turned out and proved excellent players.' This
was the first band the Mashonas had heard.

Brass banding in the Central Africa Territory has been maintained
mainly in and around Salisbury (Rhodesia). As this is the territorial
centre the European corps has been able to count on the help of
missionary officers and Salvationist musicians from western countries
working in the city.

Bandmaster David Connel was in charge of the Salisbury Citadel
Band for twenty years, retiring in 1958 after thirty-two years' service
(he was Bandmaster at Kilmarnock Riccarton, Scotland, before
settling in Rhodesia).

The week-end visit of Johannesburg City Band, South Africa, to
Salisbury in 1954 made history. Major Ron Cox, then the Commanding Officer at Salisbury Citadel, recalls: ' The visitors had journeyed

720 miles in approximately twenty-three hours by coach, a long enough journey on good roads but a real bone-shaking experience over the 300 miles of Rhodesian roads, which finally brought them from the border to Salisbury. Within two hours of the end of the journey the band was in place for the first festival!' There is no doubt that the section from South Africa made a wonderful impression on the citizens of Salisbury, both European and African.

In 1963 Salisbury Citadel Band became the first Rhodesian section to play in South Africa.

Salisbury Citadel bandsmen have shown a practical and devoted interest in the African bands of the territory. When, at the conclusion of a ten-year instrument scheme, twenty-two new instruments were presented to the band in 1948, the discarded 'old faithfuls' were passed on to the Salisbury Location Band, later to become Harare.

There has been a band at Harare for some thirty years, and it has remained the only African band in Rhodesia. After Brigadier Fred Lewis heard the band in 1939 he reported to *The Musician*: 'I was not expecting to hear such a good version of " Whither Pilgrims? " (in march time) and " If the Cross we boldly bear ".' Eighteen years later the band, having undergone many changes of personnel, learned to play its first march, 'The great call'. Up till then the only music possessed by the band was the Band Tune Book. Since then the Unity Series has been secured and has proved extremely useful.

The band has had a champion in Lieut.-Colonel Railton Graver, one time in charge of the Central Mashona Division and now General Secretary. As the result of his interest whilst in England on homeland furlough in 1958, a number of instruments were donated to the band; these were taken back by the Colonel and presented to the band when the Territorial Commander, Colonel (later Commissioner) Carl Richards, was welcomed to the Central Mashona Division.

When the International Staff Band had a new set of festival tunics for its tour of the U.S.A. and Canada in 1957, the discarded uniforms were sent to Africa, some to the Johannesburg African Central Corps and the rest to Harare. Another African band to have benefited by such practical generosity is Bulawayo, which still parades resplendent in festival tunics sent out by Oldham Citadel Band.

Some years ago a Bulawayo bandsman put up for election to the Native Location Committee. Several copies of an election address were roughly printed with pen and ink and distributed. It read: ' Vote for Josiah J. Chikoko, Muyanga. Because he will ask municipalet to reduce rents of rooms, also for killing cockroaches in rooms. Again he will ask for more stoves for the Africans in Bulawayo Location and at Muzitikazi. Vote for him.

'He is well known in united school as a janitor, in a debating society, also as a bandsman in The Salvation Army and often as a chairman in concerts.'

An all-round candidate!

East Africa

NOT long after the commencement of Salvation Army work in Kenya in 1921 attempts were made to introduce brass bands. This was not easy, for the African has his own inherent means of making music on a variety of instruments centred around the fascinating rhythmic consistency of the percussion.

The military band of the King's African Rifles set a high standard of efficiency and it was to emulate this popular group that Salvationists were persuaded to learn brass instruments.

In the early 1930s there was a small group of players functioning in Nairobi, chiefly for the purpose of assisting in meetings conducted by territorial leaders and international visitors. This was organized by Headquarters but was claimed by the corps as well.

Special arrangements were made to suit the band's instrumentation. A simple and soft style of playing was adopted and occasionally a vocal chorus was introduced. Later string and woodwind sections were added, forming an orchestra which reached a good standard.

A shifting population and changes of appointment brought about the end of this group all too soon. From time to time since then a band, organized by Territorial Headquarters and formed from members of the staff, has taken part in meetings in the city.

The first official corps band in East Africa was formed in the Thika Division in 1959. The Divisional Commander, Brigadier Cyril Woods, who served as Bandmaster at Attleborough and Norwich 2, Norfolk, before becoming an officer, appealed to his home division for some instruments. The response from six corps made it possible for the Brigadier to return to Africa from homeland furlough with a number of instruments presented to him in a central holiness meeting in Norwich.

The only other regular band in the territory is that at the Thika School for the Blind and this is a unique combination. 'To bring sightless African children into an Army setting is to provide a rich soil for the production of music,' declares Major Gordon Swansbury, the Principal.

A flute band had been in operation for some years but when it was learned that the brass instruments of a defunct local town band were to be sold an offer on behalf of the school was accepted.

For fourteen weeks a number of boys from Standards 5 and 6

attended band practice for the purpose of mastering the intricacies of Braille music notation. This had to be adapted for brass band music. And then, with instruments at last available, the boys went into action.

When General and Mrs. Wilfred Kitching visited Thika on August 22, 1958, the band made its first public appearance, playing hymn tunes. Courageously the difficulties were overcome. All instruments from tenor horn downward were suspended from the shoulders by a leather strap. This enabled the player to have his left hand free to read the music, written in Braille symbols and clipped to his ' stand ', which was strapped to his left knee.

It was a birthday surprise for General Kitching to witness the first public appearance of this unique band and when later asked to describe his reactions he said: ' I experienced the desire to shed tears to relieve my emotions; tears of sorrow as I considered the sadly afflicted young people and tears of joy that there could be this added interest for them.'

In the years of National Service following the end of the Second World War many British Salvationists were stationed in Kenya and added their quota to Army activity in Nairobi. On one occasion the lads contributed sufficient money for a set of harmonicas to be purchased and presented to cadets of the training college.

A popular feature for some years in Nairobi was the regular Sunday morning ' Listen to the Band' programme relayed over the Forces Broadcasting Station. This consisted of the playing of Salvation Army records.

*   *   *

Chosen by General Edward Higgins to open up the Army's work in Tanganyika, Ensign (later Lieut.-Colonel) Francis Dare, with his wife, relinquished the command of Holloway Citadel Corps, in North London, and hoisted the yellow, red and blue flag in the old town of Tabora on October 29, 1933. But he needed more than a cornet to make an impact upon the people.

As a boy at Southend Frank Dare had received cornet lessons from Harry Appleby, of Household Troops fame, and soon he had become an outstanding soloist. During the First World War he enlisted to serve with Salvation Army ambulances in France and became solo cornet player and Deputy Bandmaster of the Ambulance Band, which, under Lieut.-Colonel Bramwell Taylor, was one of the noted bands of those days.

After the war the band toured Britain and from General Bramwell Booth Frank Dare received a presentation cornet. This accompanied him to Germany where he became Bandmaster of the Red Shield Band with the army of occupation in that country,

He married another red shield worker and, returning to England, they settled in Blackpool, where Frank became Bandmaster of the Citadel Band.

Then came the call of God to fuller service. The way was not easy to follow, but in faith Bandmaster and Mrs. Dare stepped out, little realizing how far they would travel in accepting the challenge of officership.

Frank Dare's banding days were not over and his presentation cornet was put to use during the time he was solo cornetist and Deputy Bandmaster of the Cadets Band of the 1923–24 session and in his nine years of service as a corps officer in the British Territory.

Little wonder that after Lieut.-Colonel Dare had hoisted the Army flag in Tanganyika he should take his beloved presentation cornet from its case and press it immediately into service.

When the pioneer wanted a crowd; when he wanted to impress some 'hard-boiled' old gold miners; when he wanted to teach Africans the music of a hymn or Army chorus—he produced his cornet. In work among lepers, the blind, in the prisons and stockades, Lieut.-Colonel Dare played and prayed for the soul of Africa.

After the Second World War the Colonel took a well-deserved rest in his homeland and, following a period of divisional work, returned with Mrs. Dare (and his presentation cornet) to give the remaining years of active service to East Africa, first as Training Principal and then as General Secretary.

CHAPTER SIXTEEN

EASTERN INTERLUDE

India

THE large police force awaiting the arrival of a thousand-strong invading 'army' at Bombay received a shock when the *Ancona* docked and four Salvationists walked down the gangway. That was on September 19, 1882. Characteristically, this was no orthodox landing. The pioneering quartet marched from the boat with music, Major Frederick Tucker carrying the flag, Captain Henry Bullard playing his cornet, Lieutenant Arthur Norman beating a drum and Lieutenant Mary Thompson jingling her tambourine. Next day meetings were held in a tent they had brought with them.

The first bands formed on the India sub-continent consisted not surprisingly of drums and fifes. These instruments were in common use in the east and it was natural that as the various Salvation Army settlements were opened on the Movement's oldest mission field such groups should be formed.

These were not Salvation Army sections in the accepted sense; rather were they bands formed among the people benefiting from the pioneer social, medical and educational services. In 1909, a year after work had begun among the criminal tribes, a drum and fife band was in action at one of the settlements, the hangman being the Bandmaster. Madras and Trivandrum could also boast a band.

Western officers appointed to India invariably encouraged the formation of brass bands and one of the first must have been that recruited at Simla in 1908. The name of 'Staff Band' would appear to be rather pretentious, but this title probably pin-pointed the personnel's identification.

The Trivandrum Band was formed in 1907 and, with their red coats and white dhoties, the boys attending the Army's boarding school at this centre soon attracted attention. The Bandmaster was a member of the Maharajah's State Brass Band and sought to teach the boys along the same professional lines. It was through his influence that the band received an invitation to play before the Maharajah in 1909. At that time it was unheard-of for such an exalted personage to entertain at his palace children of low caste.

Army scholars, with their instruments, played an important part in the Durbar Coronation Celebrations of 1911. The Bapatla Drum and Fife Band did so well and added to the success of local celebrations so

greatly that the leading Brahmins voted thirty rupees to purchase a
gold medal for the band to commemorate the occasion.

In 1912 Commissioner Booth-Tucker—who led the Bombay
'invasion' thirty years before—reported that there was only one
brass band in India, at Nagercoil. This, again, was formed of boys
attending the Army boarding school in that city, instruments and
drums having been sent out from England.

Soon after the Army had accepted the request to manage a leper
hospital for the Cochin State Government in the 1920s, the Superin-
tendent, Adjutant Edwin Francis, energetically set himself the task of
securing brass instruments and teaching the patients to play. When
General Edward Higgins visited the settlement in 1933 he was greeted
by a smartly dressed section playing efficiently. Although described
as ' the band that never marches ', for obvious reasons, this group made
a great impression in government circles and had a wide influence in
South India. Early in 1936 Adjutant Francis, who had taught the forty
bandsmen who had served in the band since its formation, assembled
his musicians to hear for the first time an Army band on the radio—
Chalk Farm on the Empire wavelength from London. ' Once or
twice ', reported the Bandmaster, ' we could even hear the bandsmen
blowing water out of their instruments.'

                    *   *   *

In 1953 the Madras and Andhra Territory (then Madras and
Telugu) needed 182 brass instruments. After unsuccessful appeals for
help had been made to two other Indian territories, a friend in Madras
discovered a quantity of brass, but it had to be shipped to Bombay.

Eventually the consignment arrived at Territorial Headquarters
and a search was made for a craftsman in the city. A first-class
mechanic with a vice, hacksaw and a brace and bit put to work his
natural gifts of copying, and within a few days had ' manufactured '
the required instruments, all in tune and ready to play—all for the cost
of £45.

This expert craftsman was not setting up in competition with the
Army's own instrument factory in England: he had produced brass
flutes. Thirty corps in the territory were the grateful recipients of
augmentations to their flute bands, one of the most efficient sections
being the corps cadet brigade flute band attached to the Army's high
school at Bapatla.

The three-day visit of Madras Central Band to the Bapatla High
School and neighbouring institutions in 1957 was a venture of faith.
In planning such a campaign it had to be remembered that the hot sun
would prevent much action during the day, that travelling over rough

ground during the week-end would cause transportation difficulties, and that the sound of brass bands is strange and potentially offensive to Indian ears.

The band, fourteen strong, played in the criminal settlement, at the leprosarium, in the crowded bazaar, to the high school staff and students, on the veranda of the hospital at Pennur, to the students of a training college, at three village corps and in the managers' club of a nearby factory—an assortment of audiences to be envied by any band!

Reported Captain William Metcalf, then on the staff of the high school: ' The campaign concluded at 1.30 in the morning when an unconcerned-looking train steamed in three hours late to take the tired bandsmen home to Madras, 220 miles away. . . . The whole plan was an experiment in spiritual warfare in India.'

An officer whose work in this territory will never be forgotten is Brigadier Richard Nuttall, who as General Secretary was promoted to Glory in 1946. Twenty-seven years before, Bandmaster Nuttall, of Blackpool Citadel, and his wife, a gifted singer and the corps Songster Leader, followed the will of God to become Salvation Army officers. Later came the call to missionary service and in 1923 the Nuttalls sailed for India. The Brigadier will be remembered by the melody that bears his name, by the march, ' Blackpool No. 2 ', and by the song, ' Sunshine, sunshine, shining along our pathway '.

*　　　*　　　*

In the Western India Territory there are brass bands at Bombay Byculla (Central) Corps and at Anand Hospital and Corps. Commissioner Joseph Dahya is a former bandsman of the Bombay section which can include among its Bandmasters Lieut.-Colonel Arthur Hook, the present Secretary of the International Staff Band, Colonel Leslie Russell and Colonel Donald Smith. At one time the band was unique in that all its members were sons of officers. The corps timbrel group is also a popular attraction.

*　　　*　　　*

No story of Army endeavour in India could be complete without a reference to Colonel Edwin Sheard who, with Mrs. Sheard, served there for thirty-five years, more than twenty of them among the criminal tribes. Converted during a visit of the International Staff Band to Blackpool in 1903, Edwin Sheard became a bandsman and top tenor in the male voice party. It was after Bandsman and Mrs. Sheard saw a *War Cry* advert for ' consecrated, devoted, married couples for service overseas ' that they offered and were accepted.

Lieut.-Colonel Bernard Watson wrote in *The Musician*: ' When men who had been kept in chains for two years were placed under his care on the Andaman Islands, and Sheard was warned that he should carry a gun for safety's sake, he ordered the chains to be struck off the "crims". He had no gun.

'Nor did he ever need one. Men born and steeped in crime learned to love him. What policemen failed to do the bandsman called by God from Blackpool accomplished.'

When Edwin Sheard retired from active service, decorated twice by his king, he returned with his wife to their beloved Blackpool, where he played baritone in the band and served as Band Sergeant for ten years. He was promoted to Glory in 1963.

A few weeks before his passing, as he was leaving a Saturday festival given by Croydon Citadel Band, the Colonel felt guided to speak to a man in the foyer of Blackpool Citadel about his soul. The result was that the two men entered the empty hall and the missionary hero knelt with a needy soul helping him to find the power he so much desired. Edwin Sheard loved the souls of men.

Pakistan

LAHORE (Pakistan) Central Hall Band came into being in 1924 mainly as a result of the enthusiasm of Adjutant John Charles, who had been a Bandmaster in England before entering the training college. In an early photograph of the band may be seen two future Territorial Commanders, Lieut.-Commissioner Arthur Hughes and Colonel Charles Green, and a future Chancellor of the Exchequer, Commissioner C. Herbert Mitchell, who served as Bandmaster for some time. Other members of the band who rose to territorial leadership were Colonel Edwin Sheard and Lieut.-Colonel Frank Mortimer.

Ceylon

LACK of permanent leadership has made it difficult to maintain Ceylon's only band—at Colombo Central. In the 1930s valuable pioneer work was put in at the Slave Island Corps by Captain (later Lieut.-Colonel) George Lovegrove and when that band was later without a Bandmaster Major Hilda Gardiner took charge, playing solo cornet herself.

The Major soon learned that the drum was indispensable in open-air meetings, but sometimes discovered that it was either damaged or worn out. With an absence of surplus money there was only one thing to do—to learn how to repair drums herself. She soon earned a reputation in this art and demands for renovations came from corps all over the island.

The opening of new corps called for new drums and, with zinc centres from the coppersmith, wooden rims from the carpenter, goat skins from India, rope from the hardware stores, and leather lugs from the shoemaker, she fashioned drums for more than a dozen corps.

When, in 1937, Major Gardiner was transferred from Colombo she commenced a band in Moratumulla.

The revival of musical interests on the lovely island of Ceylon can be dated to 1947, when the band and songster brigade in Colombo were re-formed. The former section presented the greater difficulty. Sometimes there would be as many as seventeen players and then suddenly, owing to changes of work and appointments, the band personnel would be down to eight. But there were always a few to keep the Army playing.

The appointment of Bandmaster John Rodie, originally from Ayr, Scotland, marked the beginning of a new era in the band's history. The occasional arrival of a new instrument served to encourage the comrades. In 1958 a euphonium, a gift from the North Sydney (Australia) Band, was presented by the Territorial Commander, Lieut.-Commissioner Gwendoline Taylor.

Another cornet, presented in 1959, had an interesting history. When Lieut.-Colonel James Stobart, living in retirement in South Africa, decided to part with the cornet that had been his companion throughout his officership, he sent it to Ceylon, where his son, John, was the Territorial Commander. Colonel John Stobart not only presented the cornet in a festival at Colombo but joined Bandmaster Rodie in a cornet duet.

Burma

BURMA's only band, at Tamwe, Rangoon, took a new lease of life in 1960 when eight new instruments were donated by the U.S.A. Central Territory. The instruments were presented by the Officer Commanding, Lieut.-Colonel Edward Robinson, to Major Clifford Bowes, the Commanding Officer, who trained and led the band whilst in charge of the Tamwe Corps and Boys' Home. Earlier he had served as Bandmaster at Lahore, Pakistan.

Japan

ACKNOWLEDGED to be in the forefront of aggressive evangelism in Japan, The Salvation Army has also led the way in the progression of religious music. With the introduction of Western educational methods and their cultural development there has grown up an appreciation of the Western form of music. That is probably why Army bands, although existing in a limited way, have enjoyed consistent popularity over the years.

The pioneers in Japan quickly introduced the drum into early-day

Army meetings, and it was this instrument that in 1900, five years after the Army had commenced operations, played an important part in what was perhaps one of the most remarkable victories in Salvation Army history.

The consciences of Salvationists in Japan were stirred by the scandal of licensed prostitution. In Tokyo alone there were five licensed quarters, the largest of which, Yoshawara, boasted 5,000 prostitutes and was known the world over. A police regulation forbade any of the girls to leave such an establishment without written permission of the brothel keeper and the manager of the licensed quarter.

Following the courageous example of an American Methodist missionary, Colonel (later Commissioner) Henry Bullard, then in charge of Army work in Japan, decided to rally his forces to march on the most notorious quarter in Tokyo to inform the girls that there was a clause in the law under which they could be released and to offer them the shelter of a Salvation Army rescue home.

In Tokyo the Colonel summoned his officers—fifty in all—and after a night of prayer led them into action with the flag flying and drum beating. Attracted by the drum and the singing, the girls came running into the streets where copies of a special 'Rescue Number' *Toki-no-Koe* (*The War Cry*) were handed to them.

Hooligans in the pay of the brothel keepers went into action with a brutal attack. The flag was torn to shreds; the drum was smashed. The result was almost disastrous for the Salvationists. But this was the beginning of the end; not of The Salvation Army in Japan, but of the social evil its soldiers were fighting.

Within two months—weeks of cruelty and indescribable hardship —the Emperor signed a decree permitting any prostitute desirous of freedom to make her wishes known at the nearest police station. More than 12,000 girls availed themselves of this amendment in the law in the first year. The battle was won, a battle in which the drum had played a part.

★   ★   ★

When the Founder visited Japan in 1907 a band was organized for the occasion. A report in *The Bandsman and Songster* stated: 'Our one great Japanese brass band assisted in welcoming the General to Yoko-hama.' Musicians attached to the headquarters were enlisted for the purpose and this group could have formed the nucleus of the Terri-torial Staff Band which came into being on a permanent basis in 1916.

As in other missionary countries Western officers helped to lay the foundations of Army banding and to maintain interest and standards. Japan has been blessed with a number who gained experience in their

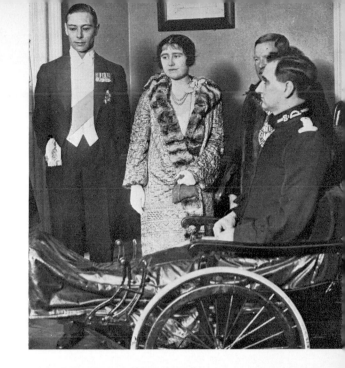

At the Composers'
Festival, 1928,
with the
Duke and Duchess
of York

The Household
Troops Band
at Margate

Chalk Farm Band playing to the President of Finland in Helsinki, 1934

The International Staff and Earlscourt Bands leaving Buckingham Palace, 1965

Salvationists march in Osaka, Japan

homeland territories before arriving in ' The Land of the Rising Sun '. One of the founder members of the Japanese Staff Band was Captain (later Colonel) Henry R. Pennick and one of the first Bandmasters was Ensign (later Lieut.-Colonel) Herbert Climpson.

The band, small but rendering useful service, was a victim of the earthquake which brought widespread devastation and heavy loss of life to Japan in 1922. The instruments and music were destroyed with the headquarters and two of the bandsmen, Brigadier Sashida and Staff-Captain Sakai, were among the fatal casualties.

The Army's role in bringing relief to the injured and homeless included dispensing cheer and comfort to those being accommodated in large refugee camps in Tokyo and Yokohama. The Territorial Commander, Commissioner William Eadie, realizing the necessity of music in this ministry, gave his attention to forming a Staff Brass Quintet.

Some weeks passed before the necessary equipment could be secured. Then instruments began to appear from various sources. To replace the music one member brought out from the bottom of his trunk a couple of bandmaster's scores and odd journals. Another produced copies of *The Musical Salvationist* containing brass quartets and quintets. A brave attempt was made by one of the group to arrange simple melodies and marches and in due course the quintet made its appearance.

The leader of the quintet was Major (later Commissioner) Ernest Pugmire, who played euphonium. Others were Staff-Captain Climpson and Staff-Captain (later Commissioner) Ernest Bigwood.

Three years later the Territorial Staff Band was re-formed with Major Pugmire as Bandmaster and reinforced by more Western officer-musicians, among them Brigadier (later Lieut.-Commissioner) Victor Rolfe. Thus began a period of service which remained unbroken until the Second World War.

Brigadier Rolfe, who later became the Territorial Commander, served as Bandmaster for a time before being succeeded by a gifted young Scottish musician who arrived in Japan in 1930 to become Private Secretary to Commissioner Gunpei Yamamuro, the Territorial Commander. Captain Charles Davidson served as Staff Bandmaster for some years and was appointed the territory's first Secretary for Bands in 1935 with an assignment to inaugurate twenty-five corps bands during the year and to seek to enrol 100 new bandsmen.

Apart from an appointment in Malaya, subsequent internment during the Second World War, and a period of service in the U.S.A., Charles Davidson served in Japan until December, 1964, when, as a Commissioner and Territorial Commander, he left the Orient to take command of the New Zealand Territory.

Adjutant (later Lieut.-Commissioner) George Grattan and Major (later Lieut.-Colonel) Arthur Best were also members of the Staff Band during that period. A short while before sailing for Japan in 1930 the last named made his final appearance with the International Staff Band at Regent Hall, playing a euphonium solo, ' Land beyond the blue '. Appropriate indeed!

In 1935 the Japanese Staff Band conducted a campaign in Manchukuo. This undertaking was carried out during the coldest season and many small centres were visited along the Trans-Siberian railway route. The band played in Seoul, Korea, on the return journey.

Following the outbreak of the Second World War it was not until 1952 that another headquarters band was formed. This was in preparation for the visit of General Albert Orsborn, and three practices a week were held under the leadership of Brigadier (later Lieut.-Commissioner) Arthur Long.

Eighteen in number, the band made its first public appearance at the congress gatherings, wearing beautifully tailored uniforms. The men earned the warm commendation of their International Leader.

Later that year the band accompanied the General's representative, Commissioner John Bladin, on several of his campaigns in Japan. Said the Commissioner: ' I appreciated the valuable musical services of the band, but I valued even more highly the men's spirit of devotion and soul-winning zeal.' Without exception the bandsmen ' fished ' in the prayer meeting and dealt with seekers at the Mercy Seat.

Due to a great extent to the personal interest of General Bramwell Booth, who arranged for brass instruments to be sent to Japan, many corps bands were formed in the territory in the middle 1920s. Asakichi Osuga, who had been sworn-in as a Salvation Army soldier in 1901, although no longer a young man, learned to play a cornet.

Having mastered the difficulties, this comrade became Bandmaster at Shibuya, Tokyo, and is today one of Japan's outstanding local officers. Nearly eighty years of age, he still conducts the band and is also a member of the Territorial Staff Band.

China

ALTHOUGH all overseas Salvationists were required to leave China in 1951 and there is no international Army now functioning in that land, sufficient musical progress was made between 1916 and the above-mentioned year to merit a place in this survey.

Band history in China focuses mainly on the Headquarters Staff Band in Peking in the early 1920s. The arrival of Adjutant (later Brigadier) James Sansom, solo cornet player in the International Staff

Band up to the time of his sailing, meant the real beginnings of things musical in the territory.

By 1922 a Staff Band was in existence with Adjutant Sansom as Bandmaster. The personnel included Colonel (then Adjutant) Arthur Ludbrook, in after years to become the Territorial Commander for China North, and Brigadier (later Colonel) Robert Chard.

James Sansom—gracious, kindly, handsome and sincere—enjoyed his well-earned homeland furlough in 1935. Invited to play with the I.S.B. again, he took up 1st cornet with the enthusiasm he had always shown as the band's sweet-toned soloist, and at Regent Hall made an indelible impression with his earnest appeal to his listeners to be ' Christ centred '. In that summer he went with the unique London Band on campaign in Sweden as its Leader.

Shortly afterward he left London to pioneer Army work in South China. In March, 1936, he was promoted to Glory at the height of his powers.

Hong Kong

BEGUN in 1930, Army work in Hong Kong was first directed from Peking and then became part of the newly formed South China command in 1935.

Any musical history that this area might have dates from the end of the Second World War. Among R.A.F. personnel which arrived to occupy Hong Kong on September 4, 1945, were seven Salvationists. In the Young Men's Christian Association's building they met for a meeting led by Lieut.-Colonel William Darby and were joined by Major (later Lieut.-Colonel) Harold Littler, who with his wife and children had just been released from internment.

On the following Sunday the servicemen attended Kowloon City Corps and, although no instruments were available, they took part in the meetings, greatly to the joy of their Chinese comrades.

Two years later Salvationist servicemen stationed in Hong Kong were able to form a band, thus re-establishing the musical forces.

It was a British bandsman, Clifford McTighe, of Hucknall, serving with the Royal Navy, who inspired the formation of a band at the King's Park Children's Home, Hong Kong. Seeing the great need for instruments, he wrote to his home corps, explaining the position. Soon nine instruments were on the way with a promise for more to follow. McTighe was appointed Band Instructor and continued to give valued service while serving in the Crown Colony.

Malaysia

THREE years after Army work began in Malaysia the first band was formed—at Singapore Central. An officer, writing to London at that time, said: 'We are in no sense pioneers, but rather consolidators of previous efforts, and among other things the advent of a band is still an expected event.'

Made up mostly of European officers, the band found a great champion in the Officer Commanding, Brigadier (later Commissioner) Herbert Lord. Adjutant (later Lieut.-Commissioner) Fred Harvey was a member of that first band.

Then came the Second World War. It was left to Salvationist servicemen, as at Hong Kong, to rekindle an interest in brass banding. These enthusiasts spent patience and time in teaching Chinese Salvationists of both sexes to play instruments. Gradually they took their places in the Singapore Central Band.

As recently as 1956 six of the bandsmen made history when they travelled 155 miles to conduct a campaign in Malacca. At the conclusion of the Sunday morning meeting the party journeyed thirty miles to Batang, where Army work had but recently started and where a clinic was already in use. The musicians were the first Christians to hold an open-air meeting in the village.

The Philippines

ALTHOUGH there is not as yet a brass band functioning in the Philippines—lack of instruments is the main reason—there is a great love for music among the wonderful Salvationists scattered throughout the many islands in this area. The need is being met by the use of guitars which in some places are being augmented by banjo, one-string petrol-can bands, ukulele and concertina—and, of course, the drum!

Korea

THE first Salvationist brass instrumentalist in Korea was Captain (later Lieut.-Colonel) Charles Sylvester. Arriving in Seoul late one Saturday night, he made history the next morning when he took an old brass cornet to the hall.

A few days later cadets began to arrive for the first training session in Seoul. Among them was a Korean from Hawaii who could not raise the modest fee required for his training, but was willing to hand over four instruments he had brought with him. The value of the instruments was assessed and they were accepted.

The following Sunday morning, February 13, 1910, a Salvation Army band marched along the main street of the Korean capital for the first time. The band consisted of Colonel (later Commissioner) Robert Hoggard, the Territorial Commander, who supplied the bass part on a euphonium, his teenage son, Robert, who also became a

Commissioner, Captain (later Commissioner) Herbert Lord, Captain Sylvester and the Korean cadet.

This pioneer group did not operate for long; the cadet was commissioned, Captains Lord and Sylvester farewelled for appointments in other parts of the country and the younger Hoggard left for Japan. When Captain Sylvester returned to the capital city in 1915 he gathered a number of Korean learners around him and began to teach them scales. Soon a second band was functioning.

When it became almost impossible to maintain a corps band it was suggested that the boys cared for under the Army's roof should be taught to play instruments. The progress made was remarkable and with Captain Sylvester as its conductor the band was in great demand.

During this period the Boys' Home Band became the first brass band to broadcast over the Korean radio. Shortly afterwards Captain (later Lieut.-Colonel) William Novell arrived from England. He was appointed to the home and became the Bandmaster, serving in this capacity until he was transferred from the territory, where the leadership was undertaken by a Korean comrade, Major Kwon.

The day after the capture of Seoul during the Korean war of 1950, the invaders ordered the boys to parade with their instruments, and then marched them northward. They have not been heard of since.

But there is still a band at Seoul Boys' Home. A new group was formed and when General and Mrs. Wilfred Kitching arrived at the airport to commence their Korean campaign in the autumn of 1961 the band greeted them with music.

Indonesia

THE first bands formed in Indonesia were attached to the leper colonies which, at the request of the Dutch Colonial Government, were being managed by The Salvation Army. This was in 1909.

When Commissioner Johannes de Groot visited the Pelantungan Leper Colony four years later he was accompanied by Brigadier William Richards, who provided a detailed description of the band.

Each of the fifteen men ' played their music with zest and enjoyment that could not have been beaten by an English band ', the Brigadier reported. The eldest of the group was forty, the youngest fourteen, and all were stricken with the dread disease which in those days could be nothing but fatal.

The Bandmaster, with nose, mouth, ears and tops of fingers already beginning to disappear, was the saddest sight of all. With the drum before him on a stand, the drumstick in his right hand and a cymbal in his left, he led the band in perfect time, conducting with the drumstick while he played the cymbals, and using the cymbal as a baton when a drum part was required.

This story could have been repeated about other colonies at this time. Bands at Kalawara, Central Celebes, and the Semarang Leper Colony were formed in 1932 by Adjutant Johannesson, a Norwegian officer, who proved himself a brass band enthusiast. Another was Brother Oey, the owner of large estates who wanted to form a band among his 3,000 employees. He secured the services of a converted military bandmaster who had just left the Queen of Holland's army, and employed him solely for this purpose. He was later commisssioned Bandmaster at Krengseng Corps.

In the mid-1920s a Menadonese school-teacher, who taught in one of the Army schools opened by Lieut.-Colonel Leonard Woodward, pioneer missionary in Mid-Celebes, made a flute out of bamboo from the bush. A good player himself, he experimented with his home-made instrument until he was satisfied with its efficiency. He then sent the boys into the bush to collect bamboo and gave them instruction in the making of a flute.

He measured each bamboo cane for length and wind holes and then left it to the boys. As each instrument was completed it was tested and destroyed if not up to standard.

Work went on until each boy possessed a flute of required merit. The flutes were called sulings, some ' small ' and others ' great ', the difference in size denoting a variation in pitch of an octave. In this way was formed the first flute band in Indonesia.

The news quickly spread. Children in other schools took up the idea, and soon groups of woodwind players were being introduced all over the area. As the bands developed, the instruments became more pretentious. The plain bamboo cylinders were adorned with floral designs artistically carved with chopping knives, the first three inches of which were extremely sharp and served the additional purposes of shaving and cutting hair.

To play a flute is part of school ritual in Celebes. Half an hour of playtime every day is devoted to band practice. It is not unusual for the children to play to and from school. The boy who lives the farthest away leaves his village early in the morning, playing his flute, and is joined at points along the road by others, until a gigantic band is functioning by the time school is reached.

All these children are attached to corps, which means the local flute sections reach a high standard, being divided into adults, young people and children. The corps bands play before and after meetings and march through the villages, rallying the soldiers at given points and playing them to the hall.

They make a picturesque scene, these Salvationist musicians whose grandfathers had been murderers and headhunters, fearing and worshipping the devil.

CHAPTER SEVENTEEN

MUSICAL AMBASSADORS

IN 1905, three years after its ten-day tour of Scotland, Chalk Farm Band accepted an invitation from the Territorial Commander for Holland to tour in that country. No British corps band had travelled abroad up till then.

The eleven-day campaign was a tremendous success, the enthusiastic welcome accorded the visitors at every place thoroughly justifying the venture. In this way the north London band, under its renowned leader, Bandmaster Alfred W. Punchard, set the pace for exchanged musical campaigns which have become regular and frequent happenings.

Two years after that first overseas tour Chalk Farm Band returned to Holland and crossed the frontier into Germany, where Essen, Cologne and other cities were visited.

Interrupted by the First World War the musical ambassadors were off again in 1920, this time to Sweden and Denmark, covering the 2,100 miles by sea, train and motor coach. Each continental campaign became more ambitious than its predecessor and in 1927 the tour included four countries—Belgium, Germany, Switzerland and France. In Paris Bandmaster Punchard was invited to sign the famous ' Golden Book '.

Three years later a fifteen-day tour was undertaken through Sweden and Norway, the band journeying more than 2,500 miles, playing in cathedrals and State churches in both countries and at exhibitions in Stockholm (Sweden) and Drammen (Norway).

Finland, as well as Sweden and Denmark, was visited in 1934, the band playing to the President outside his palace in Helsinki.

The most extensive continental tour of all took place in 1936 and included six countries—Holland, Germany, Czechoslovakia, Austria, Switzerland and France. In Utrecht on the first day of the campaign the Bandmaster was greeted by the Young People's Sergeant-Major of the No. 1 corps, who had been won for God through the band's visit twenty-nine years before. A tribute to the spiritual impact of such tours!

In Berlin great crowds greeted the British Salvationists most enthusiastically and Bandmaster Punchard laid a wreath at the National War Heroes' Memorial. A day later Prague Salvationists happily welcomed the first Army band from Britain to visit their land.

When the band crossed the frontier into Austria, the Bandmaster was the recipient of congratulations on entering the eleventh country outside Great Britain in which he had led his band—a record that will take long to surpass. In Austria Vienna was the scene of a memorable open-air festival given to several thousand citizens from the steps of the stately New Palace.

Six days were spent in Switzerland and the historic tour concluded with a visit to Paris, a long march through the boulevards preceding the festival. The Captain in charge of the hostel where the men billeted revealed that the band's visit nine years before—particularly its discipline and spirit of joyous service—had led to his becoming a Salvation Army officer.

Chalk Farm Band has continued its globe-trotting since the Second World War with campaigns in Sweden in 1948, and Switzerland in 1961.

*   *   *

Inspired by the example of the Chalk Farm campaigners, other British bands cast longing looks toward the continent of Europe and when the cross-Channel route was reopened after the First World War opportunities were presented. In 1920 Harlesden Band visited Belgium, bringing encouragement to the people of that land amidst the ruin and devastation caused by four years of war.

Two years later, following visits by Derby 2 (Central) and Gillingham Bands, Dinnington Band was invited to campaign in Belgium. It was an excited Bandmaster J. W. Tomlinson who discussed the possibilities of such a tour with his band.

As most of the bandsmen in this Yorkshire mining village were employed at the colliery it was decided that the Bandmaster should see the agent, a Christian man, to seek permission for the men to take their holidays at the same time. After reading the letter from National Headquarters and learning the estimated cost of the travelling, the agent gave his support to the venture, promising to help with the finances as well. He personally raised £78 toward the expenses.

Bandmaster Tomlinson reports: ' The whole village turned out to give us a glorious send-off, workmates from the colliery lending a hand to load our cases on to the bus which was to take us to the station.' Eleven thrilling days were spent in Belgium, the band being augmented by Staff-Captain (later Commissioner) W. Alex. Ebbs, who was stationed in that country and who played the Bandmaster's euphonium throughout the tour.

Dinnington Band became a victim of the industrial depression of 1931 when, among the 800 miners who found themselves out of work, were several of the band's key players. One became an outstanding euphonium soloist at Kettering; another gave excellent service for many years as a solo cornetist at Coventry City.

* * *

Such bands as Lausanne (Switzerland) and Utrecht (Holland) have conducted campaigns in Belgium, but visits are not too frequent. Following Chelmsford Band's tour of 1949 thirteen years passed before another band from the United Kingdom visited the country. This time the honour fell to Shaw Band from Lancashire, which also became the first British corps band to fly to the Continent for a week-end engagement.

The visits of British bands to France have been equally rare, Southsea, Salisbury and Watford being among the few. Earlscourt (Canada) Band visited France in 1965. The Men's Social Work Headquarters Band also campaigned in France at Easter, 1939, but this was confined to the Paris area.

Bands from territories other than the British have always been appreciated by the Salvationists of Germany. The close proximity of a number of continental countries have enabled bands from Denmark, Switzerland and Holland to make frequent visits.

* * *

There were significant campaigns in the years immediately following the end of the Second World War. Bandmaster Henning Petterson, of Huskvarna (Sweden), long thought about the best way of celebrating the golden jubilee anniversary of his band in 1948.

He had dreamed of a trip to England, or France, or Holland, but in the end he decided on an Easter tour which would serve to cheer and bless Salvationists in Germany. Eighteen months before the tour a savings club was launched in the band and every man was thus able to put away 100 kroner toward the expenses.

In addition every man was required to provide food for himself for the entire campaign, which took up a great deal of luggage space. The band also carried over 100 kilos of food to be distributed in the corps they were to visit.

The band left Huskvarna on a Friday night and gave two festivals in Denmark *en route*. Sunday night found them in Padborg, sleeping for six hours in the station waiting-room. The next day, overcoming tiredness of body, they fulfilled a festival engagement in Bremen.

* * *

Ten years after the English midland city of Coventry suffered death and destruction from the sky, Coventry City Band visited Germany.

The climax of the tour came in Berlin. When the band arrived at an early hour at Charlottenburg Station, the Berlin Philharmonic Brass Orchestra of thirty-eight players was on the platform to provide a musical welcome. The two thrilling days spent in the capital were marked by flowers and friendship.

Cordons of police controlled the crowds when five thousand people gathered for an open-air festival in the Hermannplatz, and all traffic was stopped for the march along the broad Berliner Strasse.

Travelling with the band, Lieut.-Colonel Ernest Rance reported: ' With a complete understanding of the significance of the visit, the Territorial Commander (Lieut.-Commissioner S. Carvosso Gauntlett) established a relationship between the German people and the men from Coventry which produced many tender and moving scenes.'

Lieut.-Commissioner Gauntlett said: ' Coventry has come to mean something new over here. The whole campaign was a triumph. From the German side we are deeply grateful for magnificent playing, grand comradeship and a spirit of Salvationism and dignity of deportment beyond praise.' Further evidence of the Army's effective frontier-leaping, no-barrier internationalism!

In the summer of 1964 a band from the U.S.A. visited Germany for the first time. Hollywood Tabernacle Band conducted a week's tour in Great Britain, then broke its journey from Groningen (Holland) to Copenhagen (Denmark) by giving a festival in Hamburg. The memory of that evening was blurred three days later when two of the bandsmen—Jan van Dalen and Frank Moulton—lost their lives in a car accident outside Bremen and a third, John Wielmaker, was seriously injured.

* * *

The Netherlands has always been a ' happy hunting ground ' for British bands. As long ago as 1891 the Household Troops Band accompanied Commandant and Mrs. Herbert Booth on a visit to that country and between the two world wars several overseas sections were welcomed.

The honour of being the first British band to visit the continent of Europe after the Second World War belongs to Boscombe. In 1947 this band became the first to play at the British Airborne Cemetery at Arnhem, where a wreath was laid on the memorial by Bandmaster Herbert Mountain, a custom that has been followed during all subsequent visits of British bands.

The visit of a British band to Holland has become almost an annual event and sections from Switzerland and Sweden also have toured in the land of dykes and windmills.

* * *

Bands from Sweden have journeyed far from their homeland to proclaim the gospel message in music, perhaps none more so, in recent years, than Tranås. England, Switzerland, Holland, Germany and France have heard this excellent group, as have large audiences in the U.S.A. and Canada. Stockholm 7 is another band that has travelled extensively on the continent of Europe and Stockholm 5 and Jönköping String Bands have campaigned across the Atlantic.

*   *   *

Owing to its isolation, Finland has received only few visits from touring sections, although the Swedish Staff Band campaigned there in 1910 and 1911. Occasionally a Swedish band spreads its wings to encompass this 'outpost' of Europe and three British bands— Chalk Farm in 1934, Croydon Citadel in 1960 and Edinburgh Gorgie in 1963—have conducted memorable campaigns.

*   *   *

The birthplace of the Army particularly has attracted overseas bands and the International Congresses of 1904 and 1914 and the Centenary Celebrations provided Salvationists in Britain with the opportunity of meeting musicians from many countries.

Before the First World War visits were confined to such international events and between the wars only a few bands toured in England, among them Hague Congress Hall (Holland) in 1929, the Danish Staff Band in 1932, Zürich (Switzerland) Central Band in 1935 and Basle 1 (Switzerland) a year later.

As in other countries, modern transport facilities have aided the speeding up of the international exchange and, following the campaign by Rotterdam Congress Hall Band in August, 1946, sections from Sweden, Denmark, Holland and Switzerland have been warmly welcomed. Scotland, Northern Ireland and Wales have been included in a number of these campaigns.

*   *   *

When the International Staff Band celebrated its coming of age in 1912 an article in *The Bandsman and Songster* referred to the 'flying crusades' it has conducted in all parts of the United Kingdom. (By that time the band had also toured in Switzerland, Holland, Italy, France, Belgium and Germany.) The possibility was hinted at of a visit to the United States and Canada, but almost immediately the idea was dismissed with the comment: 'Perhaps this is waiting for the perfection of aircraft.'

That was a distant dream. Bleriot had flown the English Channel only three years before, but seven years and a war were to pass before Alcock and Brown made the first crossing of the Atlantic Ocean in an aeroplane.

Nevertheless, the dream did come true—forty years after the prediction. In 1952 the I.S.B. conducted a month-long coast-to-coast tour of Canada, making the return crossing by plane and flying extensively to and from appointments within the Dominion.

Arriving at Montreal Airport, the band emplaned for Ottawa where the Governor-General expressed an official welcome. Following a greeting by the Prime Minister at the famous Peace Tower of the Parliament Buildings the campaigners, escorted by 'mounties', marched to the National War Memorial.

Thus began a triumphant and breath-taking tour which took the men through centres in Ontario to the West Coast, history-making gatherings being held at Victoria (Vancouver Island), the capital city of British Columbia, and Vancouver. The return journey, in hops, included stops at Calgary, where the bandsmen were welcomed at 5 a.m. by officers and bandsmen in cowboy regalia, Banff, where an aged Indian chief welcomed 'the good white brothers who made big music', Regina and Winnipeg.

After participating in the annual *Empress of Ireland* memorial service and the spring festival in Toronto the band continued its journey eastward, concluding its tour at Halifax, Nova Scotia.

Five years later the band made its first visit to the U.S.A., covering a distance of almost 21,000 miles, 17,000 of them by air. Beginning with a week-end in New York City the band then visited such centres as Washington, D.C., Philadelphia, Miami (Florida), Pittsburgh, Akron, Cincinnati, Chicago, Los Angeles, Kalamazoo, Cleveland, Niagara Falls, Toronto (Canada), Montreal (Canada), Boston, Hartford and Newark. The band was invited to take part in the Easter sunrise service in the Hollywood Bowl, its playing being heard by an estimated audience of a hundred million. From the Atlantic to the Pacific, from the Gulf of Mexico to the Northern Lakes the Staff Band had carried its dedicated music.

In 1962 a third visit to North America was made when Canadian cities were visited for a second and third time and the band took part in the Army's eightieth anniversary celebrations in London (Ontario). During this tour the bandsmen again took part in the Hollywood Bowl Easter morning event and visited San Francisco for the first time. A last-minute cancellation of a flight from Montreal due to inclement weather prevented Newfoundland from being visited.

Other territories in which the Staff Band has campaigned since the

First World War are Holland (1926 and 1949), Sweden (1950),
Switzerland (1954) and Norway (1964).

*   *   *

Only in recent years has the exchange of visits between bands in the
U.S.A. and Canada become a regular feature. In 1909 the New York
Staff Band carried out a 1,279-mile tour in Eastern Canada (the
Dominion was then divided into two territories) and twenty-eight
years were to pass before the band visited Toronto for a second visit.
Kingston and Hamilton (Ontario) have been scenes of New York Staff
Band campaigns since 1961.

In 1937 the Chicago Staff Band celebrated the thirtieth anniversary
of its formation by visiting Canada for the first time, Earlscourt
(Toronto) being the corps at which the week-end campaign was
conducted.

When, five years later, this band visited Winnipeg Citadel, it was
the first band from the U.S.A. to play in Manitoba's capital city.
Band Sergeant J. R. Webster, faithful international reporter of
Winnipeg events for many years, recalls: ' We had long looked for the
visit of a band from " across the line " and when we greeted the
Chicago Staff Band a cherished ambition was realized. The bands of
the Royal Canadian Air Force and the Princess Patricia's Canadian
Light Infantry paraded the visitors to the City Hall for a reception by
the Mayor and Aldermen.

' The band's personnel included Adjutant (later Brigadier) Cyril-
Everitt, Captain William Stevenson and Lieutenant (later Major) Ron
Rowland, whose cornet trios were exhilarating. Adjutant (later
Colonel) Douglas Norris, who was the staff Bandmaster, Captain (later
Brigadier) Howard Chesham and Bandsman Jack Nielson made up a
delightful horn trio. In the trombone section was Bandsman Ray Ogg,
composer of the " Chicago Temple " march, who was later to write
another popular march, " Rousseau ".' A contemporary report says
that 2,500 people were unable to gain admission to the Sunday afternoon festival.

One of the most widely travelled corps bands is that of Hollywood
Tabernacle, California. A trip to Vancouver in 1958 provided this
section with the honour of being the first Californian band to campaign in Canada. In 1960 Los Angeles Tabernacle Band, as it then
was, completed a ten-day tour of 10,000 miles which began with
participation in the annual spring festival in Toronto. West Toronto,
Toronto Temple and East Toronto Corps were visited before the band
continued its tour, working westward via Niagara Falls, Buffalo,
Detroit, Chicago and St. Louis (Missouri), to Kansas City.

In many areas in Canada it is easier and more convenient for bands
to exchange visits with their American counterparts than to 'special'
in their own territory.   Corps in such close proximity as Detroit
(Michigan) and Windsor (Ontario) frequently unite to provide a
programme with an international flavour.

It is equally true that campaigning in eastern Canada by western
Canadian sections is still something of an event, especially in view of
the great distances to be covered.   When Winnipeg Citadel Band
travelled to Toronto to take part in the spring festival in 1961 it was
the band's first visit to that territorial centre for twenty-seven years.
When Halifax Citadel Band, Nova Scotia, was featured in the 1963
spring festival it was making its first trip out of Nova Scotia.   Playing
in the same festival was Grand Falls Band, the first from Newfoundland
to visit Toronto.   Two years before, Corner Brook East Band became
the first from Newfoundland to 'special' on the Canadian mainland
when it visited Glace Bay, Nova Scotia.

Thanks to ever-developing transportation facilities the distance to
the New World is certainly shrinking and it is no longer unusual for
Hamilton (Ontario) Citadel Band to be the guest section in congress
meetings conducted by the Chief of the Staff in Los Angeles; a
Toronto band to campaign in Miami; Vancouver Temple Band to
play at a World Fair in Seattle (Washington) and San Francisco, or for
Oakland (California) Band to travel 500 miles by road to take part in
congress meetings led by the General at Long Beach.

Bearing this in mind, it is surprising to realize that the New York
Staff Band did not make its first visit to California until 1958, a year
after the International Staff Band had visited Los Angeles.

*   *   *

The first corps band from Europe to tour in North America was
Tranås, Sweden.   A touch of international camaraderie was added
en route by a spontaneous incident.   When the Scandinavian Air Lines
plane carrying the Swedish bandsmen to New York landed at Prest-
wick, Scotland, for refuelling just before midnight in early April, 1954,
Ayr Band was at the airport to play ' So we'll lift up the banner ' as
the aircraft touched down.

Although the Scotsmen did not receive much warning that the
Tranås Band would be making a ' flying ' visit, urgent phone calls and
speedy arrangements made the gesture possible.   As the passengers
alighted Ayr Band gave a typical welcome with ' Ye banks and braes '.
Greetings were exchanged and by request ' Petone Citadel ' was played.
Bandmaster Gunnar Borg conducted 'Auld lang syne '.

After being presented with a sprig of white heather each, the

bandsmen boarded the plane and were airborne to the strains of
' Crimond '—at one o'clock on a wet morning!

Soon after arriving in New York Tranås Band began its extensive
history-making campaign by participating in the biennial music
leaders' congress. When Dr. Edwin Franko Goldman, the eminent
American composer and conductor, heard his march, ' Kentucky ', he
said: ' Ladies and gentlemen. You are hearing tonight one of the
greatest brass bands of non-professional musicians I ever have heard
. . . and that takes in a lot of territory. These men are wonderful!
Any of the brass players in any of the symphony orchestras could not
play any better than these men. I do wish all school and college bands
could hear them.'

The month-long tour was a tremendous success. With the
Japanese Cherry Blossom Festival in Washington, D.C., serving as a
colourful background, the programme in the Constitution Hall
thrilled a large audience, more than half of which was hearing a
Salvation Army band give a programme for the first time. At the
conclusion Bandmaster Borg was presented with a key to the city of
Washington as a memento of the visit and in honour of the band's
service to the cause of music.

Easter week-end was spent in the Swedish-American city of
Jamestown, New York, where, naturally enough, a popular item was
Erik Leidzén's ' First Swedish rhapsody '.

On Palm Sunday morning a broadcast from Akron, Ohio, was
heard by one of the largest radio audiences ever to listen to a Salvation
Army presentation. The Armed Forces Network included radio
stations in Ecuador, Tangiers, Greenland and Korea. Its potential
audience ran into millions.

In addition, tape recordings of the programme were distributed
throughout the United States and parts of Europe including Germany,
Denmark, Finland, Norway and Sweden. The Tranås bandsmen
heard the programme broadcast from a Stockholm station two weeks
after returning home.

The only festival given on Canadian soil took place in Toronto's
Massey Hall. At Buffalo, New York, three eminent Salvationist
composers—Colonel Bramwell Coles, Erik Leidzén and Emil Söderström—were present to hear their writings featured on the programme.

*   *   *

The second band from Europe—other than the Household Troops
and International Staff—to visit the U.S.A. was the Netherlands
National Band. In 1959, coinciding with the 350th anniversary of the
opening of the Hudson Valley by the Dutch pioneers, the band carried

out a month's campaign which included the spring festival in Toronto (Canada) and a visit to Montreal.

Upon its arrival in Washington, D.C., the band was received at the Netherlands Embassy by the Netherlands Ambassador and consular staff. The tour of the city included a visit to the White House while President Eisenhower and his family were in residence.

*　　*　　*

In 1923 Bandmaster A. W. Punchard received an invitation from Commissioner Charles Sowton, then a Territorial Commander in Canada, for Chalk Farm Band to visit the Dominion, the proposal being that the tour should also include some calls in the U.S.A. This project required much consideration, especially in view of the time necessary for the band to be absent from England.

Interviews with shipping companies (air travel was not even remotely contemplated in those days) and negotiations regarding the expense led to the proposal being accepted in principle, but International Headquarters considered such a tour inadvisable at that time. The idea was reluctantly abandoned—'for a while'. Thus Chalk Farm Band was deprived from adding yet another 'first' to its long record.

Forty-one years later—in April, 1964—Tottenham Citadel became the first corps band from the British Territory to visit Canada and the United States, its seventeen-day tour beginning soon after the band arrived by air at Montreal. The first festival was given in Ottawa, and the next morning the bandsmen were received on behalf of the Canadian Government at Parliament Buildings.

In Toronto the band shared the sixtieth anniversary celebrations of Dovercourt Citadel Band, a festival in the Massey Hall highlighting these events. After a visit to Peterborough, Ontario, the band crossed the border into the States, calling at Syracuse, Boston, Hartford, Philadelphia, New York, Scranton, Pittsburgh and Cleveland. The stay in New York City was planned to coincide with the music leaders' councils, the partnership festival with the New York Staff Band proving a memorable occasion.

Returning to Canada at Niagara Falls, where a programme was given, Tottenham Citadel became the first British band to play at Stratford-on-Avon, Ontario, Canada's Shakespeare town, before appearing as the guest section in the Toronto spring festival. The thrill-packed tour ended with Sunday meetings at Hamilton.

*　　*　　*

American Salvationists have also shown a high regard for Scandinavian strings bands. In the summer of 1957 the Stockholm 5

K

(Sweden) String Band was invited by officers responsible for Scandinavian work in the U.S.A. Eastern and Central Territories to campaign for a month.

Proudly bearing the new flag presented to them on the eve of the tour by King Gustav VI Adolf of Sweden, the thirty members crossed the Atlantic by plane to be enthusiastically received in New York City. That night the Swedish lasses, neatly attired in maroon and blue uniforms, attended a crusade meeting conducted by Dr. Billy Graham in Madison Square Gardens. They were recognized publicly by the noted evangelist and warmly acclaimed by the crowd.

The next day the campaign opened with a festival given at New York Citadel (Scandinavian) Corps.

In September, 1964, a second Swedish string band visited the U.S.A.—from Jönköping. The first half of the month was spent in the Central Territory. Many cities, including Chicago and New York, were visited and the band's presence attracted large audiences of Scandinavians.

Forty-two of the seventy-five members of the band made the trip. Each paid her own fare, many taking on extra employment in order to cover the costs. Also, most of the women forewent their holidays.

*   *   *

In June, 1960, the New York Staff Band paid its third visit to Britain (previous occasions were for the International Congresses of 1904 and 1914). That the New Yorkers meant business was proved when, within forty-five minutes of its arrival at the International Training College, Denmark Hill, from the airport, it had embarked on a two-hour practice. The next evening the visitors were plunged straight into the bandmasters' councils festival at the Royal Albert Hall and on the day following participated in the councils conducted by General Wilfred Kitching.

Taking to the road, the band's first stop was at Nottingham, where William Booth's birthplace was visited before the evening festival in the Albert Hall.

In the U.S.A. some critics had suggested that touring with a brass band in Great Britain was like 'taking coals to Newcastle'. That familiar saying was perpetuated in the City Hall of the northern city of this name when the Executive Officer of the Staff Band, Colonel William Maltby, presented the Divisional Commander with a sizeable piece of coal from the North-East Pennsylvania coalfield, especially glazed and embossed with a Salvation Army shield and bearing an inscription to mark the occasion. Mrs. George Marshall, widow of the famous composer, met the band before the festival.

Upon arrival in Edinburgh the campaigners were welcomed to the Palace of Holyrood House by the Lord Provost and the United States Consul-General, both of whom addressed the band at lunch. An afternoon programme in the Ross Bandstand in Princes Street Gardens was followed by a festival in the Usher Hall.

Crowds in Manchester, Liverpool, Birmingham and Oxford were equally vociferous in their welcome and the tour reached a triumphant climax with a farewell festival at Clapton Congress Hall presided over by the Chief of the Staff (Commissioner William Dray). The historic occasion concluded with ' The King of kings ', and the echo of the majestic final chords had not died upon the air before the audience had risen to its feet to display evidence of approbation seldom seen in Army circles in Britain.

*　　　*　　　*

Hollywood Tabernacle Band continued its extensive travelling (already referred to) when it became the first corps band from North America to visit Great Britain for fifty years.

From its initial appearance at the bandmasters' councils festival in the Royal Albert Hall the men from California won the hearts of British Salvationists with their sincere evangelism and technical excellence. At Regent Hall a memorable Sunday's activity made a tremendous impact on the corps and the unique district. The band's rapid marching step and fine martial bearing attracted great crowds to accompany it through the West End streets.

On their journey north the campaigners made stops at Coventry, Birmingham, Nottingham and Newcastle before crossing the border. In the Usher Hall, Edinburgh, the bandsmen made an unexpected entry with tartan tammies in glorious Technicolor. Said a reporter: ' The representative Scottish audience really relished this modest piece of American showmanship which set the pattern of a bright and buoyant festival.'

The British part of the tour ended with a week-end at Manchester which resulted in ten seekers being registered.

Crossing the North Sea, the Hollywood Tabernacle Band brought further blessing to enthusiastic audiences in Amsterdam and Groningen (the Netherlands), Hamburg (Germany) and Copenhagen (Denmark). It was following the final week-end in the Danish capital that the accident occurred in which two of the bandsmen lost their lives.

*　　　*　　　*

The first band from the U.S.A. to visit Scandinavia was Rockford Temple, from the Central Territory. In 1963 the men crossed the Atlantic by air to participate in the Swedish Congress gatherings in

Stockholm and to give a festival in Norway. A year later the Northern New Jersey Division Youth Band campaigned in Denmark and Sweden.

This talented group was 'adopted' by the State of New Jersey during the twelve months of 300th anniversary celebrations, and the trip to Europe was officially sponsored by the State authorities.

*   *   *

History was made in 1948 when Hawthorn Citadel became the first Australian band to visit New Zealand and to campaign outside the Commonwealth. Among the centres visited were Foxton, Palmerston North, New Plymouth, Hamilton, Putaruru, Opotiki, Wairoa and Napier (North Island) and Lyttelton, Ashburton, Dunedin, Timaru and Christchurch (South Island). Week-ends were spent at Auckland Congress Hall and Wellington Citadel.

At Wellington, Petone, Wellington South and Wellington Citadel Bands united with the visitors for a 'wonder week-end', the musical highlight of which was the festival in the town hall when the programme closed with the playing of the 'Hallelujah' Chorus by massed bands and grand organ.

Ten years later the Melbourne Staff Band fulfilled a long-held ambition by carrying out a seventeen-day tour of New Zealand. After stopping for a programme at Sydney Congress Hall, the band crossed the Tasman Sea to begin its campaign at Auckland. Ten days on the North Island was followed by visits to centres on South Island including Gore, Invercargill and Wellington. Sydney Congress Hall (1952) and Brisbane Temple Band (1964) have also campaigned in New Zealand.

*   *   *

The first New Zealand band to visit Australia was Wellington Citadel in 1949, when, during three weeks, the principal cities of both territories were included in the campaign. Vast distances were covered by exhausting rail travel.

Fifteen years later a similar tour by the same band was accomplished in half the time, thanks to the advancement of air transport.

The campaign began in Melbourne and continued to include Brisbane, Inverell, Newcastle (New South Wales), Sydney, Dulwich Hill and Petersham.

The only other New Zealand band to visit Australia is Auckland Congress Hall which, in 1958, conducted a three-week tour. The full itinerary included visits to Wollongong, North Sydney, Goulburn, Wagga Wagga, Norwood, Unley and Horsham.

Easter week-end was spent in and around Adelaide and the band participated in the Territorial Congress in Melbourne.

★ ★ ★

Unique in the history of Salvation Army campaigning was the London Band. It was formed solely for the purpose of conducting a continental tour and, with the fulfilment of that assignment, ceased to exist.

In 1935 Commissioner Charles Rich, then Territorial Commander for Sweden, suggested a visit to his territory of a small British band. Other bands, notably Chalk Farm and Tottenham Citadel, had visited Sweden, but the Commissioner was anxious to demonstrate the potentialities of a comparatively small ensemble more the size of the average Swedish band of that period.

So the London Band came into being. About a dozen of the players were members of the International Staff Band, the remainder, with one exception, being selected from corps in the London area. Colonel George Fuller, then International Staff Bandmaster, was the conductor, and Brigadier James Sansom, who was on furlough from missionary service in China, acted as leader.

The trip was arranged so hurriedly that rehearsal time was limited. The uniform problem was solved by the purchase of plain red tunics, which, adorned with the Union Jack, the bandsmen were required to buy themselves.

In nine days the band gave twenty festivals and travelled more than 1,000 miles. The playing of Tom Giles on cornet, Cyril Brisley on trombone and Captain Bernard Adams on saxophone was featured on the various programmes.

A humorous interlude typical of band tours concerns Adjutant (later Lieut.-Commissioner) Gösta Blomberg, who acted as interpreter for the London Band. At the commencement of a festival the Adjutant would introduce the band, and then explain that the personnel included two sons of the Territorial Commander—Adjutant Victor Rich and Captain Wesley Rich, both of whom have since become Colonels.

The Swedish comrades were naturally anxious to identify the brothers, and Adjutant Blomberg would then call upon the Commissioner's sons to stand up, which they dutifully did. This developed into quite a routine until one day, when the inevitable request was made, the entire band stood up in response. None enjoyed the joke more than the Commissioner, who was touched by the hidden tribute and often referred to the bandsmen as his sons. A member of the band said: 'We all appreciated the kindly and almost paternal interest the Commissioner displayed in us.'

*   *   *

What might have been the most extensive campaign in the history of Army music was announced by General Bramwell Booth at Bandmasters' Councils at Clapton in January, 1921—but it never took place! Toward the end of the afternoon session the General made known his decision to send a band formed of capable British bandsmen around the world.

The General explained that the men selected would have to be efficient players and singers, with a love for souls as well as music. They would have to be prepared to be honorary members, receiving no remuneration for their services, although all expenses would be paid. The tour would probably be across the United States and Canada to Hawaii, Fiji, New Zealand, Australia, Japan, Ceylon, Port Said, Genoa, across the continent of Europe to Paris and then to London once more. It was suggested that conscription would not be needed for membership of the 'World-Tour Band', the leader of which, said the General, was already in mind.

The cause of the dropping of this ambitious plan is unknown, and the majority of places named are still awaiting the first visit of a band from Britain.

CHAPTER EIGHTEEN

BEHIND THE NOTES

FOLLOWING the campaigns conducted by the Fry family in many parts of Britain a wave of musical enthusiasm swept the land. Bands sprang up everywhere and, naturally enough, they needed music.

As most of the special arrangements used by the 'Hallelujah Family' were carried out by the eldest son, Fred W. Fry, the help of this talented pioneer was enlisted by the enterprising early-day Bandmasters. He sought to meet the demands for accompaniments to songs, often working in trains, trams or billets as well as carrying out the campaign responsibilities.

Soon there were too many bands for Fred Fry to oblige and the task of providing music was left to the individual Bandmasters. Those who were not able to prepare copies for their men—not all were aware of their deficiency!—obtained music from a variety of sources. Much of it, secured from outside circles, was totally unsuitable for Salvation Army purposes, and several wide-awake music publishers, sensing money in the business, began producing compositions advertised as 'Just the thing for Salvation Army bands'.

This and other experiments soon produced a state of complete chaos. As far as popular song arrangements were concerned there was a sad lack of uniformity, and this was revealed to a pathetic degree when bands gathered for divisional and area events. United playing, which later became a feature of Army musical activity, was out of the question, for the arrangements were at variance one with another in matters of pitch and harmonies.

Although there had never been any thought of bands as a separate musical force in the mind of William Booth—they were viewed purely and simply as an aid to congregational singing—with the phenomenal growth of brass banding came the conviction that a distinct branch should be formed, under proper oversight, to ensure that bands should play the same kind of music in a uniform way.

In September, 1881, Fred Fry, private secretary to Commandant Herbert Booth, at that time in charge of the men's side of the officers' training home at Clapton, was appointed to produce music to meet the growing needs of corps brass bands. This responsibility was in addition to his existing duties.

To encourage the composer in his task the Army purchased a

second-hand printing press, some letter type and two founts of pied music type which no printer would put in order.

In *Father of Salvation Army Music*, Lieut.-Commissioner Arch R. Wiggins states:

> The acquiescent Fry was given instructions to put the type into the correct cases and find out how to set it up ready for printing Salvation Army music and song, both in staff and tonic sol-fa notation.
>
> Although he had been unacquainted with the work of a compositor, Fry set himself the task, almost entirely unaided, of mastering this specialized and most difficult branch of printing, and with commendable success. . . .
>
> His ingenuity again came to the rescue of this man of many parts. He drew a plan of the cases and then a copy of each piece of music type. These were divided into sections and placed in the two cases in the positions in which he thought they would be most convenient for him to handle. Some years afterward, Fred Fry visited a music publishing house and, to his surprise and gratification, found very little difference in the order of the various pieces of type from that which he had adopted.
>
> Fry fixed his setting stick at the proper length, started to build up his puzzle and then found that he had reached the end of the line whilst still in the middle of a bar. What was he to do? A happy thought occurred to him. The line was divided into ems—the printer's measure—and all that was necessary was for him to write under the top line of his copy the number of ems each chord, etc., should take. If it did not come right at the end of the line he could add or subtract, in pencil, sufficient of them to make the line of the required length. He had no more trouble with spacing the music.
>
> By such crude methods did The Salvation Army produce its first printed music . . . and it will always owe a debt of gratitude to Fred Fry, the man who was never at a loss in finding the way through a problem.

Ten months after Fry took up his duties, band music for The Salvation Army was being published, printed on stiff cards, each set containing eight tunes and sold at sixpence per instrumental part. Between then and March, 1883, seven such cards were issued, but the venture was not considered successful. Some of the bands had by this time become so accustomed to playing music of a more advanced order that they did not take too kindly to the idea of having to make what they considered to be 'retrograde progress'. They had, they said, made more advance than playing merely song tunes. This controversy led to the publication of a regulation forbidding the use of all 'outside' music.

In September, 1882, a young infidel, Richard Slater, was converted at Regent Hall, London. A musician of outstanding ability who, as a member of the Royal Albert Hall Amateur Orchestral Society, had played first violin under Sir Arthur Sullivan and other notable conductors, Slater, with his dedicated talent, proved the man for whom William Booth was seeking. The Founder had come to the opinion that the Army should have its own Music Department.

This was established on October 22, 1883, at Clapton under the personal supervision of Commandant Herbert Booth. The three members of the staff were Richard Slater, Fred Fry and Henry Hill, who were given the rank of Bandmaster and recognized as officers. They were together for three years.

Henry Hill, from Hull, was a police sergeant and had served for a considerable time with the police band in that city. He had also been Bandmaster at Hull Icehouse Corps and, on moving to London, took up a similar appointment at Clapton Congress Hall. Because of his experience he was a useful man. His love for the Army, and especially his interest in its musical development, was proved by the fact that he gladly forfeited a pension (the time for qualifying for this was drawing near) to take up a full-time post in the Music Editorial Department, as it later became known, where he remained until 1888.

These then were the men who laid the foundation of the Army's musical edifice. Their initial production was *Salvation Music*, Volume 2 (most of the verses were to popular secular melodies), the first collection to be issued of original Army songs with music. This was in December, 1883, barely two months after the department's formation.

In less than a year the first issue of *The Salvation Army Brass Band Journal* was published in a cheaper form than were the earlier stiff cards, and at more regular intervals. The idea caught on and proved successful both from a business standpoint and as a means of meeting the needs of the ever-growing musical side of Army activity.

No time was lost in preparing a band book in which eighty-eight congregational tunes were arranged for accompaniment purposes. This was published in November, 1884, and was the most important musical work to be issued up to that time. By the end of that year Band Journals 1 to 5 had been released.

In addition to their editorial duties, Slater, Fry and Hill were required to travel with the ' Singing, Speaking and Praying Brigade ', led by Herbert Booth. They composed and arranged much of the music used by the brigade.

The efforts of the department to provide compositions for the ' Singing, Speaking and Praying Brigade ' were so successful that copies were in great demand. It was natural that those who heard the popular songs should wish to sing them, and to meet the growing need these were reprinted in leaflet form and sold at one penny each. Later they were collected in one volume and issued as *Favourite Songs of the Singing, Speaking and Praying Brigade* and in this way the Army's first original vocal music appeared.

Greater publicity was given to these new compositions during the first International Congress held in London in May, 1886, and the outcome of this extended interest was the introduction of *The Musical Salvationist* two months later. This publication has regularly appeared since then and has ever sought to provide material for the Army's vocalists and to encourage the musical-poetical gifts of Salvationists.

With the establishment of the *Band Journal* and *The Musical Salvationist*, Staff-Captain Slater (his promotion to that rank from that of Bandmaster was not long in coming) and his two valued assistants were kept busy ensuring a steady flow of compositions, both vocal and instrumental, although it must be emphasized that the latter still consisted of simple arrangements of song tunes for the main purpose of accompanying singing.

It became apparent that the Army's musicians, apart from being supplied with material to sing and play, needed some technical instruction. A small scale sheet was published in May, 1887, and tutors for the various instruments in use in Army bands followed, that for the cornet being the first of the series. This was on sale for the first time at the Army's Silver Jubilee Celebrations at the Crystal Palace on July 15, 1890.

By this time Henry Hill had left the department to become a corps officer and Slater's only assistant was Staff-Captain Fred Fry, who continued to serve this branch of Army activity until appointed to Canada as private secretary to Commandant Herbert Booth, the Territorial Commander.

On October 14, 1892, Fry's successor began work in the department. He was Captain (later Colonel) Frederick G. Hawkes.

Richard Slater chose well and wisely. This was no hasty appointment. Young Fred Hawkes had become known as the able euphonium player in the Household Troops Band. For five years he travelled with this noted combination, not only proving himself an accomplished instrumentalist but also finding time to study various branches of the art of music, including harmony and composition.

In April, 1891, Fred Hawkes's first song—words and music— appeared in *The Musical Salvationist* and it is evident that this and other early experiments created a favourable impression upon the music chief. More than a year later the young trooper, to his surprise, received a number of letters from Richard Slater, inquiring as to his line of musical studies.

This interest was obviously worth while for, when the vacancy caused by Fry's transfer needed to be filled, another Fred received the appointment.

A month before Fred Hawkes joined the staff the first full band score had been published with Band Journal 201. This was printed by lithography from hand-written copies made by Staff-Captain Fry, a responsibility which immediately devolved upon the new assistant. Speaking of this exciting and historic period, Colonel Hawkes recalled the many times he suffered from writer's cramp and aching eyes as he slowly and carefully committed the myriad notes and signs to sensitized paper, using lithographic ink—a greasy, sticky fluid—and a small mapping pen.

This tedious work, though extremely trying to the young beginner, proved invaluable experience and taught him many things. His laborious duties forced his attention on inner detail and gave him a minute knowledge of full scores, which were then unknown outside the Army.

The first score for which Hawkes was responsible was the Christmas, 1892, issue of Band Journal 205–208. It is of historical interest that the first band scoring the Colonel was required to do after entering the department was arranging the bass solo in the march, ' A Full Salvation' (B.J. 212). In this way he had a hand in producing the most advanced Army music to that time, for this was the first song published in march form.

Whether Bandmasters of those days were not sufficiently progressive to keep pace with the opportunities presented them or whether they could not see the need for wanting to know what was happening in the band, it is a fact that, after appearing consecutively until Band Journal 270, the full score was dropped as not being a paying proposition. But with ever-mounting evidence of wisdom and enlightenment, wielders of the baton later began to clamour for the discarded publication and in June, 1899, a fresh start was made in a new form with Journals Nos. 367–370. Full scores have appeared ever since.

The earliest issues of *The Musical Salvationist* contained Army pieces arranged for various instruments such as the piano, violin, string bands, concertina bands and drum and fife bands, as well as concerted items for brass instruments. In addition its pages included educational articles (this was before the publication of *The Bandsman and Songster*), which were highly appreciated by enthusiastic Salvationists; and *The Musical Salvationist* became not only a collection of new songs from which band arrangements could later be made, but it was accepted as the Salvationist musicians' textbook as well.

The earliest numbers of the *Band Journal* were, of necessity, of simple arrangements. They were, in the main, faithful transcriptions of already popular vocal music, for at that time the sole function of a band was to assist the singing both on the march and in the meetings. As with the progress of any healthy project, composers, performers and listeners were not content with this for any length of time, and

step by step music expanded. The tunes became more developed
with a more varied harmonic construction.

On September 4, 1901, a memorandum containing the Music
Board's proposals for revising the policy was placed before William
Booth. The result was that the Founder decided to permit the use of
band music for which no words had been composed or intended. He
also agreed that, subject to certain conditions, the Music Board could
give further latitude to instrumentation and arrangement, the piece
not necessarily being confined to the melody.

Slater was commissioned to submit specimen types, three of which
were approved for publication: the marches, ' The morning hymn '
(B.J. 411), ' Our Battalions ' (B.J. 415) and ' Festival ' (B.J. 422). These
compositions represent the earliest pieces written expressly for Army
brass bands and therefore mark an important milestone in Salvationist
musical history. Other early pieces in this form were ' Spanish
Chant ', ' Vesper Hymn ' (both by Colonel Hawkes) and the ' Swedish
March '.

The first selection, ' Old song memories ', appeared in January,
1902, and was given away to bands as an advertisement. It occupied
two pages and was not included in the *Band Journal*. Other new forms
were gradually added.

The publication of Slater's festival arrangement, 'Lead, kindly
Light ', caused something of a sensation. A florid semiquaver arrangement for the cornet in one section was the cause for complaint.

' Actually, it was the Army's first air varié, although that designation was then forbidden,' says Lieut.-Commissioner Wiggins in *Father
of Salvation Army Music.* ' " Lead, kindly Light " was a precursor of
what is now generally known as the meditation form,' writes Colonel
Hawkes. Air varié or meditation, there is no doubt that this Slater
production set the Army banding world talking.

*   *   *

In 1915 General Bramwell Booth instituted a commission to
inquire into matters relating to Salvation Army music and the regulations and administration governing bands and songster brigades. Part
of the commission's terms of reference was to consider and report on
how far, in its judgment, the development of Army vocal and instrumental music during the past ten years had been of advantage to:
(1) the supreme importance of efforts for the salvation of the people
and the building up of a simple and zealous soldiery; (2) the desirability
of Salvation Army music; and (3) the extent to which the vocal and
instrumental music now issued is suited to the abilities of Salvationist
executants.

The Council of Inquiry consisted of:

Commissioner John Carleton (*Chairman*).
Commissioner Edward J. Higgins.
Commissioner John Lawley.
Commissioner George Mitchell.
Commissioner Charles Jeffries.
Lieut.-Colonel Samuel Hurren.
Lieut.-Colonel John Hillary.
Lieut.-Colonel Herbert Jackson.
Lieut.-Colonel George Holmes.
Major Catherine Booth.

In order to make the basis of inquiry as broad as possible the following were called in to give evidence:

One Divisional Bandmaster.
One Divisional Songster Leader.
Seven Corps Bandmasters.
Four Corps Songster Leaders.
Six Field Officers.
Four Divisional Commanders.

In addition information was also given by the Chief Secretary for the British Territory, Brigadier Richard Slater, Major Fred Hawkes, Major Arthur Goldsmith and Band Inspector Edward Hill.

In order to keep procedure strictly confined to the terms of reference, as set forth in the Minute, a list of over sixty leading questions for each section of witnesses was drawn up by the council, that for Bandmasters and Songster Leaders, for instance, differing slightly from those put to Divisional Commanders and field officers. While the main questions were put by the chairman, any member of the council was free to interrogate witnesses on points arising out of the answers given. As those giving evidence had no previous knowledge of the questions, the answers were unpremeditated and spontaneous.

A verbatim report of the answers was taken and typed copies were later supplied to each member of the council.

The first sitting was held on October 26, 1915. In all, twenty sessions were held, each of about three hours' duration.

On March 23, 1916, the council presented a completed report, one of a full and detailed character dealing not only with faults and weaknesses, but also making recommendations for improvements. Many suggestions were adapted almost immediately; others, of a long-term character, were introduced later.

A brief extract of the findings read: ' The commission . . . has given careful attention and consideration to the views of the comrades who have given evidence. It has also endeavoured to keep well in mind the main purpose of Salvation Army music, both vocal and instrumental, and which, in its opinion, are of a threefold character, viz.: (1) to attract, (2) to accompany congregational singing and (3) to speak directly to the hearts of the people.

'The commission is of the opinion that the recent development of Army music, both vocal and instrumental, has been of advantage to the Army, from each of these standpoints.'

Here was direct evidence in favour of the way being opened to a more advanced style of music, developed as a result of Richard Slater's interview with William Booth in 1901.

The report also included some amount of criticism and recommendations for improvements but, on the whole, it was distinctly reassuring and confirmed Army leaders in their musical policy and its administration.   *   *   *

Although certain modifications, alterations and additions have been made from time to time, the composition of the brass band, so far as instruments are concerned, remains practically as it was at the introduction of the first issue of the *Band Journal*, the flugel horn being the only additional instrument introduced.

In the early days there was no restriction on the type of musical instrument used. The first groups were composed of a mixture of brass, woodwind, whistles, concertinas, accordions and fiddles, but the formation of the band gradually took shape and by the time the *Band Journal* was first issued the following plan of instrumentation was agreed upon: B♭ and E♭ clarinets, 1st and 2nd cornets, 1st and 2nd tenor horns, 1st and 2nd baritones, 1st, 2nd and bass trombones, solo euphonium, B♭ bass and E♭ bombardon, side and bass drum.

The reason the B♭ and E♭ basses here stand in reverse order to the present system of grouping is that for some years the E♭ bombardon was the largest and deepest bass instrument in general use, the B♭ bass part being played on the euphonium. It was not unusual for a large band to have three solo euphoniums and three bass euphoniums. In due course, however, the latter dropped out of use and BB♭ monstre basses were gradually introduced. By the summer of 1895 the Musical Instrument Department reported the sale of five monstres.

For a number of years clarinets were featured in Army bands. At the end of 1895 there were seven at Bristol 1, five at Nunhead, and four in the International Staff Band and at Portsmouth. As late as 1899 there were six at Penge, where Colonel Hawkes was the Bandmaster. The woodwind instruments slowly disappeared and by 1902 their use had become so small that it was considered unwise to go to the expense of engraving and printing the music parts. Bands still wishing to use woodwinds could improvise effectively from other band parts. Swindon I, Exeter I and Warrington Bands had saxophones well into the twentieth century, and Chalk Farm until Bandmaster Punchard's retirement in 1938.

*   *   *

During the thirty years that Richard Slater was in charge of the Music Editorial Department he had four assistants. Three of them— Fry, Hill and Hawkes—have already been mentioned. The appointment of the fourth, Staff-Captain (later Colonel) Arthur Goldsmith, marked a new era in Salvation Army band history, for he began to produce music more advanced than instrumentalists had encountered up to that time. Thus they were provided with a fresh impetus and gained a vision of higher standards.

Born in Poplar, young Goldsmith began work at International Headquarters in 1888 and much of his early theoretical study of music was done whilst walking between his home and Queen Victoria Street.

When the Junior Staff Band was formed Arthur Goldsmith, then the youthful Bandmaster at Poplar, became a member, later playing in the Home Office and Trade Headquarters Bands before joining the International Staff Band in 1901. For twenty-eight years he played in the Army's premier band, becoming renowned for his prowess as a soprano cornetist.

When *The Bandsman and Songster* (forerunner of *The Musician*) was published in 1907 Staff-Captain Goldsmith became its first editor. A year later he joined Brigadier Slater and Staff-Captain Hawkes in the Music Editorial Department, where he remained for thirteen years, serving jointly with Colonel Hawkes as music editor from 1913 until 1921.

Goldsmith dabbled in composition from his earliest years and had his first song published in 1895. Eleven years later he was successful in securing two first prizes in an international music competition. The first was for an original melody to the song, ' We're travelling home to heaven above ', which now appears in the *Tune Book Supplement* (No. 627) under the title of ' Goldsmith '; the second award was for his ' Prize Selection No. 1 ', later renamed ' Mercy '.

There is no doubt that this selection, the Colonel's first composition, published in Band Journal 534, made a great impression upon Richard Slater, as well as on the Army's musical following of that day, and it came as no great surprise when the composer was appointed to the already overworked department.

During his years in the department the genius of Goldsmith the composer reached its zenith. Selection followed selection in amazingly rapid succession interspersed now and then with a march or a sheet of

favourite congregational hymn-tune arrangements. Practically all of
his eighty published compositions for bands were written in this time,
including such Army classics as 'My Guide', 'My Light', 'Rock-
ingham', 'The banner of liberty' and 'Conquering Faith'.

Colonel Goldsmith had a conviction about the purposes of Army
music which sometimes led to his being misunderstood. When he
was the guest of honour at a 'Goldsmith Night' at Clapton Congress
Hall in April, 1939, he said: 'I have never written a selection without
having the Army and its demands always in mind. I always ask
myself: "Is this suitable for Salvation Army requirements?"'

These were no idle words, for the spiritual appeal to be found in his
compositions is sufficient confirmation of his unwavering opinion. So
strongly did he feel about the matter of suitability that when the idea
of a Festival Series Journal was first mooted, he vigorously opposed the
suggestion, fearing that the music likely to be written for the new
journal might tend to lead away from the supreme purpose of Army
banding. It is significant that no piece in the Festival Series Journal
bears his name.

Although it will probably never be known if he lived to regret this
decision, it is a fact that when Colonel Goldsmith was the conductor
of the Men's Social Headquarters Band some of these more developed
compositions were among his favourite programme choices.

Arthur Goldsmith was thirty-three years of age when he became a
member of the Music Editorial Department and forty-six when he left
it. With a few minor exceptions nothing from his once virile pen
saw the light of day after that time. This was surely too early for a
creative composer of his calibre to dry up! He was promoted to Glory
in 1948.   *   *   *

During the period that Colonel Fred Hawkes was in charge of the
Music Editorial Department (1913 to 1936) the solid foundation laid
by Richard Slater was built upon and the influence of Salvation Army
music became even more widespread.

The second Head was a progressive architect and under his direction
there was a consistent pressing forward to supply the ever-growing
need of Army bandsmen, not only in the matter of output but also in
the type of music demanded by advancing enthusiasts.

This led, in 1923, to the publication of the *Festival Series Band
Journal*, the first piece in which was Colonel Hawkes's arrangement of
'Gems from the "Messiah"', the first of many such productions
from his pen. Two years before, a *Second* (later renamed *Triumph*)
Series Band Journal had been issued to meet the need of smaller bands
and the increasing number of young people's instrumental sections.

Soloists were not overlooked in this attempt to provide music for progressive musicians within the Army's ranks and instrumental albums began to appear containing a number of solos for various instruments, all with pianoforte accompaniment. Some of these had been published previously with band accompaniment in the journals, but the albums made it possible for soloists to feature their favourite items without the band being present.

Some consternation was caused when the first theme-with-variations solo was published, but this popular style has become such a feature of Salvation Army musical life that one cannot imagine a time when the Army was without it. The same could be said of the air varié and other forms which were introduced during Colonel Hawkes's responsibility for Army music.

Although Richard Slater relinquished responsibility in 1913 (with the rank of Brigadier) he had by no means spent his last days in the department. Ten years later, when Colonel Hawkes suffered a serious breakdown in health, the ' Father of Salvation Army Music ', at the age of sixty-nine, was recalled to take temporary charge of affairs. On August 25, 1923, General Bramwell Booth accorded Richard Slater the Army's highest honour by appointing him a member of the Order of the Founder. The citation read:

> Whereas it has been reported to me that Richard Slater, a Lieut.-Colonel of The Salvation Army, rendered invaluable service in the Army's ministry of music, as a composer, also for many years as director of the musical publications issued by International Headquarters, and whereas it seems to me that the service of the said Richard Slater as above recorded was in itself and in its spirit and purpose such as would have especially commended him to the attention and approval of our beloved Founder, now I hereby appoint the said Richard Slater a member of the Order of the Founder and direct that his name be inscribed on the roll of the Order.
>
> W. Bramwell Booth.

This quiet, unassuming man, to whom Salvationists owe so much, made Army history by being promoted in rank whilst in retirement. Nineteen years after becoming a Brigadier and soon after returning to Judd Street, he was sent for by Commissioner Richard Wilson, then in charge of Salvationist Publishing and Supplies, Ltd., and, following an interview, emerged from the office a Lieut.-Colonel. He was to enjoy many more years of retirement before being promoted to Glory in December, 1939.

When Colonel Hawkes retired in 1936 he had completed forty-four years in the department and twenty-three as its head. He was promoted to Glory in November, 1959, nine months after celebrating his ninetieth birthday.

*   *   *

Upon Lieut.-Colonel Slater's return for his second period as head of the department Ensign (later Colonel) Bramwell Coles, then a member of the Editorial Department at International Headquarters, was appointed to assist him and remained in this emergency capacity until August, 1925.

Colonel Coles was then transferred to editorial work in Canada, where he remained until appointed to succeed Colonel Hawkes in 1936. He held that position until his retirement sixteen years later, when he returned to Canada. The Colonel was promoted to Glory whilst visiting England in the summer of 1960.

The name of Bramwell Coles has been synonymous with Salvation Army music since, as a young Chalk Farm bandsman, he gained awards in international music competitions with more than one rhythmic march. When his 'Prize March No. 3' was published Slater's comment was: 'The writer has melodic invention (the highest of all gifts a composer can possess) so that if he works hard enough to master the technical laws of composition, there is hope for him in the future.' 'Chalk Farm', 'Under the colours', 'The Conflict' and 'Active Service' are still recalled by older bandsmen, while the present generation delights to play 'Victors Acclaimed', 'Danforth Citadel' and 'The King's musicians'. Other marches from his pen include: 'Under two flags', 'Undaunted', 'The flag of freedom', 'In the firing line', 'The glory of the combat' and 'Departed Heroes'.

When Colonel George Fuller retired from the Bandmastership of the International Staff Band in 1942 he referred to Colonel Coles as 'the writer of some of the finest marches the world has known'. This was no exaggeration, for Bramwell Coles may well be recognized for all time as the Army's Sousa in the realm of composition.

The Colonel's selections cannot be overlooked, for he has many masterpieces to his credit, among them 'Atonement', 'The Man of Sorrows', 'Discipleship', 'When I survey the wondrous Cross ("Wareham")', 'The divine pursuit' and 'Portraits from Paul's Epistles'. His two outstanding arrangements, 'Moments with Tchaikovsky' and 'Treasures from Tchaikovsky', have also become classics in Army music.

It is inevitable that the story of such a fascinating facet of Army music-making should, to some extent, be a parade of personalities. In paying tribute to the five officers who have given such distinguished service as Heads of the Music Editorial Department it is impossible to forget the contribution made by the many who have assisted them during the long years.

*   *   *

Among those who gave valued help to Colonel Hawkes was Lieut.-Colonel Arthur Bristow who, appointed to the department from the command of Darlington Citadel Corps, served in it for three years. He was later Manager of the Musical Instruments and Musical Publications Department. The Colonel says: ' Those three years were of untold help to me and I feel indebted to Colonel Hawkes for the guidance and instruction I received at his hands! '

Henry Hall, a young bandsman from Nunhead, who has made a name for himself in other musical circles, was a junior assistant during the early part of the First World War, and among a number of former members of the staff is Bandmaster Phil B. Catelinet, of Pittsburgh (U.S.A.). Bandmaster George Marshall also lent greatly appreciated assistance for a number of years.

A member of the department for twenty-four years until April, 1944, Eric Ball has made an inestimable contribution to the band journals and gained a world-wide reputation. Included in his works that have survived the years and will continue to live are ' The King of kings ', ' The triumph of peace ', ' Exodus ', ' The old wells ', ' Constant Trust ', ' Songs in exile ' and ' The Kingdom triumphant '.

On November 29, 1926, Adjutant (later Colonel) Albert Jakeway joined the staff of the Music Editorial Department. ' When I was a young bandsman ', he recalls, ' I used to look upon Colonel Hawkes and Colonel Goldsmith as stars in a very distant sky; musicians whom I should never have the opportunity of knowing, let alone working alongside, as has been my privilege.'

Shortly after entering the training college in August, 1914, the young musical enthusiast came into close contact with Bramwell Coles, a fellow cadet, from whom he gathered tips on the composition of music that proved of great value.

While stationed at South Shields, Albert Jakeway enjoyed the further advantage of close association with Bandmaster George Marshall, from whom he learned much.

The Colonel's expert knowledge of the brass band (he was a member of the International Staff Band for nearly twenty years) and his close study of scoring for this medium enabled him to become one of the Army's most effective arrangers, ' The Great Physician ', ' Gems from Gounod ', ' Gems from Beethoven ', ' Where duty calls ' and ' The vision splendid ' being among his outstanding compositions.

When Colonel Jakeway joined the department the *Band Tune Book* (published in 1928) was being prepared and his first task was to copy the tune, ' For I'm going! ' He remained in the department for thirty-two years and in 1952 followed Colonel Coles as the Head. The *Unity Series Band Journal* was introduced during the period he was in charge, meeting a great need among smaller bands and instrumental groups.

Lieut.-Colonel Charles Skinner was appointed to succeed Colonel Jakeway in December, 1958. He had become a member of the Music Editorial Department in 1945 after making a considerable impression with the efficient workmanship shown in what few compositions he had written, among them being several prize-winning entries in the 1939 International Music Competition.

As a brass instrumentalist Charles Skinner made his mark as a soprano cornet player with the Men's Social Headquarters Band. Later he played solo cornet and flugel horn in the International Staff Band. In 1955, after an interval of nine years, he returned to serve a second term in the band—as Deputy Bandmaster.

If the Colonel's output has not been as prolific as some would wish, his work for bands possesses the hallmark of quality. 'Heroes of the faith' and 'Let songs abound' are two of his better-known compositions, while the march, 'Amsterdam Congress', is an international favourite. His arrangement of Grieg's 'Homage' March is equally popular. Lieut.-Colonel Skinner is also assured of a place in Army music history for his many fine songs.

Captain Ray Steadman-Allen joined the staff soon after his release from the Royal Navy in 1946, entered the training college two years later and returned to the department as an officer-member in May, 1951.

The Captain, who is one of the few Salvationist Bachelors of Music, was established as a gifted composer of a highly original character from the time his first two compositions—the march, 'Gladsome Morn', and suite, 'The Bethlehem story'—appeared in the band journals and his already prolific output has enhanced his reputation.

'Lord of the sea', 'The holy war' and 'The Emmaus journey' are masterpieces in their respective spheres, while his trombone solo, 'The eternal quest', the deeply devotional selections, 'In quiet pastures' and 'By love compelled', together with numerous vocal works, reveal the versatility of the writer.

Another young composer of exceeding promise, Captain Leslie Condon, was appointed to the department in 1957 after five years as a corps officer. The creations from his able pen are mounting, 'Universal Message', 'The temple vision', 'The call of the righteous' and 'Easter Glory' being among the best. Bandmaster Michael Kenyon, of Hadleigh Temple, Songster Leader Michael Babb, of Regent Hall, Bandsman Terry Camsey, of Upper Norwood, and Bandmaster Brian Bowen, of Staines, have also given valued assistance to the department in recent years, as did Songster Leader Donald

Osgood, of Southall Citadel, prior to his being called up for service in the Royal Air Force in the Second World War.

It has already been stated that the first home of the Music Editorial Department was at Clapton. Here it remained for several years before moving to a pleasant north London suburb to be near Herbert Booth's residence. This was a most agreeable arrangement for the members and certainly one conducive to creative impulse. The absence of the noise and rush usually associated with Salvation Army centres was ideal for musical work.

After a while it was found necessary to transfer the department to a more central position. The venue decided upon was the Trade Headquarters at 98 Clerkenwell Road—on the top floor at the rear of the building, in close proximity to the peak of a large factory chimney from which belched volumes of choking smoke, burning rubber, sulphur and various forms of disagreeable effluvia. Frequently it became necessary to close the windows when the wind blew from a northerly direction!

In late 1896 another move was made, this time to International Headquarters, 101 Queen Victoria Street. The department occupied several offices during its stay on 'the building', as '101' was affectionately termed, the most suitable being a room on the top floor overlooking the Thames. The Surrey hills were visible in clear weather; the Crystal Palace glittered in the sunlight. The delightful distant scenery, together with the ever-moving and even somewhat murky waters of Father Thames, proved a fruitful source of inspiration.

When the Trade Headquarters transferred to new premises at Judd Street, King's Cross, in 1911, later becoming Salvationist Publishing and Supplies, Ltd., the possibility of housing the Music Editorial Department under the same roof was soon a matter for serious discussion. This resulted in the 'M.E.D.' taking up residence there the next year.

There is a tradition in the department which has been preserved and respected. The methods, policies and routine systems have changed little since the old days and there is no short cut to acquaintanceship with these recognized virtues. Experience is the only teacher.

*   *   *

Before 1904 all the band compositions and arrangements published were the work of members of the Music Editorial Department. The first complete composition published from the pen of a writer outside the department was a march by the youthful Deputy Bandmaster Herbert Twitchin, of Regent Hall.

Other young writers took encouragement from this success and submitted their humble compositions to Lieut.-Colonel Slater, who never ceased to inspire them. International music competitions, introduced in 1905, brought to light new writers—among them Robert McNally in Australia, Bramwell Coles and Edward Hill in London, Arthur Young in New Zealand. Later were to come Henry C. Goffin, Harry Otway and William Broughton.

Few of these early music-makers had the opportunity of studying, a privilege enjoyed by their modern counterparts. Some could afford to enlist the expert help of a teacher or instructor; others had to be content with the occasional textbook, in many instances at some cost and personal sacrifice.

George Marshall was in the latter category. When he left school he went to work down the mine. The ability to think music came as second nature to the boy and often, when working at the coal-face as snatches of melody would rush to his mind, he hurriedly wrote his inspiration down in chalk on the wall, a tub, or even on the wide back of the miner's shovel. Many Salvationist composers who have had similar inauspicious beginnings have later delved laboriously into books on harmony and its attendant complications.

George Marshall had his first march, ' The Citadel ', published in 1912, and continued to submit works which created a great impression in Army banding circles. The story of his accident in a mine disaster and his subsequent partial recovery is told in detail elsewhere but here it must be recorded that for thirty-eight years, from a wheel-chair, he produced music with meaning that has a place all its own in Army history.

Some of those Marshall pieces were before their time and were not fully appreciated until years after they were published. ' Army of the brave ', ' Horbury ', ' Great and glorious ' and ' Behold the Man ' are among Salvationist classics. Army musicians felt that none more worthy could have been so honoured when, in 1951, General Albert Orsborn admitted Bandmaster George Marshall to the Order of the Founder. The beloved Bandmaster passed to his heavenly reward in January, 1956.

The *Band Journal* published from the Army's international centre has benefited from the dedicated service of a number of international composers, men like Territorial Band Inspector Harold Scotney, of Australia (formerly a Bandmaster in New Zealand), Bandmaster Jules Vanderkam, of Belgium, Bandmaster Norman Audoire and Deputy Bandmaster Percy Merritt, of Canada, and Bandmasters Harry Kirk and Herbert Mountain, of England.

Salvation Army music, especially the Scandinavian expression of it, owes much to Lieut.-Colonel Klaus Østby. Richard Slater had been working in the Music Department in London for seven years when Østby became a Salvationist in Oslo, Norway, and a friendship developed between them which lasted until Slater's death in 1939. His friend was promoted to Glory the following year.

They had much in common: both were devotees of Wagner and both were humble, hard-working, loyal Salvationists. They admired each other greatly, a fact revealed by the numerous letters they exchanged. Slater once said that in his early days Østby was the most thoroughly studied music theorist in the Army. They thought alike. On one occasion the Scandinavian composer wrote a tune which he hesitated to publish. 'I am glad I did not publish it,' he said later, 'for soon afterward *The Musical Salvationist* contained a tune by Slater which contained exactly the same motif as my melody!'

Klaus Østby was most industrious. He carefully pruned his own music, often producing several forms of a composition before he was satisfied. The famous 'Kabelvarg' march exists in at least six different versions. This interesting composition, written in the winter of 1891, marked a departure from the early-day style of marches; it is descriptive music. The Norwegian Staff Band, of which Østby was the Bandmaster, was campaigning in the far north and due to visit the fishing town of Kabelvarg. The journey was required to be covered by boat and the elements were not at all kind; in fact, the party was prevented from landing for some time.

During the delay, when most of the bandsmen were feeling very much 'under the weather', the unperturbed Bandmaster was recording his impressions on manuscript paper. When the bandsmen arrived safely in harbour this march, depicting a storm at sea and the bandsmen's reaction to it, was the first rehearsal piece. It became a favourite, but did not appear in the *Band Journal* until more than forty years later!

'The Father of Salvation Army Music in Scandinavia' will be remembered as a composer chiefly for his masterpiece, 'Princethorpe', a meditation based on a hymn tune he discovered during a visit to England. This composition was played for the first time in public by the International Staff Band at the Bandmasters' Councils Festival in London in the summer of 1908. Slater called it 'the Army's severest test'. 'Princethorpe' remained unpublished for fifteen years, until the introduction of the *Festival Series Band Journal*.

For forty years and more Erik Leidzén and Emil Söderström have been household names to Army bandsmen. Endowed with gifts above the average, they produced compositions which have been eagerly awaited and have tested the ability of the most progressive bands.

After settling in the U.S.A. as a young man and experiencing varying fortunes, Swedish-born Erik Leidzén became established as a highly respected professional musician and the country's foremost band arranger. For some years he was closely associated with Edwin Franko Goldman, for whose musical groups he was the permanent arranger. With all these commitments Leidzén found time to provide pieces for Army bands and to maintain his soldiership at the Scandinavian Corps in New York City. Toward the end of his life—he died suddenly in December, 1962—his writings were prolific. 'The night cometh . . .' was his explanation.

Such compositions as 'The Saviour's name', 'None other name', 'On the way Home', 'The Cross' and 'Fling wide the gates' will not easily be forgotten or laid aside.

Danish-born Emil Söderström also settled in the U.S.A. as a youth and played in the Chicago Staff Band for a while. For twenty-five years he was staff arranger for the National Broadcasting Company in that city, reaching the height of his profession. His compositions for Salvation Army bands, many of them written by request for specific events, include 'Fighting for the Lord', 'Southland Memories', 'Deep Passage', 'On the sea' and 'Song of Israel'.

A New Zealand-born son of an English father and Scottish mother, Major Dean Goffin attracted the attention of Salvationist musicians when, in the years immediately following the end of the Second World War, outstanding compositions from his pen began to arrive at the International Music Editorial Department and, following their approval by the Music Board, were played by the International Staff Band. 'The Light of the world' and 'The shadow of the Cross', inspired by famous paintings by W. Holman Hunt, were among the earliest. 'Symphony of thanksgiving', Prelude and fugue, 'Arise, my soul, arise!', Themes from the 'Italian' Symphony and 'My strength, my tower' are among his many brilliant works. He is a Bachelor of Music.

The post-war generation of Army composers now almost encircles the globe. The most promising include Corps Sergeant-Major Thomas Rive, of Auckland Congress Hall, New Zealand, holder of the Doctor of Philosophy degree for music; Bandmaster Morley Calvert, of Montreal Citadel, Canada; Captain Stanley Ditmer, of New York, U.S.A., and Young People's Band Leader Erik Silfverberg, of Gartnergade, Denmark.

General Wilfred Kitching was already a well-established composer and arranger of brass band music when he was elected to that high office in 1954. One of the few band pieces from his pen published during his term of office was a meditation on General Evangeline

Booth's song, ' I bring Thee all '. His immediate predecessor, General Albert Orsborn, is the composer of the stirring hymn tune, ' Brantwood ', which has an honoured place in the Army's treasury of band music.

Commissioner John J. Allan, who served General Orsborn as Chief of the Staff, was the composer of ' Memories ', published in the *Festival Series Band Journal*, a cornet solo which he himself featured with the New York Staff Band many years before.

In 1948 Mrs. Brigadier Leonard Adams, of the U.S.A. Western Territory, as Captain Ruby Palm, became the first woman Salvationist to have a band arrangement published. It was not until 1964 that the talent of a second woman composer—Diane Martin, of Jamaica, New York, a former pupil of Erik Leidzén—was similarly recognized and rewarded. Both compositions appeared in the American *Band Journal*.

The present-day composers of Army brass band music are proving worthy successors to Slater, Hawkes, Østby, Goldsmith and the other pioneers. If the idiom of expression has changed with the passing years, the music is as sincere and its message as clear.

*   *   *

In 1896 William Booth felt that a special board should be formed to administer and control musical output and to be directly responsible to him for this and other aspects of musical activity. A Memorandum from the Chief of the Staff (Bramwell Booth) issued in the October of that year brought into being the International Headquarters Music Board, as it was named, with Commission John Carleton as Chairman.

The board was created as a permanent authority to regulate and pass all music issued by the Publishing Department. The music requiring the attention of the board was prepared in the Music Editorial Department under the direction of Major Richard Slater, who himself sang the original songs to his fellow board members, accompanying himself at the organ. The assistance of the International Staff Band was sought in presenting band compositions for approval.

This I.H.Q. board continued to operate for some twenty-five years, its illustrious members including Commissioners T. Henry Howard, who became the second Chief of the Staff, George Mitchell, James Hay, Richard Wilson, John Laurie and William Eadie. Brigadier (later Commissioner) Albert Powley was appointed Secretary to the Board in 1898, remaining so for nearly a quarter of a century. The second officer to hold that position, Lieut.-Colonel John Aspinall, served the board for fifteen years.

In 1921 the position was reviewed, with the result that a Minute was issued to the effect that:

> The General has decided to establish, at National Headquarters, a Board known as the National Music Board, which shall be the permanent authority for regulating the music to be used in the British Territory and to be supplied by Salvationist Publishing and Supplies, Ltd.
>
> The Board will be responsible for the regulation, classification and approval of all music, both vocal and instrumental, and of all tutors, text-books and general musical literature proposed to be issued for Salvation Army purposes in the British Territory.
>
> The Board is empowered to reject or amend the words of any song which, in its judgment, are unsuitable for Salvation Army use.
>
> The Board is empowered to permit, on such conditions as it may decide to be wise, the use of outside music, which it has approved and which, because of copyright or other reasons, cannot be published by The Salvation Army and to which approved words are attached.
>
> The Board has the authority for considering and deciding upon all requests for the use or publication of any Salvation Army copyright songs or music, but not of Band Journals.
>
> The Board is empowered to decide as to the necessity or otherwise of reprinting, in the same way or in a different form, any music or song already published by The Salvation Army. It will also decide all matters relating to the general form of music or musical literature, etc.
>
> The Board will regulate arrangements relating to musical composers' competitions and examinations and will make the awards.

The first Chairman of this newly constituted body was Mrs. Bramwell Booth, then British Commissioner.

A further change in designation took place in November, 1936, when the *International* Music Board was established by General Evangeline Booth to regulate music—both vocal and instrumental—used in the British Territory and in other territories ' not having a Music Board or Department '. With eleven members and a secretary this was the largest controlling group yet appointed and consisted of: Commissioner Charles Rich (British Commissioner and Chairman), Commissioner George Jolliffe (Secretary for Trade and Publisher), Lieut.-Commissioner Frank Barrett (Territorial Commander for London and Southern Territory), Colonel Henry Gore (Secretary to the Chief of the Staff), Colonel George Fuller (Bandmaster of the International Staff Band), Colonel Arthur Goldsmith (noted composer and former member of the Music Editorial Department and the International Staff Band), Colonel Railton Howard (Leader of the Assurance and Harrow Songster Brigades), Brigadier Bramwell Coles (Head of the Music Editorial Department), Major Arch R. Wiggins (Editor of *The Bandsman and Songster* and song-writer), Adjutant Edward Saywell (National Band Inspector), Territorial Bandmaster Alfred W. Punchard and Major James Morgan (Private Secretary to the British Commissioner and Secretary to the Board).

From this formidable list it will be clearly seen that appointment to the Music Board in the majority of instances was because of positions held. The British Commissioner remains the Chairman and the membership, of practical necessity, includes the Publisher, the Secretary to the Chief of the Staff, the Head of the International Music Editorial Department, the Staff Bandmaster, the National Secretary for Bands and Songster Brigades and the National Bandmaster.

In January, 1949, the Board extended its personnel to include four representative corps Bandmasters—Albert Munn, of Kettering, John Lyons, of Harlesden, Donald Osgood, of Southall Citadel, and Herbert Mountain, of Boscombe, to serve in rota. This proved a success and the representation at corps level has been retained and was even extended when a corps officer was appointed to the Board.

Since the formation of the first board in 1896 the International Staff Band has borne the brunt of responsibility for preparing and presenting all music intended for the Band Journals. At times in the board's history this burden has been shared by the Salvationist Publishing and Supplies Band and, during the years of the Second World War, ' Rosehill '.

For a while vocal music was presented by the Salvation Singers but in the absence of a permanent Headquarters songster brigade songs have been played to the Board by a member of the Music Editorial Department. Music earmarked for *The Musical Salvationist* and allied vocal publications are heard and passed by the International Music Sub-Board, which has a corps officer and songster leader among its members.

In recent years Territorial Music Boards have been set up in Australia, New Zealand, Canada, the U.S.A., Sweden and the Netherlands and, in some instances, separate journals are published, but in the main overseas musicians play music from the *Band Journal*, published in London and authorized by the International Music Board.

CHAPTER NINETEEN

ADMINISTRATION AND MISCELLANY

CONDUCTING Bandmasters' councils in London in December, 1905, the Chief of the Staff (Bramwell Booth), sprang a surprise by announcing the appointment of Brigadier Richard Slater as ' Secretary at National Headquarters of the Bands and Songster Brigades '. ' We have reached a new and important stage—perhaps an epoch—in our musical warfare,' said *The War Cry* in reporting the event.

After making the announcement the Chief of the Staff continued: ' For the present the Brigadier will retain the oversight of the Musical Department and have a seat at the Musical Board (*sic*). He will travel about the country and his special care will be the Bandmasters.' At this reference there was a ' ringing volley '.

Responding to the ovation which greeted him, Brigadier Slater referred to the ' unexpected announcement ' and characteristically expressed the hope that he might be able to make ' both ends meet, the musical and the spiritual ', so far as the bands and brigades were concerned.

Nothing further was heard officially of the matter. In a letter written seven months later to his old friend, Lieut.-Colonel Klaus Østby, in Stockholm, Slater referred to the appointment of ' Secretary for Musical Affairs ' which ' for several reasons ' he was not able to take up.

Some years later, with the end of the First World War and bandsmen resuming corps activity so cruelly interrupted four years before, General Bramwell Booth again sensed the need of a central administration to advise and guide not only the returning servicemen, but those officers and local officers responsible for their spiritual welfare. The formation of a Bands Department at National Headquarters was announced in January, 1921.

The choice of Colonel Alfred Braine as the first National Secretary for Bands was a happy one. He had given a full life to the Army's musical interests, dating from the day, forty years before, when he had become the seventeen-year-old Bandmaster at Battersea I. His service had included a period as a member of the International Staff Band and as leader of the Salvation Singers. As ' Publisher Braine ' he issued the Army's first tune book. His recent service on relief work in Central Europe had also provided him with an understanding of some of the problems inevitably connected with rehabilitation.

For four years the Colonel directed the interests of bandsmen in the British Territory and then it was announced that Lieut.-Colonel (later Lieut.-Commissioner) Fred Adams, the father of Lieut.-Colonel Bernard Adams and at that time Assistant Chief Secretary at National Headquarters, would be responsible for band affairs. A year later Staff-Captain Wilfred Kitching was appointed Assistant Secretary for Bands, assuming the full responsibility some months afterward.

At this time the Staff-Captain's selection ' My Jesus ' was very popular, having just secured first prize in an international competition, and the bandsmen of the territory acclaimed the composer with a touch of possessive pride. He was ' their man ' and it was with energetic enthusiasm that they followed his virile lead in those halcyon days of the late 1920s. Little did they—or he—realize that one day Staff-Captain Kitching would be the General.

In 1930 Major (later Commissioner) Charles Durman succeeded to the appointment. As the first Bandmaster of the Men's Social Work Headquarters Band and Songster Leader at Ilford his interest in music had been of a front-line character. A glance at *The Bandsman and Songster* of this period reveals that the Major was frequently referred to as the National Secretary for Bands and Songster Brigades, which gives an indication of the ascendancy of vocal sections at that time. When, two years later, a Songster Leader was appointed a member of the corps census board, the place of the brigade in Army service was established.

Major Durman's link with the Bands Department lasted for six years. Although he became Secretary for Special Efforts in 1933, the two departments were merged with the Major in charge.

The year 1936 saw an upheaval at National Headquarters with the dividing of the British Isles into four separate territories—London and Southern, Scotland and Ireland, Wales and Western, and Northern. *The Bandsman and Songster* for November 21, 1936, carried a news paragraph announcing that band and brigade matters would in future be referred to the Chief Secretary of each territory. The Territorial Band Inspector, Captain (later Senior-Major) Edward Saywell, however, would continue to serve in that capacity with the designation of National Band Inspector and have the added responsibility of acting as liaison officer with the B.B.C.

Five years later, by which time three of the territories had reverted to a central administration, Adjutant Saywell was appointed National Secretary for Bands and Songster Brigades, a position he held throughout the difficult years of the Second World War and until he was succeeded by Senior-Major (later Lieut.-Colonel) Ernest Rance in May, 1950.

When the Colonel, a well-known composer and song writer, had completed a record period of ten years in this capacity, Major Dean Goffin took up the important appointment in January, 1960, after serving as National Bandmaster for three years.

The problems that come to the National Secretary's desk are many and varied. *Orders and Regulations for Bands and Songster Brigades* are required to be observed and, while such cases happily are few and far between, vital disciplinary decisions have to be made.

In such a voluntary organization, and with such diversities of social and educational background, clashes between personalities are bound to arise, chiefly through local circumstances. It is very true that ' a healthy band is a spiritual band '. All Army administration must have a spiritual basis.

Much of the work of the Bands Department is routine. The National Secretary is the liaison officer between The Salvation Army and the B.B.C. and all requests for auditions and broadcasts should reach his desk. Proposed broadcast programmes must also be submitted for approval.

A considerable portion of the department's time is taken up with running the Bandsmen's Widows' Gratuity Scheme. This was outlined by the Chief of the Staff (Bramwell Booth) in Bandmasters' councils in January, 1907.

The fund is supported by a levy upon each band participating whenever there occurs the promotion to Glory of a person in respect of whom a gratuity is payable. It is estimated that in the British Isles two bandsmen die every week.

The scheme is for the benefit of (a) the widow of a bandsman and any children under the age of eighteen years, provided they are still at school and dependent, or (b) the widowed mother of an unmarried bandsman, provided she was solely supported by him. Relatives other than those provided for sometimes mistakenly regard the gratuity fund as a family insurance. It must be remembered that levies are paid from the bandsmen's fund where such exists, otherwise from the band fund.

The successful National Secretary for Bands and Songster Brigades needs to have a flair for organizing for there is much to occupy his time in that direction. Arranging the periodical Bandmasters' and Songster Leaders' councils in London is a gigantic task. A venue for the Saturday festival such as the Royal Albert Hall has to be booked well in advance. Catering firms also require plenty of notice and months of preparation include arranging for the printing and issuing of invitation cards, planning the programmes, selecting the participating bands and soloists and supervising the welfare of the hundreds of delegates whilst they are in London. All this requires to be carried out in detail, and when the councils are followed by a training course a great deal more has to be done.

This routine to a lesser extent has to be followed in connection with the national songster festival and the popular inter-divisional councils which have been a feature of post-war interests.

Three months after the announcement of the formation of the Bands Department with Colonel Braine as the first Secretary, the bandsmen of the British Territory learned that Bandmaster A. W. Punchard, of Chalk Farm, had been appointed Territorial Bandmaster.

The Army Press of those days suggested that the creation of this new office and the man selected to fill it would be the subject of discussion in Army musical circles 'from Land's End to the Cheviot Hills'.

Twenty-eight years before, young Fred Punchard, not yet eighteen, had become Bandmaster at Chalk Farm and already his band had earned a name for pioneer tactics which had marked 'A. W. P.' and his men as Salvationist pace-makers. More honours were still to come their way in the years that lay ahead.

The Territorial Bandmaster was to be closely associated with the National Secretary for Bands in an honorary and advisory capacity in all matters which concerned the spiritual and musical progress of the musicians of The Salvation Army in the British Territory. Bandmaster Punchard brought all his talents to this new responsibility and maintained that close link until his promotion to Glory, in October, 1950, twelve years after he had handed his baton to another at Chalk Farm and joined the ranks of honoured 'retireds'.

One of his chief public duties was to conduct massed bands at great national festivals. The number of Salvationist bandsmen who saw National Bandmaster Punchard in action at the Crystal Palace, Alexandra Palace, Royal Albert Hall, Queen's Hall and other well-renowned buildings is rapidly diminishing.

A business man with a genius for organizing, A. W. P.'s flair for administrative detail made his counsel particularly welcome in matters concerning Army bands and bandsmen. His practical experience as the leader of a section, which remains to this day one of the best-known corps bands in the Army world, gave him authority which earned the respect of all.

When Commissioner William R. Dalziel, then the British Commissioner, conducted Bandmaster Punchard's funeral service in the Chalk Farm hall he described the promoted warrior as the 'Pattern Bandmaster', a qualification which ensures the name of Britain's first National Bandmaster being remembered so long as there is a Salvation Army.

There was a Band Inspector for the British Territory some years
before the Bands Department was created. In 1907 Bramwell Booth
(then Chief of the Staff) appointed Bandmaster Edward H. Hill, of
Southall Citadel, to that position. His duties were to include conducting special practices, in which he would be prepared to give any
information, tuition and advice that, in his judgment, were called for;
advising the Bandmaster on technical and other matters relating to
choice of pieces, care of instruments and band finance; discussing the
spiritual health of the bandsmen and assisting, where possible, to give
help in this direction. Before leaving each corps the Band Inspector
would examine every instrument and all accessories.

'Being an old Bandmaster,' commented *The Bandsman and
Songster*, 'the Band Inspector has often felt the need of help and
encouragement, so that, by the grace of God, he is quite prepared to
lay himself out to do his utmost to help, encourage and strengthen each
band in its work for God and the salvation of souls.'

And so the convert of twenty years before, who practised writing
music on the bricks he handled in his daily work, accepted the challenge
of this venture and began to move up and down the British Isles,
proving himself not only a link with London, which was most appreciated by the hundreds of bandsmen visited, but a spiritual father to
many who sought his words of counsel.

'Ted' Hill was a giant among men. For eighteen years he carried
out his responsibilities with untiring enthusiasm and dedicated purpose.
The coming of Band Inspector Hill to a band practice was an important
occasion. Instruments needed to be cleaned until they shone like new
and every man was expected to attend.

In December, 1925, Divisional Bandmaster Edward V. Saywell, of
Gillingham, was announced to succeed Band Inspector Hill and
continued the good work where his predecessor had laid it down. He,
too, became known and loved in all parts of the British Territory and,
although dogged by ill health on numerous occasions, served the
interests of Army musicians in this capacity until assuming the heavier
responsibilities of the National Secretary for Bands and Songster
Brigades in 1941. He was an officer from 1933.

The 'Territorial Band Inspector' became 'National Band Inspector' when the British Territory was divided into four separate commands in 1936. Territorial Bandmaster Punchard's title became
changed in the same way.

When conducting Bandmasters' and Songster Leaders' councils in
London in June, 1955, General Wilfred Kitching intimated that he
intended to fill a position which had been vacant for fourteen years
and that he had the 'right man in mind'. Some months later it was

announced that Captain Dean Goffin, a corps officer in New Zealand, had been appointed National Bandmaster for the British Territory.

The change in name was noted and some, at first, thought that the Captain was to succeed Bandmaster Punchard. It was soon made quite clear, however, that Captain Goffin was to follow in the wake of Band Inspector Hill and Senior-Major Saywell and that his duties, in the main, would follow closely the pattern already designed.

When Major Goffin was promoted to be the departmental head Captain Norman Bearcroft became the National Bandmaster in October, 1960.

Senior-Major Saywell was a valued member of the Bands Department for thirty-four years. In retirement he continued, at home, to serve the interests of Army musicians in a positive and worthwhile capacity. He was responsible for the Band Training Correspondence Course until his passing in March, 1959.

Leaders of music sections and those serving with them who wish to gain technical proficiency have always been encouraged in the Army, although it has been continually stressed that such efficiency should not be a musician's sole determination or the paramount qualification for leadership.

In April, 1907, examinations in music for Bandmasters, Songster Leaders and bandsmen were announced. Several showed interest in the venture and were successful in the tests, which were continued with graded difficulty for a year or so. But it was not until 1927 that a systematic course was devised. This was known as the Bandmasters' Correspondence Course and was designed mainly for baton-wielders.

The course, revised by Senior-Major Saywell in 1934, was comprehensive and ideally suited to the need of Salvation Army music leaders. It included the theory of music, first lessons in harmony, band training, doctrine, orders and regulations and Salvation Army history. Students who were successful in the intermediate and advanced examinations were required to take a final practical test before a board of examiners. Those who came through this gruelling experience were awarded the Bandmasters' Efficiency Badge, to be worn on the left sleeve of the tunic.

The first Bandmasters awarded the badge were Harry Kirk, of Leeds, and William Major, of Coventry. Many followed their example and the coveted badge began to appear in all parts of the world. It was, however, a ' domestic honour ' and not recognized by any of the colleges of music.

Each student was required to (1) teach part of an Ordinary (later General) Series selection that he had previously studied; (2) conduct a Second (later Triumph) Series selection chosen thirty minutes before

M

the examination; (3) conduct a tuning test with a small group of instrumentalists; (4) take part in a short oral examination. To be awarded the badge the students were required to gain 150 marks out of a possible 200.

With the outbreak of the Second World War difficulties arose which made it impossible for the final practical examination to be held, although the course was not suspended. By 1945 the names of those 'queueing up' for the badge made a lengthy list and it was decided to abandon the award.

In recent years the replacement of the old designation by that of Band Training Course has offered a far wider influence and appeal. Although there is no longer the glamour of a badge to entice eager students, the interest is just as great and Salvationists from all parts of the world, at a most reasonable inclusive fee, enrol every year. The course is of eighteen months' duration.

It was again revised in 1962. While the *Handbook of Doctrine* and *Orders and Regulations for Bands and Songster Brigades* were retained, more modern text books on the rudiments of music and harmony were introduced.

Convalescent home

FOLLOWING an announcement made by General Bramwell Booth to Bandmasters in council at Clapton in February, 1922, a convalescent home for bandsmen recovering from illness or an accident was opened by the British Commissioner (Mrs. Bramwell Booth) at Great Yarmouth, on the English east coast, in June the next year. The proceedings were presided over by the Mayor (Councillor E. J. Middleton), who was a bandsman at the local corps. Brigadier and Mrs. Thomas Read were appointed to take charge. (Their twin sons, Stanley and Harold, were later to make history by each marrying a daughter of a Staff Bandmaster: Dora Mitchell and Hilda Fuller.)

Standing in its own grounds of about an acre, which were laid out in lawns, shrubs and trees, situated about one minute's walk from the sea front and within easy reach of the railway station, 'Seafield' was taken on a fourteen-year lease. The use of the home for the stated purpose was shortlived, however—a tribute to the physical fitness of Salvation Army bandsmen! The premises were retained by the Army for some time and were put to good service as a social work centre.

Instrument-making

THE rapid development of Salvation Army brass banding in the 1880s naturally provided difficulties in the securing of suitable instruments. These were procured from a variety of quarters and left much to be desired in the way of tone and tuning.   Sensing the need for a standard-ization in this direction, in May, 1889, the ever-realistic Commissioner John Carleton, then in charge of the Trade Headquarters, sought permission to commence instrument-making.

The first ' factory ' was a small room partitioned off for the purpose at No. 56 Southwark Street, London, premises occupied at that time by the Trade Headquarters. The staff consisted of a ' maker ' and a ' polisher '. Two months later an apprentice, Jack Furness, was added. His indentures were signed by General William Booth and he became known throughout the trade as an expert valve-maker. He was Bandmaster at St. Albans for twelve years and from 1919–39 was Manager of the Musical Instrument Factory in the same city.

Instrument-making was on a modest scale at first, concentration being placed upon the construction of cornets and repairs. The limited space available precluded the making of large instruments. The styles of other makers were followed at first but gradually there appeared distinctively constructed models designed to meet the rigours of Army warfare.

The removal of Trade Headquarters to more spacious premises in Clerkenwell Road, in 1890, marked a progressive step in instrument-making. Army instruments became popular and several first-class men from leading instrument manufacturers joined the staff. Around this period a Printing Works Band was formed with Staff-Captain Cusden as Bandmaster. It became merged into the Trade Head-quarters Band.

In 1894 the first full set of instruments was completed, specially manufactured for Luton II (now Luton Citadel) Band. The instru-ments were used for the first time at the Crystal Palace festivities that year. Two years later, states Alfred Philpot, an early-day apprentice, a full set of silver-plated instruments, at a cost of £400, was made for Oldham II Band.

This, the latest development in Army instrument-making, was to have been displayed at the exhibition in the Royal Agricultural Hall, Islington, in 1896, but William Booth saw the instruments during his inspection of the stands before the official opening and was greatly displeased.

' Is this the way the bands waste their money while I go around the world begging for the " Darkest England " Scheme? ' he asked Philpot, who was in charge of the stand. It is said that the instruments had to be hidden from sight.

A number of years later Bramwell Booth, realizing the economy involved in the long run, gave permission for the factory to make silver-plated instruments. Regent Hall claims to have had a 'silver band' (nickel-plated) in August, 1882.

Immediately following the exhibition the factory was moved to Fortess Road, Kentish Town, which building did not prove at all suitable for the purpose. After a five-year stay in this north London suburb the manager, Major (later Colonel) Clifford Grinsted, the father of Commissioner Edgar Grinsted, pressed for the factory's removal to premises which had recently been taken over by the printing works at St. Albans. The move took place on November 5, 1901.

During the twenty-four years that Colonel Grinsted was in charge of the instrument factory he personally tuned every instrument produced—20,000 of them. This responsibility has now devolved jointly upon the Manager of the Musical Instruments Department at Salvationist Publishing and Supplies, Ltd. (who also has the oversight of the Instrument Factory), and the Head of the Music Editorial Department.

The early-day 'Reliance' instruments gave way to 'Triumph' models when larger premises were secured. After the First World War the 'Triumphonic' family was introduced and later models have included the 'Bandmaster' and 'Herald' cornets and the 'Festival' trombone. Despite the setback caused by two world wars and the shortage of skilled labour, the high standard of manufacture has been maintained and now The Salvation Army is one of two instrument-making establishments left in Britain.

Arthur Carrick, senior charge hand for thirty years, served the Instrument Factory for double that period, and Charles Palmer, who was head of the valve section from 1919, had completed forty-nine years' service in the factory when they both retired in March, 1952. Carrick commenced working for the Army a month before his thirteenth birthday—as office boy to Commissioner Carleton at Clerkenwell Road. Palmer, rejecting an offer to be apprenticed to the 'Tea-Tasting Department', was given employment at the Army's Cycle Department at Kensal Rise, with written instructions placing in his special care Bramwell Booth's own cycle. With the advent of the combustion engine and William Booth's refusal to allow the Trade Department to launch into the motor-cycle industry, the lad joined the staff of the Instrument Factory.

On the three occasions when Army instruments have been entered for an exhibition they have won gold medals. These events were at Christchurch, New Zealand, in 1907, the Franco-British Exhibition at the White City, London, in 1908, and at the International Exhibition of Wind Instruments held at the Hague (Holland) in 1951. At the last-named exhibition the 'Bandmaster' cornet gained the gold award, the

'Triumphonic' four-valve euphonium and 'Triumphonic' E-flat bombardon receiving second place in their respective classes.

Not all The Salvation Army's experiments in instrument-making have been successful. Some years ago a new form of slide trombone mechanism was introduced by the invention, at the St. Albans factory, of an E-flat bass trombone, similar in pitch to the E-flat bombardon. This was fitted with a double slide, part of which worked automatically in the opposite direction from behind the player's shoulder. This ingenious invention had its drawbacks. There was the danger of meeting some obstruction behind the player; the spring device which worked the rear section was of so delicate a nature that the slightest accident would be liable to put it out of action. Another disadvantage was that no music was provided for it, the player having to use the E-flat bombardon part, thus making the performance too sustained for the special instrument.

The making of Army instruments was demonstrated at the British Empire Exhibition held at Wembley in 1925. Ten years later a set of instruments, made for the band at Ashburton, New Zealand, was on show at the Army's youth day at Alexandra Palace. In 1949 the instrument factory was featured in the popular B.B.C. series, 'Down your Way', when Richard Dimbleby visited St. Albans. After being initiated into some of the mysteries of instrument manufacturing and listening to Lieut.-Colonel Arthur Bristow, then Manager of the Musical Instruments Department, play the flugel horn, Mr. Dimbleby attempted to broadcast a 'tune' himself!

Band uniform

In August, 1878, at the first War Congress held after The Christian Mission had became The Salvation Army, Elijah Cadman, who had already introduced the use of military titles, declared: 'I would like to wear a suit of clothes that would let everyone know I meant war to the teeth and salvation for the world.' Without waiting for instructions, the more enterprising of the men officers began to wear various types of helmets and military caps adorned with home-made badges.

Second-hand military attire appealed to bandsmen and a variety of uniforms began to appear. Commandant George Felton, an early-day bandsman at Plaistow, London, remembered the Bandmaster's buying at the Petticoat Lane market a set of cast-off Hussars' uniforms consisting of yellow-braided tunics, tight-fitting trousers and pill-box caps. The Hussars being a tall regiment meant that most pairs of trousers had to be shortened! When General William Booth visited Glasgow in 1883 the six bands taking part in the meetings all wore full military uniform, but of *different* styles.

Two women Salvationists of the Chelsea Corps, working at a Pimlico military clothing stores, agreed to make a set of uniforms for the corps band. These were red twill jackets decorated profusely with yellow braid.

Colonel Fred Hawkes and his brother bought their first band uniforms in 1886. They had been spending a week-end at Battersea II, where their sister was a soldier, and a visit to the Trade Headquarters in Southwark Street was arranged for the purpose.

'The purchase of that tunic was a memorable event for me,' said the Colonel. 'I was seventeen years of age. It was not a very striking-looking garment. The trimmings consisted of some red braid on the cuffs, a red collar with wide black braid and, most conspicuous of all, some half-dozen brilliant brass buttons, embossed with prominent S's.

'Seeing this was supplied over the counter, and not by bespoke order, I presume it was the standard band uniform of that period. I cannot say the fit was perfect, for the lower buttons fastened only with difficulty and some effort was required to make the " two ends meet "! Still, that was quite a small matter. I now possessed a real Army-made band tunic, and it was worn with pride, the brass buttons being kept brightly polished.'

As a member of the Household Troops Band for five years the Colonel was called upon to wear successively several types of uniform, each style influencing the choice of other bands.

As the bandsmen were out in all sorts of weather, summer and winter, it was decided to provide them with a special variety of lined mackintosh. The first supply looked very attractive, but later, after being submitted to a heavy downpour of rain, something wrong was discovered with the 'proofing' material employed in their manufacture. On being dried out the 'macs' became as stiff as boards.

'Our venture with band uniform overcoats was not a great success,' the Colonel admitted. 'Later they developed another defect and turned purple!'

The Troopers' next complete set of uniform was the style that was eventually adopted for universal use: blue tunic, faced with black braid and lined with narrow red trimmings. This pattern was used until the band was dissolved.

Colonel Alfred Braine claimed that Penge Band was the first to be supplied with this style. This could well have been seeing that the Colonel was Bandmaster at Penge at that time and also a member of the Trade Headquarters staff. Commissioner John Carleton, then in charge of the Trade Department, was also a bandsman at Penge, as were several other members of the staff. The band did, in fact, act as the official band for all musical engagements carried out in connection with the Trade Headquarters and special consideration would be accorded on this account.

A Trade Department advertisement appearing in *The War Cry*, November 11, 1890, stated:

> We have made special arrangements by which all our bandsmen may get into proper Salvation Army uniform and hope that our endeavour to meet the interests of our comrades will be generally appreciated. We are prepared to send our cutter to take measurements and orders, and with sample suits from which selections may be made, to any corps on the following conditions:
>
> If 10 suits are ordered we will send 100 miles.
>
> If 15 suits are ordered we will send 150 miles.
>
> If 20 suits are ordered we will send 200 miles.
>
> We can make and trim to any sample approved by your D.O. (Divisional Officer) and shall be pleased to forward a sample suit or suits for inspection to any corps FREE OF CHARGE.

Chalk Farm was the first corps band to obtain a set of uniform overcoats with a monogram on the epaulets. In 1930 the Salvationist Publishing and Supplies Band became the first, apart from the International Staff, to wear Model 'C' coats, up till then reserved for officers.

Tottenham Citadel Band first had red tunics in 1885 and other early-day sections to wear similar patterns were Carlisle Citadel and Highgate. These were not reckoned to be additional jackets as may be worn today.

Musicians' own paper

ON a Sunday afternoon in February, 1907, 450 Bandmasters and Songster Leaders, gathered in council at Clapton, heard the Chief of the Staff (Bramwell Booth) announce that the musicians of the Army were to have their own paper. Although musical matters had been given generous space in *The War Cry* (the 'Band Chat' column was always a popular feature) and latterly in the monthly publication, *The Local Officer*, the need had long been felt for a domestic journal of the ever-growing army of music-makers. The enthusiasm with which the news was received was a sure sign of the popularity of the step and an indication of its future success.

The Bandsman and Songster was launched in April of that year with Staff-Captain (later Colonel) Arthur Goldsmith as its first editor. Sixteen pages for one penny! With the exception of a period toward the end of the First World War this periodical has appeared ever since, changing its name occasionally—it was *The Bandsman, Local Officer and Songster* in the early 1920s—until it became *The Musician of The Salvation Army* with the first issue of 1938.

Staff-Captain (later Lieut.-Commissioner) Arch R. Wiggins was appointed editor in 1933 and remained in that position until 1946, thus qualifying for the record of longest serving editor. Brigadier George Stevens occupied the chair from 1908 until his retirement twelve years later. Other well-known musical personalities to hold this appointment were Lieut.-Colonel Bramwell Taylor (1920–21) and Lieut.-Colonel Thomas Tucker (1926–33).

Three years after the launching of *The Bandsman and Songster*, *The Local Officer and Bandsman* was issued in Australia to serve the musicians of that country. After the end of the Second World War a revival of interest led to the publishing of an Australian *Musician* which is now issued fortnightly. At one time an attempt was made to run *The Musician* in the U.S.A. but the venture was short-lived.

The Musician, issued from International Headquarters, is unique in that it is the only periodical published by The Salvation Army that accepts paid advertisements. This break with tradition occurred when it was realized that *The Bandsman and Songster* could render a valuable service to Army musicians who were in need. Through the advertisement columns unemployed bandsmen in one area were able to find work in another part of the country. Particularly was this service useful during the depression years of the early 1930s. Later the privilege was extended to include the buying and selling of articles and the advertising of suitable holiday accommodation.

Some years ago a request reached the *Musician* office from Hamilton (Ontario), Canada, for an advertisement to be inserted announcing the visit of Flint, Michigan, U.S.A., Young People's Band to that corps. This was considered to be an excellent means of previewing the event!

Young people's bands

IN *The War Cry* dated April 14, 1888, the Field Secretary's Notes, a weekly feature, stated: ' The first junior soldiers' brass band appeared at Clapton Congress Hall on Easter Monday and did well.'

Although this group is not specifically said to have belonged to the Clapton Congress Hall Corps, it is safe to accept the idea for, in *The Coming Army*, a report on young people's work published in the same year, mention was made of ' The Clapton Junior Soldier Corps ' and a print was published of the youngsters on the march, aided by a number of instrumentalists following the flag.

The first junior bands were not of brass instrumentation. There was a drum and fife band in action at Folkestone in 1884 and similar groups were formed at Tunbridge Wells, Hammersmith and Wood Green, the first-named section being known as a ' little soldiers' band '. Other early-day bands, presumably all brass, were formed at Folkestone and Portsmouth, and there was a Bristol Divisional Junior Band in 1889.

An historic photograph, published in *The Musician* for August 28, 1948, shows a band 'formed of young men from Exeter and Plymouth about 1888'. The 'young men' are holding a variety of brass instruments and wearing smart small-peaked pill-box hats, with the exception of a good-looking cornet player who is majestically clad in something remarkably like a policeman's helmet.

'The Clapton Junior Soldier Corps' on the march, 1888

The formation of the Junior Staff Band in 1889 did much to encourage corps sections, although the early attempts were only partially successful. Wrote Richard Slater at the turn of the century:

> Junior brass bands are more difficult and more expensive than drum and fife bands, and more risk is attached to boys playing brass instruments, but such bands are of wider usefulness for Army purposes and offer excellent opportunities for training lads for the more extensive work of senior brass bands.

Boscombe Corps claims to have possessed the first commissioned young people's band—in 1908—but an explanation is necessary. It is probable that 'junior bands' became 'young people's bands' in that year and it could be that this section was the first to be formed under the new title. The leader was commissioned 'Young People's Bandmaster', a title immediately withdrawn.

Canada had a Boys' Brass Band attached to its Territorial Headquarters, Toronto, in 1908. Major Wilfred Creighton was responsible for this group of twenty-five players who wore 'knee pads and special uniform'.

Because some Salvation Army territories have no brass band background the regulation governing the formation of young people's bands is elastic: 'The instruments may be brass, reed, string or drums and fifes.' This gives a place to the efficient string bands of Scandinavia, the guitars of Central Europe, the flute bands of Indonesia, the fifes of India, and the percussion of Africa. It is surprising, however, how many eastern territories have taken up the brass band idiom.

Huskvarna (Sweden) Young People's Band made history in 1960 by becoming the first overseas youth section to visit Great Britain. In connection with the British Congress of that year the band carried out a ten-day tour extending from Newcastle upon Tyne to Brighton. In 1964 the New Jersey Divisional Youth Band became the first section from the New World to visit Europe when they campaigned in Sweden and Denmark.

The influence of young people's bands cannot be fully assessed. More than forty years ago a band was formed in a south of England corps. As a result a boy was converted and seventeen members of his family were brought to know Christ because of that initial contact. The boy himself became a Divisional Commander. When Colonel George Higgins was the Commanding Officer at Hendon, north London, in 1936, he looked around at the many fine boys attending the meetings and decided to re-form the young people's band. Five of that group became Salvation Army Bandmasters and four Staff Bandsmen, among them Roland Cobb and Derek Smith, who earned names for themselves as cornet soloists with the International Staff and New York Staff Bands respectively.

Flint Citadel, one of the best-known young people's bands in the Army world and formed in 1920, is justly proud of its record of ' successes ': thirteen officers, a Territorial Music Director, a Staff Bandmaster, three corps Bandmaster and a number of Bandmasters and Songster Leaders serving in other corps.

A few years ago a Nigerian law student was attracted by an open-air meeting being led by a young people's band on a street corner in south London. He followed the boys to their hall where he knelt at the Mercy Seat at the conclusion of the meeting. Today he is serving his own people as a Chief Magistrate and earning a reputation for fair justice and Christian influence.

The first young people's band in Denmark was formed by Adjutant (later Lieut.-Colonel) Ernst Söderström in Copenhagen in the early 1900s. Of the twelve foundation members, four—Erik Leidzén, Emil Söderström, Kristian Fristrup and Viktor Hedgren—became internationally known. Details have already been given of the first three. Hedgren was a member of the Chicago Staff Band and composed a number of pieces published in the American Band Journal. A cornet solo from his pen, ' Heavenly Rejoicings ', appeared in the General Series Journal issued from London.

At Asbury College in Wilmore, Kentucky, a unique Army band has operated since 1956 when Paul Rader and fifteen other Salvationist members of his class decided to form a music ensemble. This group soon became a thirty-piece band with Rader as Bandmaster.

Of necessity the personnel changes with each graduating and incoming year, but a fine standard of efficiency has been maintained. A highlight was the band's participation in a music congress in New York City. The bandsmen and bandswomen represent only half the Salvation Army Students' Fellowship at the college.

There are few more rewarding appointments in Salvation Army service than those to do with youth work, and a Young People's Band Leader is high on this honoured list. His is a specialist's task, and gifted indeed is the man who fulfils all the demands made upon him. *Orders and Regulations for Bands and Songster Brigades* states: 'The person appointed should possess the skill and perseverance needed to train the members musically; also be qualified to command their respect and develop them as true Salvationists.'

Many men have been happy to dedicate themselves to this task, even though it may have meant sacrificing service in the senior section. Theirs is a job second to none in the Army world, and their success, to quote General Wilfred Kitching, is governed by their losses—to the senior band.

Music camps

THE introduction of music camps throughout the Army world marked the beginning of a new era of enthusiastic youth musical activity and the credit for this inspiration must go to the U.S.A. Eastern Territory.

The first was a young people's camp held in the old Metropolitan Province at Long Beach, New Jersey, in August, 1921. The Provincial Young People's Secretary, Staff-Captain (later Commissioner) John J. Allan, with Mrs. Allan, organized and directed the enterprise. Forty-five young American Salvationists made the trip to the seaside camp and the success of the venture was hailed with enthusiasm. Seventy per cent of the students attending that first camp became Salvation Army officers.

But music camps were not yet a permanent part of the Salvation Army youth programme in the U.S.A. It was not until 1935 that the big move forward began. The great success of high school bands springing up across America had much to do with this new wave of enthusiasm.

That summer saw the inauguration of territorial music camps in the Eastern and Central Territories—at Star Lake, New Jersey, and at Wonderland, Wisconsin. In addition, divisional camps were established one by one from the Atlantic seaboard to the Pacific coast. In 1942, under the leadership of the Territorial Commander (Commissioner Allan), who had pioneered the Long Beach camp and organized the first territorial event at Star Lake, the Central Territory's music camp at Wonderland was revised and renamed the Central Music Institute, with an advanced curriculum and a three-year study course leading to the presentation of diplomas. The presence of Professor Irwin Fischer, of the American Conservatory of Music and for many years a member of the celebrated Chicago Symphony Orchestra, and other outstanding musical friends of the Army, has made this institute one of the finest of its type inside or outside The Salvation Army. In recent years international personalities have been invited as the guest conductor, among them Bandmaster Phil B. Catelinet, Major Dean Goffin, Eric Ball and Lieut.-Colonel Bernard Adams.

In 1946 a Territorial Advanced Musicamp was instituted at Star Lake for the more proficient students and potential music leaders of the Eastern Territory, this in addition to the regular Star Lake camp. The names of Brigadier Richard Holz and Erik Leidzén will for ever be associated with this camp.

In that same year Commissioner William Arnold founded a territorial music camp for Salvationists of the Southern Territory at Junaluska, North Carolina. Because of the great distances involved it has not been found possible to organize a territorial music camp in the Western Territory, but a number of divisional events are held. Sacramento Citadel, California, in 1956 sponsored a corps music camp for elementary, intermediate and advanced training. Some seventy young people gathered at a lakeside setting in the High Sierra, close to the area where gold was discovered in 1849. Forty classes were held daily. So successful was the experiment that this unique camp became a regular feature of the corps' annual programme.

In 1940 Canada followed the example of the American territories and held its first music camp at Jackson's Point, Ontario, fifty miles from Toronto. This was very much a territorial event, students travelling from as far west as Saskatoon, Saskatchewan, and as far east as Moncton, New Brunswick. There were sixty-eight in all. This became an annual event throughout the days of the Second World War.

The suggestion, in 1945, that the territorial camp in Canada should be disbanded resulted in separate camps being held in the Newfoundland Province and in each division throughout the Dominion. Bermuda followed suit in 1960.

When Commissioner Allan, as Chief of the Staff, took up residence in London, his stories of the North American music camp programme enthused youth leaders in the British Territory, and Britain's first camp was held at Hadleigh, Essex, in August, 1947. The week proved more than a musical experience for the boys, for many are Salvationist music leaders today and can date their spiritual progress to the night they knelt in dedication at a bench in a hut at Hadleigh. Several of the students became Salvation Army officers.

The next year Kenley Royal Air Force Station, a noted Battle of Britain fighter base associated with ' the few ' and nestling beneath the lovely Surrey hills, was the home for a week of the 166 boys attending the second British music camp. The R.A.F. was still in residence and it will remain a mystery how a high-ranking Air Ministry official allowed a persuasive Assistant National Young People's Secretary to talk him into agreeing to such an unheard-of proposal! A sergeant and eight airmen were posted to the camp to care for the needs of the boys and their instructors. Those privileged to be there will not easily forget the varied experiences: availing themselves of the Station Commander's invitation to share the camp facilities (including the NAAFI stores and billiard room), carrying the advantages to excess by stripping the trees in the orchard in record time, dodging the aircraft landing and taking off, and mustering outside the main gate to march smartly past the sentry at thirty minutes after midnight following a three-mile walk from the nearest railway station after a festival at Croydon. The next year the music camp was back at Hadleigh!

Despite difficulties in securing suitable premises, the music camps in Britain have continued to function. The National Music Camp (renamed Summer School of Music in 1959) moved from Hadleigh to Tylney Hall, Hampshire, in 1956. In addition, there have been a number of divisional camps, the first being organized by the Northampton Division at Grendon Hall in 1950. The first Scottish territorial camp was held in 1948 and in 1964 the first Welsh event attracted many enthusiastic young musicians of the Principality. In 1949 General Albert Orsborn became the first International Leader to visit a music camp when he spent an afternoon with the Hadleigh students.

Music camps are now a regular feature of Salvationist youth activity in all parts of the world. At Adelboden, high in the Bernese Oberland, Swiss young people meet for brass and string band instruction; Sweden's camps usually precede the annual congress gatherings in Stockholm, at which the youthful musicians, fresh from their week's course, play an important part with highly developed technical skill; the Belgian and French camps often attract Salvationists from other parts of the Continent, including students from the British Isles anxious to improve their linguistic powers.

Norway's first territorial music camp was inaugurated in 1949 and

held at the Army's log-hut site—the ' Gronnlia '—outside Oslo.
Seventy young people's band members attended. To reach the camp
from the nearest point on the bus route the boys were required to
ramble through the forest for half an hour.

When the first camp for string band members was held in that
territory ten years later, the importance that the Norwegian Government attached to this innovation was revealed by the fact that the
State Youth Council donated 25,000 kroner (approximately £1,250)
toward the venture.

This event was held at Skien, and some of the pioneer students
came from north of the Arctic Circle, a journey which necessitated
travelling two days and nights by express steamer and 1,000 miles by
train.

Denmark's first camp of sixty delegates was held in 1947 at
Gilleleje, a seaside resort fifty miles north of Copenhagen.

The first music camp in the Australia—Eastern Territory was held
in 1949 at Collaroy, overlooking the Pacific Ocean. Forty boys
attended.

In the Australia—Southern Territory the first camp took place in
1957 at Mount Evelyn, in the Dandenong Ranges. Since that time
territorial camps have been held annually at the Parkdale Youth
Centre, a beach location in a Melbourne suburb. Other such events
for young people of the States of South Australia and Victoria have
also been conducted at intervals during recent years.

New Zealand has had a territorial music camp since 1960. Held
at Akatarawa, some thirty miles from Wellington, this is staffed by
Salvationist professional musicians. The sponsoring by corps of
promising young musicians has become a feature, and recent extensive
developments include the organizing of divisional camps.

In some territories music camps have gone beyond the limit of
youth interest. A bandsmen's camp was inaugurated in the Netherlands in 1947. At Plön, in Schleswig-Holstein, a camp for bandsmen
of the Northern Germany Division was commenced in 1961. Three
years later the function of the camp was expanded to include bandsmen
from all over Germany.

Concertinas

THE potential effectiveness of concertinas was realized early in the
Army's history. In 1887 Captain Thomas Kyle was summoned to
appear before the magistrates at Torquay for playing in the streets ' an
instrument not strictly known to the musical profession and called a
concertina '. Since the instrument had been invented by Sir Charles

Wheatstone in 1829, it is surprising that it took such a long while to be recognized!

Mr. Herbert Booth helped early-day officers by issuing a book describing the minimum of chords necessary for ordinary playing.

The first concertina band was formed at Bristol Citadel in 1884 and received a great welcome at the first Crystal Palace day six years later as it marched past the saluting base playing ' Saints of God, lift up your voices '. The Founder waved his top hat in delight. It was the playing of ' For you I am praying ' as a solo by one of the members that led to the boyhood conversion of Hugh Redwood, later to become well known and respected as a religious editor in Fleet Street and tireless auxiliary worker for the Army's cause. Other concertina bands were inaugurated at Plymouth Congress Hall, Sheffield Citadel and Doncaster.

The Army drum

IT is hard to imagine The Salvation Army without its ' big bass drum '. This symbol of vigorous religion is recognized the world over. Next to the Army flag the drum is the best-known emblem of militant Salvationism. Even where there is no band one can be almost sure to find a flag and a drum.

William Booth loved the drum and compared its function with that of the church bell, except that the message of the drum was ' fetch 'em ' in contrast to the ' come ' of its parish counterpart. He regarded it as an instrument with a purpose and insisted upon its use in all his meetings.

Once, at Balham in 1911, the Founder, half-way through the opening song, missed the punctuating note of the drum and at the end of a verse made the pithy comment: ' I never think my meetings are complete without the drum. I believe the drum is quite as sacred an instrument as the cornet, organ or tambourine. Now I expect there is one somewhere here, and if there is no one in the corps to beat it, I shall get somebody from the platform:

> From all the doubts that have filled me with gloom . . .
> From all the fears that would point me to doom,
>   Cleansing for me.

Isn't that worth a beat of the drum? '

The Balham drummer evidently thought so, for he responded with vigour and promptitude, augmenting the drum beat with a clang of the cymbals.

The drum was not quickly accepted as an addition to the Army's brass band. When Charles Fry and his sons became the first band, at

Salisbury, their cornets, trombone and euphonium were not considered to be so much out of place, for such instruments had, for some time, been similarly used accompanying the singing in chapel services. Not so the drum, which was condemned as evil and belonging to ' the world '.

In April, 1879, however, the ' Happy Family ' added a drum to its complement and Austin Grant became the Army's pioneer drummer. The instrument, purchased for ten shillings, was curious in shape and size, of extraordinary length and not unlike an Eastern tom-tom. Because of its unusual design it was suspended from the ceiling and used solely for indoor meetings. Later the ends were cut off, heads fitted and the drum was made presentable for outdoor service.

Prejudice had still to be overcome. Because the citizens objected to the Sunday use of the drum in the streets of Salisbury, it was played on weekdays only. At last, however, the drummer ventured forth on a Sunday and his courage was rewarded. ' We had had only two or three souls each night until then,' said Fred W. Fry, ' but that night there was a break in the ranks of the sinners, and we felt as if God set His seal on the use of the drum. Wherever we went the people wanted a band, or at least a drum if they couldn't afford anything more. And so we introduced the drum into the Army.'

The drum has never lost its appeal. Thousands, responding to its rallying beat, have been led to find salvation and a new way of life. Lieut.-Commissioner S. Carvosso Gauntlett's *Into the Highways* records:

> George Manning used to tell of the outcome of his substituting for the drummer on a march of the Regent Hall Band. He started off on the wrong foot! Five beats on the drum . . . but the Bandmaster saw to it that the band did not begin to play until the five beats had been given again, this time properly.
>
> Years later, Manning heard a man give his testimony in the Regent Hall. He recalled the day when he had bought poison and gone into Hyde Park to end his life. Suddenly he had heard five drum beats—but no music following; then another five, and the sound of the band. His curiosity was aroused, he found the band and, in the Army hall, the Saviour.

A drum helped in the Army's conquest of India. Purchased at Camberwell, England, where it received its baptism of fire—and water —it was taken, in 1882, by Major Frederick Tucker and his pioneer group to Bombay. On their march from the quay Lieutenant Arthur Norman, formerly a blacksmith, beat the drum. For a time the Salvationists met much opposition and were forbidden to march the streets, but the drum was not idle for long. Pioneers found that they could sit down in an empty hall, begin to beat the drum and the place would fill in no time. It was later stated that, although Major Tucker and his party wore Indian dress and made peaceful overtures, the people would not have been attracted to indoor meetings but for the call of the drum.

One Sunday morning in 1931 the General Secretary for the East Africa Territory, Brigadier (later Commissioner) Ernest Bigwood, was standing near the Uganda–Kenya border. Of the occasion he says:

> We had been led to expect a large congregation and as we stood, bewildered but not afraid (we had only recently arrived), the silence was broken by the sound of distant drums, first from one direction, then from another, almost like an echo. Suddenly colour lent enchantment to the scene—a splash of red, a flag, our beloved yellow, red and blue, and the hills seemed to break into song as one group after another picked up the refrain of a popular Army chorus. And so we received our earliest and most lasting thrill of our first Sunday in Africa. Those drums! They captivated us.

From the earliest days of the Army the drum's supreme function has been its use as a Mercy Seat in open-air meetings. When for some months in the 1880s the Highgate Corps, north London, was without a hall and all meetings were held in the streets, no gathering concluded without the drum being placed on the ground and the invitation given for convicted sinners to kneel in penitence and seek forgiveness. At this time and by this means a revival broke out. When Field Commissioner (later General) Evangeline Booth visited the corps no fewer than forty penitents knelt at the drumhead.

On the Roll of the Order of the Founder is inscribed the name of Thomas Hodge, an Australian bush driver who was a heavy drinker until, at the age of forty, he was marvellously converted. When his corps at Nyngan, New South Wales, closed, Hodge, already an old man continued the fight alone for another eight years. Without the aid of a motor car he travelled the seven miles into the town and took his stand in the street. Three times on Sundays and on several evenings a week, in full uniform with a Bible and a drum, he proclaimed the glad tidings of salvation.

What must be a unique event in Army musical history took place during 1958. To mark the Centenary celebrations of the Province of British Columbia, Canada, Vancouver Temple Band ordered a bass drum from London. But this was to be no ordinary job of transportation. The centennial drum was presented by General Wilfred Kitching at a festival given by the International Staff Band at Camberwell. Thus the Staff Band drummer had the honour of playing it for the first time in public.

Two days later the drum began its long journey. It was played in festivals in Cardiff, Edinburgh and Belfast, before crossing the Atlantic to Newfoundland, and in provincial capitals and other centres before arriving finally in Vancouver. Accompanying the drum was a log book for particulars and signatures of representative bandsmen.

N

The last band to use the drum before its presentation was that of Los Angeles (now Hollywood) Tabernacle from California (U.S.A.), which visited Vancouver for the Congress. As the Chief of the Staff (Commissioner William J. Dray) handed the much travelled history-making drum to Bandmaster Clifton Gillingham, he said: 'The message of the drum is to summon sinners to the Cross through the ministry of soul-saving music.'

The Army drum does not belong to the past. True, its character has changed with the passing of the years. No longer the wide, tom-tom type of 'weapon', it has been modernized, and today it is the fashion for bands to possess a tuned rod tension instrument. The music of the drum, too, has developed beyond all recognition. No longer can the instrument be regarded as the 'Cinderella' of the band, the starting point for a learner. A composer is required to give the greatest care and detailed concentration to scoring for the drum parts, for such matters as tuning and rhythmic acquiescence cannot be left to chance.

Colonel Arthur Goldsmith first saw the potentialities of the drum in Army music. As a young composer and the brilliant soprano cornetist of the International Staff Band, he had attended the memorial service of Cecil Rhodes and realized for the first time the true poetic beauty of the drum. For that impressive occasion Lieut.-Colonel J. Mackenzie (Senior Director to His Majesty's Brigade of Guards from 1900 to 1920) composed a solemn drum prelude which, opening with a soft fluttering hardly audible, rose to a tremendous thunder and then gradually faded away to a delicate murmur and final silence.

So impressed was Arthur Goldsmith by the moving effect that a year or two later, when working on his first band selection for an International Music Competition, he introduced a similar dramatic touch. This, aided by two trombone chords, gave the effect of a closing gate and a sense of awful doom. To those privileged to play the 'Mercy' selection—it secured first prize—under the composer's baton, the eerie drum part will for ever remain a thing of beauty, perhaps unsurpassed in Army band music.

The idea of seeking permission to form a Drummers' Fraternal came to Brigadier Burnal Webb in 1937, after three corps drummers had assisted him in the conducting of week-end meetings at Luton Citadel. The Brigadier had been a side drummer in Coventry City Band before entering the training college and had not lost his enthusiasm for percussion instruments. As a drum soloist he had appeared on numerous programmes.

The object of the Drummers' Fraternal was, in an unconventional yet dignified manner, to attract people to God and The Salvation

Army; also to offer percussional tuition, exchange ideas, wage spiritual campaigns and present programmes that were 'different'. The pages of *The Musician* were opened to the Brigadier, who for a number of years provided instructional articles and wrote on matters of interest to the fraternal he had founded.

This group has a record of soul-saving campaigning of which it is justly proud. A few years ago in the City of Birmingham, England, a combined drum display was being given by the fraternal in an open-air meeting in the famous Corporation Street. A man, attracted by the unusual and fascinating sight, followed the march to the citadel where, when the invitation was given, he was the first of the seekers. In the same meeting, again attracted by the drummers, a well-known bandmaster of a contesting band, a backslider for twenty years, made the decision to return to God and the Army.

Tambourines

IN the early days of The Christian Mission, when William Booth was conducting meetings in the heart of London's East End, he came to the conclusion that he needed a drum to 'beat up an audience'. When sufficient money could not be raised, his fertile mind sent him post-haste to a second-hand shop owned by Mrs. George Dexter.

On being asked to produce a drum for hire, the shopkeeper hunted the premises, to discover that the only musical instrument in stock was a tambourine. This was offered on free loan to the Founder —and eagerly accepted. It could well be then that General Booth himself was the first to play a tambourine in The Salvation Army.

But the idea was not taken up at that time. Some years later the General wrote an article on ' Miriam, a Forerunner of the Prophetesses of The Salvation Army' in *The War Cry* (February 17, 1881) and asked: ' Do not our prophetesses lead their people with music and song under the bare heavens in processions of mercy? Do they not play their music—if not timbrels—their violins, and cornets, and concertinas, and such other instruments as come to their hands?'Accompanying the article was a large illustration featuring Miriam with a timbrel in her hand.

Captain Charles Rothwell, the Commanding Officer at Mansfield, read the article, took the hint and set a fashion. He saw a tambourine for sale in a pawnbroker's shop and bought it for his wife to play. Mrs. Rothwell immediately used it in the processions which ' filled the devil with disgust, the newspapers with comments, the barracks with people and helped sinners into the fountain '!

In October, 1882, Commissioner George Scott Railton reported that 1,600 tambourines had been sold in six weeks and warned the

Army's Miriams that they should not beat tambourines without at the same time singing!

Another warning was forthcoming from the General. Conducting meetings in Scotland, he stated that when tambourines were used there should be something to balance them, ' such as clappers, bones, fifes, banjos '! In the same gatherings Mrs. Booth declared that tambourines and fiddles were as ' sacred as organs '.

At Torquay, in April, 1883, Deborah Parkins was appointed Tambourine Sergeant. Many years later, as Mrs. Commissioner Railton, she said:

> I thought tambourines a most natural means of expressing our happiness and I enjoyed banging my tambourine to the glory of God. I regarded the instrument as being just as characteristic of one sort of thing as the harmonium is of another. ... You have only to raise it before the largest possible assembly in Christendom and you banish as with a dynamite bomb all fear of public opinion.

Harmoniums were frowned upon by William Booth because of their association with chapels and consequent ' lack of attraction for the " masses " '. The day of electronic organs was to dawn much, much later! Bramwell Booth played a flutina and ' even occasionally struck a triangle '. It is stated also that Railton carried a set of bones in his pocket and, when he thought the meeting was stiff and wanted loosening up, rattled them!

Guitars

INSPIRED by the example of the Joystrings, a rhythm group formed at the International Training College, London, in the autumn of 1963, Salvationist youth has revived an interest in guitar playing and singing in the beat idiom of the period. This has proved to be an effective means of taking the gospel message to modern youth in a language they understand. The Joystrings' success in the way of gramophone recordings, radio and television appearances and soul-saving evangelism is too recent to need relating here.

Persecution

EARLY-DAY Salvationist musicians took a prominent part in facing the opposition presented to the Army's activities in many towns. Sheffield, Weston-super-Mare and Hastings saw the first rioting on a large scale and after many defeats the Army won its first legal battle of the streets on June 17, 1882, when its right to march in procession so far as common law is concerned was decided by the Court of the Queen's Bench.

The fight at Weston-super-Mare had brought matters to a head. When, two years later, an appeal was made to the Lord Chief Justice,

Lord Coleridge, against sentences passed on Salvationists at Hastings, the decision was that the defendants had not caused a disturbance in the accepted sense and should never have been convicted. Singing hymns or shouting ' Hallelujah! ' was not ' brawling ' and creating a disturbance within the meaning of the law, nor was playing an instrument out of tune an offence against the peace.

Although these findings seemed fair and clear cut it was soon discovered that special acts of Parliament forbade processions with music, other than military, in certain places on Sundays. The first town to put this prohibition into effect was Torquay. The thirty-eighth section of the Torquay Harbour and District Act, 1886, said:

> No procession shall take place on Sunday in any street or public place in the borough, accompanied by any instrumental music, fireworks, discharging of cannon, firearms, or other disturbing noise, provided that the foregoing prohibition shall not apply to any of Her Majesty's Navy, Military or volunteer forces.

On October 8, 1886, the corps officers and the Bandmaster were sentenced to a month's imprisonment. Fifteen months later the Captain was fined £2 and nine bandsmen and the standard bearer were fined £1 each, but they elected to go to Exeter Gaol. They were welcomed back to Torquay amid great public rejoicings led by Staff-Captain Eva Booth.

Opposition to Salvationist activities in Eastbourne began on September 8, 1890, eight months after the corps was opened. On that day Captain Emily Goss and some of her soldiers appeared before the magistrates for singing in the streets, an action forbidden by a craftily inserted clause in the town's recent Improvement Act. The case was dismissed. But the council was not going to take such defeat lightly. The next month Staff-Captain Harry Appleby, Bandmaster of the Household Troops Band, was brought before the court on charges arising from his being associated with a procession and a band of music, and was fined £1 in each case and 15s. costs or seven days' imprisonment.

The commissioning of a corps band in May, 1891, did nothing but ignite further ' fireworks '. During the summer of that year ' a constant stream of Salvationists flowed to and from Lewes Prison '. Nine bandsmen from Camberwell, London, who went to help their Eastbourne comrades, were roughly handled by the mob of some 1,500 hooligans and, by the personal order of the mayor, arrested and detained by the police in the town hall. On July 23rd they were committed for trial by the magistrates' court, charged with conspiracy and unlawful assembly.

The bandsmen appeared at the Sussex Assizes and later, upon the

Army's application, the case was removed to the Central Criminal Court. An astute judge, Mr. Justice Hawkins, decided that walking along carrying instruments was not unlawful and refused to accept the verdict given at the previous hearing at the Assizes.

Following this encouragement the legal battle for the removal of the offending 169th clause in the law was waged until a new Act repealing that which had caused the trouble came into force on September 1, 1892. Later that month *The War Cry* reported that the corps had made all-round progress and was marching with band playing, unmolested, every Sunday.

Not all magistrates' courts were hostile to Army musicians summoned to appear before them. In April, 1890, nine Upper Holloway bandsmen were charged with playing noisy instruments for the purpose of calling persons together in a public place, contrary to a certain section of the Police Act. The chairman of the bench dismissed the summonses, deciding that the bandsmen were playing in a band, the purpose of which was to facilitate the marching of Salvation Army processions and to accompany the singing of hymn tunes, and that they were not playing noisy instruments for the purpose of calling people together. A week or two before, the same magistrate had dismissed a summons against the Chief of the Staff (Bramwell Booth) and the Field Secretary (Major Alfred Barritt) for 'aiding and abetting' the playing of the 'noisy instruments' in dispute.

In 1911 the Hastings Town Council, after an interval of nearly thirty years, again sought to suppress the open-air witness of The Salvation Army under a by-law passed in July, 1896. As a result, Bandmaster Caleb Jeffrey appeared before the magistrates and was sentenced to fourteen days' imprisonment in Lewes Jail. On the day of his discharge the bands of Eastbourne and Hastings I and II met him at the station and marched him in triumph through the streets to the hall where a protest meeting was held. Several bandsmen later received summonses, among them Band Sergeant Bean, who served two periods of imprisonment for 'offering a prayer' at Denmark Place, a spot where the Salvationists had held open-air meetings regularly for twenty-five years.

Ten years later Hastings Citadel Band, at the request of the Chief Constable, attended the funeral of a detective, heading the procession and providing special music and song at the graveside! The drummer of that era was a member of the police force.

CHAPTER TWENTY

MUSICAL MILESTONES

THERE is ample evidence that William Booth loved music. He had a perfect sense of rhythm and delighted to put in a rolling bass part when enjoying congregational songs. Harold Begbie records that the first General, in his early-married days, sang melodiously about the house and would bound up the stairs two at a time, still singing. Bramwell Booth says: ' Army music owes much to the Founder. . . . It was he who foresaw the value of our music and determined to stamp such music with the vital and jubilant note of Salvationism.'

Councils

WILLIAM BOOTH also loved the men who made Army music and his early-day messages to them, published in *The War Cry* and *The Bandsman and Songster*, are classics of psychological understanding, good sense, sound moral advice and religious instruction. Nor can the personal interest of Bramwell Booth be overlooked. It was he who, with the General's approval, introduced bandsmen's councils. The first were conducted by him at Clapton on Sunday, December 10, 1899. Three hundred attended, representing the Army's 15,000 bandsmen, 10,000 of them in the United Kingdom.

On the Saturday 500 bandsmen took part in a musical festival, prominent in which were the items by the International Staff Band, conducted by Brigadier George Mitchell, and a string band led by Major Richard Slater.

National and territorial councils for bandsmen, with the accompanying festivals, have become a regular feature of Army musical life, developing from that humble beginning. Since the end of the Second World War inter-divisional councils have become a feature of banding life in the British Territory, the British Commissioner (Commissioner William Dalziel) reintroducing these popular events in January, 1949, with councils for the five Midland divisions at Birmingham.

The first councils for Bandmasters were held on January 17, 18, 1903. There was no associated festival on the Saturday, when delegates met in the Laura Place hall at Clapton for an informal ' get together '. On the Sunday morning the International Staff Band marched the 320 Bandmasters and Songster Leaders to the Manor Assembly Rooms, Mare Street, Hackney, where the Chief of the Staff (Bramwell Booth) led the day's meetings.

When Bramwell Booth became General he continued to meet the music leaders in council in London at intervals, and ever since the Army's General has reserved the right to conduct similar gatherings, the exception being General George Carpenter, who was deprived of the privilege because of war. The early councils took place at the Temple, Clapton, and Mildmay Conference Hall, but General Evangeline Booth saw the possibilities of the International Training College for such events when conducted in the summer with the cadets not in residence. Recent Bandmasters' and Songster Leaders' councils have been held at Denmark Hill. In 1959 it was decided that separate councils for Songster Leaders should be convened and these have alternated with those for Bandmasters as biennial events.

It is customary for national musical festivals to be held at the Royal Albert Hall. This famous building was used for the first time for such a purpose in October, 1907. Other Army demonstrations had taken place there before that date—the first in 1895—but this solely musical programme was hailed as a 'bold venture'. A reporter of the day regarded it as 'a tribute to Army music and an example of thorough Salvationism'.

The Chief of the Staff presided and the bands of the International Staff, Chalk Farm, Nunhead, Highgate, Camberwell, Regent Hall, Kennington Lane, Penge and Edmonton played unitedly under the baton of Lieut.-Colonel Mitchell. The Staff Band's solo contribution was 'Hebrew Melodies'. Other sections were Hammersmith Boys Brass Band, Edmonton Drum and Fife Band, a banjo band, a concertina band, a timbrel band (this was said to be a 'revival') and a 'singing battalion'. A male voice brigade and the Regent Hall quartet were also included. Brigadier Tom Plant provided handbell novelties and Captain Hamilton played a bagpipe solo.

While this historic festival was taking place General William Booth was discussing with President Theodore Roosevelt in the U.S.A. the value of brass bands in reaching the masses. The President said: 'There is no more effective method of evangelizing people than with a brass band. I confess I like brass bands and I like your brass bands.'

Despite the unqualified success of the 'bold venture', twenty-nine years were to pass before an Army musical festival was again held in the Royal Albert Hall. It preceded the first Bandmasters' councils conducted by General Evangeline Booth in 1936 and the bands were seated in the arena. The General presided.

The Bandmasters' councils festival was held in the same building for the next two years but, owing to days of war, no more took place there until May, 1949.

The Alexandra Palace

THE ALEXANDRA PALACE, in north London, was first used by The Salvation Army on Wednesday, July 3, 1882, to celebrate the Movement's seventeenth anniversary. Musical support was given to the celebrations, a contemporary report referring to ' the martial blast of many trumpets and thundering of many drums and cymbals and the music of concertinas and fiddles '. Five years later bands taking part in a musical demonstration were given the responsibility of playing a medley of fourteen tunes. These were listed, with numbers, and sent out to the Bandmasters with the following instruction:

> It will be well if you can arrange to meet your band, and have some practice for the above-mentioned airs. Please instruct your men to play by note as far as possible and not to manufacture their own parts. If this rule is adhered to the harmonies of the whole will be very grand. As far as possible bandsmen should play from their music, which they should bring with them.

These anniversaries were celebrated at the Alexandra Palace for the next two years, 1889—the year of the Founder's sixtieth birthday—marking another step forward in brass band presentation. The Household Troops Band provided a tune on its own to become the first solo section at such a festival.

In between the two world wars Alexandra Palace was the venue of a number of national festivals, notably in 1923 and 1926. The former marked the playing in manuscript of George Marshall's selection, ' Army of the brave ', by the International Staff Band. This was the composer's first appearance at a London festival of such magnitude since his accident. Thunderous applause greeted the playing of this hitherto unheard composition. A report of the day read: ' The Chief [Commissioner (later General), Edward Higgins, who presided] seizes the opportunity of introducing the composer; an invalid chair is wheeled to the front of the orchestra, the Staff Band at once stands in respect, every band and all the songsters following suit, and then, with a spontaneous burst of enthusiasm, the whole audience of 7,000 rises in honour of this young man, who has set so splendid an example of physical courage and intense faith in God. Rarely has such an ovation been accorded a humble Salvationist! ' Such incidents have made these occasions memorable.

Twice in the past thirty years field days have been held at the Alexandra Palace, both national youth festivals—in 1935 and 1960.

The Crystal Palace

AFTER three successful annual field days at the Alexandra Palace, the Army's twenty-fifth anniversary was celebrated at the Crystal Palace on July 15, 1890. This was the first time Salvationists had gathered at the great landmark in south London. Some years later a Regent Hall veteran bandsman, George Manning, recalled that day:

> The ' Rink ' made it a corps affair. We travelled in several horse-drawn wagonettes, the proprietor himself driving that containing the band. The horses had red, white and blue rosettes on the harness at their heads, and our driver had a tri-coloured rosette on his whip. A few weeks earlier I had taken up the G trombone and it was an eerie experience for me when we moved off *en route* for the Palace, for it was the first time I had played with the band mounted! We started off with ' Jesus is mine for ever ', which we played along Regent Street and across Piccadilly Circus. . . . When we got to Herne Hill we began to overtake Salvationist-comrades of all sorts, some on foot, others in different types of vehicles. When going up the rise of Dulwich Wood Park, near the ' C.P.', we had to disembark to relieve the strain upon the horses.
> Within the Palace one met swarms of happy people in all sorts of uniforms. Some of the men wore uniform caps with their ' civvies ', whilst others wore a red guernsey with their waistcoat over it. We could see Artillerymen's, Hussars', and other kinds of military uniforms being worn, but we were a happy people.

Manning went on to describe the details of the day. Regent Hall Band provided the accompaniment for the afternoon battle of song, led by Field Commissioner Evangeline Booth. The Household Troops and Home Office Bands were there. Woolwich Band paraded in dazzling white helmets and red plumes. Commandant Herbert Booth, who organized the day, conducted the massed items at night, with Staff-Captain Fred Fry at the grand organ, Staff-Captain Harry Appleby in charge of the brass bands and Staff-Captain Slater leading the string bands.

A year later, when 62,000 people passed through the turnstiles, the afternoon feature was ' The Biggest Band in the World—Brass, Concertina and Tambourines—10,000 instruments '. Solo bands selected to represent the British Isles and geographical areas of England were Belfast I (Ireland), Kilmarnock (Scotland), Pentre (Wales), Clapton Congress Hall (London), South Shields I (Northern England), Northampton I (Midlands), Bristol I (West), Brighton I (Southern), Norwich (Eastern), and the Home Office Band. A ' Special Tambourine Band ' also took part. At the conclusion of the festival the Household Troops Band played Herbert Booth's masterpiece, ' Promoted to Glory ', in memory of the Army Mother, who had passed away nine months before.

In 1894 the Crystal Palace was again the scene of mammoth festivals organized in connection with the second International Congress. This time it was Commissioner T. Henry Howard who, with baton in hand, led this ' tornado of hallelujah music ' in the vast central transept. Wrote a *War Cry* reporter: ' The Swedish Staff Band played a piece in which the features of their national music were well evident, but the greatest triumph, beyond a question, was won by the International Headquarters Band with the march, " A great salvation ". A veritable storm of delight burst forth at the end.' ' Promoted to Glory ' was played in every festival of the Congress.

Ten years later the National Staff Band of the U.S.A., resplendent in cowboy costume, was among the many overseas musical groups visiting London for the third International Congress. Three great festivals were held at the Crystal Palace that year—on the polo ground, in the central transept, in which 3,500 bandsmen participated in the afternoon, and a singing festival in the same hall at night.

The 1914 Congress again saw the Crystal Palace as the home of memorable festivals. That year the German and Swedish Staff Bands took part, and the U.S.A. and Canada were represented by corps bands from Flint (Michigan) and Peterborough (Ontario) respectively. In addition, the New York Staff Band made its second trip to England and the Chicago Staff Band was also present. Colonel Goldsmith's arrangement of the ' Hallelujah ' Chorus was played for the first time in public, by the International Staff Band from manuscript. The united bands, conducted by Commissioner Mitchell, played ' Promoted to Glory ' in memory of the 170 Salvationists (including all but twelve of the Canadian Staff Band) who had lost their lives less than four weeks before when the *Empress of Ireland*, bringing them to London, sank in the St. Lawrence River. In the great march past the Canadian Staff Band was represented by Kenneth McIntyre and James Johnson, two of the survivors, who continued their journey after being rescued.

Another ten years passed before the Crystal Palace once more was filled with the sound of salvation music. This began a golden decade of progress in the fortunes of Army bands. The diamond jubilee celebrations of 1925, the Founder's Centenary Celebrations of 1929, with Edward J. Higgins now the General, and the thrilling events of 1931 and 1932, with Coventry City Band setting a new standard of playing with ' The King of kings ', all had their highlights. The last day at the old ' C.P.' was held in June, 1934. Two years later it was destroyed by fire. The new Crystal Palace centre was a rendezvous for 50,000 Salvationists and friends who attended the Centenary celebrations.

Other public buildings

DURING the brief period in the 1930s when the British Territory was divided into four commands, the Queen's Hall, close to London's Oxford Circus and for many years associated with Sir Henry Wood's

Promenade Concerts, was used for the annual festivals of the London and Southern Territory. This famous home of music had also been taken by Regent Hall Corps for a number of events soon after the end of the First World War, at one of which Sir Jack Hobbs, the great cricketer, presided. It was destroyed in an air raid in 1941.

The Diamond Jubilee Celebrations of the International Staff Band in October, 1951, concluded with a programme in London's Royal Festival Hall, presided over by General Albert Orsborn. On that night compositions written especially for the notable anniversary were played for the first time, including ' Symphony of thanksgiving ', ' The eternal quest ', a trombone solo presented by Mrs. Maisie Wiggins, and ' Commemoration '.

In March, 1933, the first Army band programme to be given in the Guildhall, London, was presented by Clapton Congress Hall Band and organized by the Commanding Officer, Adjutant (later Commissioner) Edgar Grinsted. The Lord Mayor of London was in attendance.

Composers' festivals

ALTHOUGH Salvationist composers and song-writers were encouraged to submit their efforts for publication from the earliest days, gracious recognition was a long time in coming. Maybe there was wisdom in the view that publicity would not be good for the humble pioneer writers. For years composers' names did not appear either on the full score of the *Band Journal* or on the band part copies. They were not printed on the latter until 1935. Despite this accidental, or designed, playing down, hero worship has been inevitable and it has not been a bad thing for young Salvationists to find their heroes in the Army.

In January, 1927, a departure from the traditional was made with the presentation of a composers' festival at Clapton Congress Hall. The International Staff, Chalk Farm, Regent Hall, Cambridge Heath, Clapton Congress Hall and Croydon I Bands between them featured music written by Richard Slater, Frederick Hawkes, Arthur Goldsmith, Bramwell Coles, Wilfred Kitching, Herbert Twitchin, Edward Saywell and Eric Ball. All but Slater and Coles were there to conduct their contribution. The Admiral of the Fleet, Earl Jellicoe, was announced to preside but, at the last moment, was prevented from attending.

A similar event held in the same building in February of the following year was presided over by General Bramwell Booth and honoured by the presence of the Duke and Duchess of York, later King George VI and Queen Elizabeth. Hawkes, Goldsmith and Ball were there again to conduct their own compositions but this time also were included three Bandmasters—Harry Kirk, Jules Vanderkam and George Marshall. Penge Band was invited in place of Croydon I and a united songster brigade was led in turn by Major Charles Coller and Songster Leader Oliver Cooke.

Before the festival the composers were presented to the royal visitors. Recalling this highlight of his life, Bandmaster Vanderkam, from Belgium, admitted that he was nervous but the Duchess immediately put him at ease by speaking in French. Bandmaster Marshall has said: ' The Duke's royal hand-grip and genuinely sympathetic encouragement, and the Duchess's lengthy inquiries as to the cause and nature of my accident, and also the future of Mrs. Marshall and myself, were of such a nature as to touch to the utmost depths the hearts of all those assembled within that room, including a host of reporters and photographers, each of whom thought the gesture was of outstanding sincerity.'

The Duke and Duchess stayed for two hours and before their departure the General declared: ' The Duchess permits me to say on her behalf that she wishes for you and all you love every blessing of God. I think I may say, in return, that we altogether desire the same for her, and for His Royal Highness and for the Princess Elizabeth.' To conclude the programme a number of lantern slides depicting the suffering and death of our Lord were shown, to the accompaniment of ' The Man of sorrows ' played by several bands in a nearby room.

To mark the twenty-fifth anniversary of that royal occasion a third composers' festival was convened at Clapton in January, 1953. The Chief of the Staff (Commissioner John J. Allan) presided and thirteen composers and one poet were featured. General Kitching, then British Commissioner, and Bandmaster Kirk were the only participants who had been honoured on either of the earlier occasions and the scientific advances of the intervening years were unconsciously pin-pointed when the audience listened to a tape-recorded message from both Bandmaster Marshall and Second-Lieutenant Dean Goffin, who was then serving as a corps officer in New Zealand.

Composers' festivals are no longer unusual happenings. Organizers of events in New York and other great Army centres have come to realize their value.

' The Rink ' at Buckingham Palace

THE playing of the first Salvation Army band in the forecourt of Buckingham Palace came about through a misunderstanding. On Friday, May 6, 1910, King Edward VII passed away and, mingling with the crowds at the palace gates to read the final bulletin, Bandmaster Herbert Twitchin wondered if permission could be sought for

Regent Hall Band to march by the palace on the coming Sunday to play suitable music. He mentioned this to Corps Sergeant-Major Albert James, who was with him. The Sergeant-Major was manager of one of the works departments of the Westminster City Council and came into contact with the Comptroller of the Royal Household. The request was made known to this gentleman who passed it on to Lord Knollys, King Edward's Private Secretary, who thought the band wanted to play inside the gates. On the Saturday Bandmaster Twitchin received a telephone message to say that it was the Queen's wish that the band should play some of King Edward's favourite hymns in the forecourt of Buckingham Palace.

Scotland Yard was informed of the royal command and mounted police headed the procession of band and corps which left Regent Hall at one o'clock on that May Sunday afternoon. Says Bandmaster Twitchin: ' As we reached the big gates of the palace they were thrown open and we marched in. I remember the feeling of awe that came over me as I realized that we were alone in the forecourt. We were instructed to form a ring opposite a certain window of the first floor where, we were told, Queen Alexandra would be standing in the shadows. . . . We made history for the Army that afternoon.' Next day *The Times* carried a 400-word appreciation, an extract of which read: ' The band played the hymn tunes with a softness and delicacy of tone that was greatly appreciated by the listening crowds outside.'

Bandmaster Twitchin was honoured to march at the head of his band through the gateway of Buckingham Palace on four subsequent occasions—on Armistice Sunday, 1918, Peace Sunday, 1919, in March, 1932 (the fiftieth anniversary of the ' Rink ' corps and band), and April, 1946. At the conclusion of the programme in 1932 the Bandmaster was conducted to one of the state rooms to be presented to King George V and Queen Mary, with whom were their granddaughters, Princess (now Queen) Elizabeth and Princess Margaret. The party had listened from an open window and the King revealed his great interest by discussing the instruments, the men and the music played. Pointing in the especially bound programme to the title of Eric Ball's selection, ' The King of kings ', His Majesty commented: ' This piece is very appropriate.'

' I went back to my bandsmen and the waiting crowds,' said Bandmaster Twitchin, ' thanking God that He had allowed me this high honour in the fiftieth year of my connection with Regent Hall Band, and also proud of the fact that I had been able to represent Army bandsmen everywhere for the first time in the home of the English monarchy.'

The command to play in 1946 was in connection with the corps' sixty-fourth anniversary. News of the royal summons was immediately conveyed to the band's servicemen not yet released from the Forces, with the result that of the fifty-three bandsmen who marched to Buckingham Palace from Red Shield House in Buckingham Gate twenty-five had obtained special leave and wore their military uniforms. In the front rank of eight trombonists were two flight lieutenants, and among the cornetists were two officers of similar rank, with their pilot's wings up, while a Royal Army Ordnance Corps captain manned one of the euphoniums and a merchant seaman one of the basses. During the programme the Salvationists received word that King George VI and Queen Elizabeth desired to meet them in the inner quadrangle. The programme over, instruments were laid on the ground and the Regent Hall comrades disappeared from the view of the great crowd. The Bandmaster, with the corps officers, Major (later Colonel) and Mrs. Wesley Rich, were personally presented to Their Majesties, who spoke in most friendly fashion to each one. The King inquired of Major Rich where he had spent the war years and on hearing that he had been in the vicinity of London, His Majesty exclaimed, ' Then we were pals together! ' The Queen asked Mrs. Rich about the congregations at Regent Hall, and if people were being converted. On hearing the news of recent converts, Her Majesty exclaimed: ' How wonderful it must be to see lives changed like that! ' The King and Queen then descended the outer steps and entered into conversation with several of the assembled comrades, His Majesty having a special word for some of the servicemen.

That was Bandmaster Twitchin's last visit to the royal residence. A letter received by him from Balmoral Castle, dated August 6, 1951 —signed by the Lady-in-Waiting to Queen Elizabeth—in reply to a birthday greeting the Bandmaster had sent is significant. It stated: ' The Queen desires me to thank you most warmly for the message of greeting and kindness which you have sent for Her Majesty's birthday, and to tell you how greatly the Queen values the thought which has prompted it. I am to say that the Queen never forgets the happy occasions on which you have brought music to Her Majesty.'

A year later the corps' seventieth anniversary was marked by yet another invitation for the band to play at Buckingham Palace. The originally planned visit had to be postponed because of the death of the King, but on Sunday, July 15, 1952, the great gates once more opened to admit the ' Rink ' men. The Queen was suffering from a cold and the Duke of Edinburgh received the new Bandmaster, Kenneth Cook, and the corps officers, Major (later Lieut.-Colonel) and Mrs. George Wells.

In March, 1957, to commemorate the seventy-fifth anniversary,

Bandmaster Cook conducted the band through another similar pro-gramme in the forecourt of the Palace. The tune ' Aurelia ', featured in one of the pieces, ' The Light of the world ', brought back memories to veteran Band Reservist Jack Merrick, the only one present who had taken part in that first march to Buckingham Palace forty-seven years before. It was while the ' Rink ' Band was playing this hymn-tune that Queen Alexandra had appeared on the balcony and acknowledged with a hand-wave the bandsmen in the courtyard below. ' I was the Colour Sergeant then,' confided Jack Merrick between items to those standing near him, ' complete with turn-up trousers and button-up boots.' He was enjoying his seventh visit to the royal residence. Suddenly a curly head was spotted in the corner of a large second floor window above the main entrance. A face then appeared and the crowd's spontaneous intake of breath denoted that Princess Anne had been recognized. She had left her lunch table (by special permission) to see the Army band.

Bandmaster Cook, with the corps officers, Senior-Major (later Brigadier) and Mrs. Nicol Kirkwood, and other local officers, was presented to the Queen, who showed considerable interest in Regent Hall activities and in several aspects of Salvation Army banding, including the voluntary service of its members. When the Queen referred to Princess Anne's enjoyment of the programme, one of the party reminded Her Majesty that when the band played to her grand-father on the occasion of the corps' jubilee she herself was little older than the Princess. The Queen laughed happily at this reminder. ' Thank you for coming,' she said, as the Salvationists took their leave, proud to identify themselves with the band that had been summoned to its gracious Queen as their predecessors had played to her father, grandfather and great-grandmother.

Chalk Farm at the Palace

IN March, 1934, Bandmaster A. W. Punchard's completion of forty years in charge of Chalk Farm Band was recognized by a royal com-mand for that band to play at Buckingham Palace. ' As the last few bars of " Rock of Ages " were being played ', says the Bandmaster, ' a messenger approached the band, carrying an intimation that I was required in the palace, where I was greeted with the remark: " The King wishes to see you, Mr. Punchard." I just had time to ask what formalities I had to observe and to obtain a reassuring answer when I found myself ushered into the royal presence with this simple introduc-tion, " Mr. Punchard—Your Majesties ", and I was alone with the King and Queen. I had no time to be nervous, for the King, who was standing with the Queen immediately behind him, at once shook hands and expressed his pleasure at seeing me. . . . I had previously heard how everyone privileged to talk with Their Majesties was charmed by their kindly manner, and how soon one was at ease in their presence, and I can quite confirm this.'

The I.S.B. and royal occasions

THE third band to be honoured by a command to play at the palace was that of the International Staff. This honour came in connection with the band's golden jubilee celebrations in October, 1941, and the occasion was unique in that it took place in war-time. With gas respirators slung over their left shoulders the bandsmen gave a varied programme during which Princess Elizabeth and her uncle, the Duke of Kent, arrived by car. Attired in the uniform of an Admiral of the Fleet, King George VI later greeted the Bandmaster, Colonel George Fuller, and then asked to shake hands with each bandsman. Paying tribute to the memory of King George VI at the time of his death eleven years later, Lieut.-Colonel (later General) Frederick Coutts, a Staff Bandsman of that day, said: ' Royalty must be hard put to to know exactly what to say to the many different people they meet. In the palace quadrangle there were a few hesitant seconds after the first introduction—and then Colonel Fuller sailed in. The official report of the occasion said that " the King put the International Staff Bandmaster fully at ease ". One eye-witness is ready to take his oath that it was the other way round, but no one was happier about that than the King. A talking point made, conversation flowed freely, after which the King shook hands with each man, greeting Brigadier (later Colonel) Charles, the Flag Officer, as " one old sailor to another ", and chaffing Colonel Jakeway, then on BB♭ bass, as to how long the music took to go round and around from the mouthpiece and finally to come out at the bell.'

In 1951, when the band was again honoured, in the absence of the King, who was recovering from a major operation, the band's Leader, Colonel (later Commissioner) Norman Duggins and Bandmaster, Senior-Major (later Lieut.-Colonel) Bernard Adams, with the Public Relations Secretary (Commissioner M. Owen Culshaw) and Major (later Colonel) Arnold Brown, a Canadian officer representing the Dominions, were received by the Queen Consort, who was accompanied by Princess Margaret. Major Brown reported: ' The Queen seemed a little surprised that the band had not visited any of the Dominions (something this writer hopes will be rectified before long !) and congratulated Senior-Major Adams most cordially on the band's past and present standard. The presence of a Canadian naturally encouraged conversation concerning the current tour of Princess

o

Elizabeth in Canada, a subject which was evidently of pleasurable interest to Her Majesty.'

The band's third visit to Buckingham Palace was in October, 1961, the seventieth anniversary, when the Leader (Commissioner William Wotton) and the Bandmaster, with Alfred Andrews, the longest-serving bandsman, were received by Queen Elizabeth. On the opening day of the Centenary Celebrations the I.S.B., with Earlscourt (Canada) Band was summoned once again to provide music at the royal home.

These occasions do not represent the Staff Band's only royal associations. In April, 1949, during an eight-day tour in the Nether-lands, the band was commanded to play at the Royal Palace at Soestdijk, where Queen Juliana and the three Princesses stood on the terrace in the spring sunshine with the Chief of the Staff (Commissioner John J. Allan), the Territorial Commander (Commissioner Charles Durham) and Staff Band Leader (Lieut.-Commissioner Walter Rushton) to listen to the programme. The Queen congratulated Major Adams upon the playing and asked him to convey her appre-ciation to the band.

The first record of the I.S.B.'s recognition by royalty was in 1908 when the band played outside International Headquarters, Queen Victoria Street, upon the occasion when the King and Queen of Sweden passed on their way from Paddington Station to the Guildhall. The Swedish National Anthem was played as the royal visitors approached, and as the Prince and Princess of Wales (later King George V and Queen Mary) drove by the British National Anthem sounded out—at its new tempo of eighty-four crotchets to the minute (sixty was the old speed), fulfilling a request made by King Edward VII to all military bands the week before.

On the last day of the band's campaign in Norway in June, 1964, the Staff Band gave a festival in University Hall, Oslo, which was graced by the presence of King Olav, who personally thanked the Leader (Commissioner Carl Richards) and the Bandmaster.

Other royal occasions

EARLY in January, 1958, the Lord Provost of Edinburgh approached Queen Elizabeth's Secretary with a request that perhaps the diamond jubilee celebrations of Edinburgh Gorgie Band, which coincided with the completion of Bandmaster Alex Thain's thirty years' leadership, could in some way be marked during Her Majesty's stay in the Scottish capital that summer. Quickly came the royal command for the band to play at the Palace of Holyrood House when the Queen and the Duke of Edinburgh returned from the morning service in St. Giles's

Cathedral on the last day of their stay. As the programme ended the royal couple stepped into the courtyard.

'There stood the Queen and the Duke,' remembers Lieut.-Colonel Stanley Read who, as the Divisional Commander, accompanied the band. 'Her Majesty was quite relaxed and without hat or gloves. Small wonder the photographers had been excluded. This was a signal and personal honour for us. Informally and without pomp or ceremony the Queen received us and expressed her thanks to Bandmaster Thain.'

Other royal residences in Britain have echoed to the sound of Army music. In 1921 Norwich Citadel Band played to Queen Alexandra the Queen Mother at Sandringham House; in the early 1930s it was customary for King's Lynn Band annually to play Christmas carols to Queen Maud of Norway at her English residence, Appleton House.

Apart from the International Staff Band, three British corps bands have played to royalty during overseas campaigns: Doncaster to Queen Emma the Queen Mother of Holland at Soestdijk Palace in 1923; Norland Castle to Queen Wilhelmina of the Netherlands, who attended an open-air festival given by the band at the Hague in 1933; and Rugby to Queen Alexandrine the Queen Mother of Denmark, who was present at a festival in Aarhus in 1949.

On numerous occasions Army bands have provided music at civic functions attended by royalty.

In Government circles

THE International Staff Band carried out a unique and unexpected service during its Canadian tour of 1962. In Toronto at the same time as the British Prime Minister, Mr. Harold Macmillan, who was there to receive the Freedom of the city, the band was requested to provide music at his official welcome at the City Hall. Flanked by ' Mounties ', the band played to the huge crowds both before and during the official ceremony, and was afterwards thanked by the Prime Minister who, accompanied by the Territorial Commander (Commissioner Wycliffe Booth) and the Mayor of Toronto, personally greeted Lieut.-Colonel Bernard Adams.

When Sir Winston Churchill was a patient in Middlesex Hospital, London, following a fall in 1962, Regent Hall Band played favourite hymn tunes and offered prayers outside the hospital. The next day a London newspaper columnist referred to ' Sir Winston's Band '. A few days later Bandmaster Eric Rapp received a telegram from the great statesman which said: ' I am most grateful to you all.' The band also played outside the American Embassy following the assassination of President Kennedy in November, 1963.

In March, 1965, in response to the written request of Lord Morrison of Lambeth that bright and happy music should be played at his funeral, a section of the International Staff Band supplied the accompaniment to favourite hymns and provided music in keeping with the statesman's wishes. The service was conducted by General Frederick Coutts.

CHAPTER TWENTY-ONE

UNIQUE FELLOWSHIP

George Bernard Shaw

SALVATION ARMY bands have had no greater champion than George Bernard Shaw. He defended their cause in a day when they were not so well thought of as they are now. His words rang with authority, for he was a music critic before he was a critic of life and manners.

Following a journalist's reference to a horrible noise as ' worse than a Salvation Army band ', Shaw wrote a protest to the Press. The letter was brought to the notice of General William Booth, with the result that Shaw was invited to attend the next big festival to prepare a technical criticism for private circulation. The festival was held on Saturday, December 7, 1905, at Clapton Congress Hall and sections taking part were the International Staff, Regent Hall, Highgate, Chalk Farm and Clapton Congress Hall Bands. The International Staff Songsters were also included in the programme.

Writing from his home at No. 10 Adelphi Terrace, London, W.C., on March 31, 1906, ' G. B. S.' issued a comprehensive report on all that he saw and heard. In points of discipline, alertness and conscientiousness he considered all the bands ' first rate ' and paid tribute to the competent conductors who ' had evidently won their places by aptitude and efficiency '. Comments on the skill of each band were given at some length and frank, constructive criticism was levelled at the arrangers of Army music. It was suggested that the florid scoring for euphoniums was ' often far inferior in effect to broad simple chords ' and that ' exercises are not music and should be kept out of the public performances of the band '. This comment referred to the scalic semiquaver runs given to basses at the end of a movement. Arrangers were advised to score their pieces with a view to the emotional effect of the music and not to ' show off the virtuosity of their executants '.

' It is not enough for a Salvation Army band to play one of its scores technically well,' continued the report. ' You have only to hand the band parts to Mr. Sousa's band or the band of the Grenadier Guards and they will play it equally well. But there should be an emotional difference. It should be possible for a blindfold critic to say which was the Salvation Army band and which was the professional.'

During the festival the winners of the 1905 March Competition

were announced and the first and second prize numbers were played.
Shaw favoured the second piece—'Southall', by Bandmaster (later
Band Inspector) E. H. Hill—because of the 'devotional feeling' con-
tained in the trio. He urged Bandmasters to listen to the best music,
especially that 'conducted by Mr. Henry J. Wood at the Queen's
Hall'.

Colonel Bertram Rodda, living in retirement in California,
remembers, as a young Captain of fifty years ago closely associated
with the Chief of the Staff's office at International Headquarters,being
shown the sealed file with the whisper that George Bernard Shaw had
been asked to give a candid opinion of a massed festival but his findings
would be so disturbing that it was decided to keep the matter *sub rosa*.
The Colonel adds: 'I had to wait forty-five years to be allowed to
know what was in that sealed file I handled those years ago on the
second floor of the old I.H.Q.' Shaw's critique was published in full
for the first time in *The Musician*, December 3, 1960, ten years after the
author's death.

In 1922, sixteen years after the first occasion, 'G. B. S.' was invited
to attend a similar festival at Clapton to 'report progress'. He went
'to hear what changes had occurred, for better or worse, in the course
of the years which had elapsed since I astounded London by making
the heroine of one of my biggest plays a Major in The Salvation Army,
and substituted for the conventional theatrical love scene in a drawing
room a conversion scene in the yard of a Salvation barracks'. The
event took place on Saturday afternoon, February 4th, and again Shaw
gave lively and invaluable technical criticism for which he was paid a
fee. He promptly handed it back!

The critic revelled in the sonorities of the forty-three trombones,
played with 'a fervent enthusiasm that professional players can never
supply to order for their guineas'. The secrets of this second commen-
tary have been safely guarded, but without identifying the bands
referred to, perhaps the disclosure of one or two 'witticisms'—the
writer must have been in one of his facetious moods—would not be
out of place: 'Cornets want Self-Denial Week'; 'Soloist has found
the trick of playing sharp but overdoes it a little. Ophicleide wanted';
'Much better than 4' (the number of the item on the programme);
'Smashing tone used only when they meant to do it'; 'Very smart,
both playing and uniform; but not a man of them saved. Quite
secular in tone.' In a more serious vein he added that if Richard
Strauss and Sir Edward Elgar—with both of whom he had dined a few
days before—had been present they would have been sufficiently
delighted to have 'promised to compose an opening piece for the next
festival'.

When George Bernard Shaw attended his first Salvation Army gathering—a memorial service in the Royal Albert Hall in 1905—it was the music that impressed him most. He commented: ' Massed Salvation Army bands played the " Dead March " from " Saul " as I verily believe it had never been played in the world since Handel was alive to conduct it. . . . I have heard Handel's great march snivelled through and droned through by expensive professional bands until the thought of death became intolerable. The Salvationists, quite instinctively and probably knowing little of Handel, made it a magnificent paean of victory and glory that sent me—a seasoned musical critic of many years' standing—almost out of my senses with enthusiasm.' Many years later, in October, 1930, speaking at the National Brass Band Concert at the Crystal Palace, he said: ' I consider that Salvation Army bands are among the best. Because of their fervour the Salvationists get more real music out of their instruments than many professional bands.'

Shaw's greatest tribute to the progress of Army bands was paid when he wrote in *The Times* in October, 1941: ' Had the Albert Hall, the B.B.C. Orchestra and The Salvation Army's International Staff Band been within Handel's reach the score of " Messiah " would have been of a very different specification. The music would not and could not have been better, but the instrumentation would have been much richer and more effective.'

Musical personalities show their interest

THOUGH Salvation Army bands came in for much caustic comment and bitter criticism in their earliest years, the beginning of the century brought signs of the development of healthy respect. This change of attitude was undoubtedly engendered to a large extent by the public utterances of George Bernard Shaw and others who were invited to festivals and, in many cases, to preside. Sir Henry Coward attended many such events in the Yorkshire area, dating from Chalk Farm's visit to Sheffield in 1911. The unquestioning acceptance of the no smoking and no drinking ban by Army musicians was ever a cause of wonder and admiration to him.

Sir Dan Godfrey was another noted musician who made frequent appearances on Army platforms. When presiding over a festival given by the International Staff Band at Boscombe in 1937, he expressed amazement that he had once seen a Salvation Army band conducted by an Englishman in Iceland, and hoped to see something of Army activities during his forthcoming visit to South Africa. Hearing of these remarks, the Migration and Travel Department at International Headquarters advised officers at various points *en route*. Sir Dan never forgot this unexpected courtesy. His message from Port Said was typical: 'We have had a delightful day here, thanks to the kindness of Adjutant and Mrs. Victor Underhill, who are doing splendid work under difficult circumstances.'

No person did more to introduce famous musical personalities to Salvation Army music than Bandmaster A. W. Punchard. The series of 'Baths' festivals given by Chalk Farm Band in St. Pancras Public Hall between 1910 and the outbreak of the Second World War became world renowned, not only for the high standard of presentation but also for the illustrious chairmen secured. Sir Alexander Mackenzie, Sir Hugh Allen, Sir Landon Ronald, Mark Hambourg, Lieut.-Colonel J. Mackenzie-Rogan, Henry Geehl and Walter Reynolds were among that number. A unique occasion was in 1935 when 'three men from St. Paul's' shared the duties of chairman. They were Frank O. Salisbury, the artist who was then working on a painting depicting the inside of St. Paul's Cathedral at the Thanksgiving Service for the Silver Jubilee of King George V and Queen Mary, a huge canvas that was later hung in Buckingham Palace; Canon H. R. L. ('Dick') Sheppard, and Dr. (later Sir) Stanley Marchant, the cathedral organist.

In more recent years Army programmes have been enhanced by the presence and appreciated comments of such men as Sir Granville Bantock, Sir Adrian Boult and Sir Malcolm Sargent. It was after Dr. Clement C. Palmer, Organist and Master of the Choristers of Canterbury Cathedral, had heard the air varié, 'The old wells', played by an Army band that he sent the score to his friend, Sir Edward Elgar. England's 'greatest composer since Purcell' took the trouble to send a note of commendation in his own handwriting to the composer, Eric Ball. When Sir Arthur Bliss, some years ago, wrote the test piece for a National Band Contest he requested an Army band to play it through to him from manuscript, attending a rehearsal for the purpose.

Little did Salvationists realize when Dr. Ralph Vaughan Williams was invited to 'take the chair' for the International Staff Band's festival at Dorking in 1953 that this first encounter with Army bands would lead to his composing something for the band. 'Prelude on three Welsh hymn tunes' was the outcome. Vaughan Williams heard it played for the first time at a special practice held at Judd Street and later was present in the B.B.C. Maida Vale studio when the work received its initial 'public' performance. It was, however, another piece broadcast that evening, Eric Ball's Triumph Series march, 'Fight On!', that captivated his attention and inspired generous praise.

Military and brass band conductors have been no less vocal in their approval of the ever-developing standards of Army bands, among them William Rimmer, J. Henry Iles, Dr. Denis Wright, Dr. Harold Hind, Hubert Bath, Jack Mackintosh, Major G. H. Willcocks and Harry Mortimer. In his life of Herbert Booth, F. C. Ottman states that ' for several consecutive years the picked band of The Salvation Army won first prize at the annual contest for English bands '. This is not so. At no time in their history have Army bands been permitted to take part in competitive events of this nature, or in the associated concerts.

The monopoly of distinguished personalities has not been left to programme organizers in Great Britain. In the U.S.A. such musical giants as John Philip Sousa and Edwin Franko Goldman have graciously accepted invitations to attend Army gatherings. More recently Dr. Meredith Willson, famous as the composer of the stage and screen success, ' The Music Man ', has interested himself in the country's Salvationist music-making. His ' Banners and Bonnets ' was written as a tribute to the faithful service of his Army friends. This was sung by Mrs. Willson, with her husband at the piano, in the International Staff Band's afternoon programme in Pasadena, California, on Easter Sunday, 1957. Dr. Willson presided over that festival. When the New York Staff Band sang ' Banners and Bonnets ' on a television programme the composer revealed that he had started his musical career by playing drum in a Salvation Army band at Mason City, Iowa.

In Canada Sir Ernest MacMillan, Dr. Leslie Bell and Dr. Don Wright are among personalities who have taken part in big territorial events.

In civic and parliamentary affairs

GONE are the days when Army bandsmen were summoned to appear before local magistrates and often sentenced to terms of imprisonment. Gone, too, are the days when the men who played in Army bands were held in contempt and victimized by business associates, as when a bandsman was asked to resign from the Metropolitan Police Force because it was learned that he had become a Salvationist.

At Salisbury, the scene of so much early-day opposition, two Salvationists, Ernest R. Grant, a son of the Army's first drummer, and Sidney E. Chalk, have served as Mayor while Bandmasters John W. Nicholls, William J. Thomas and Albert E. Munn have held that exalted public office at Twickenham, Maidenhead and Kettering. Bandmaster Munn was elected on two occasions, a number of years separating the periods. The first Lord Mayor of Portsmouth, James E. Smith, was Bandmaster at Southsea I for a number of years, while a Salvationist Lord Provost of Dundee, William Black, was a former

Songster Leader. More recently, bandsmen have served as Mayors of Ilkeston and Warrington.

The first Salvationist mayor was Robert Archbold, of Jarrow, Co. Durham, whose election caused a sensation. There is no record of another until 1920 when Bandsman (Corps Sergeant-Major) George Dinsdale, of Brandon, Manitoba, Canada, was honoured in this way. By the time he was admitted to the Order of the Founder in 1944 he had served the community of this prairie wheat-growing centre continuously for twenty-six years as mayor, alderman and, latterly, Member of the Provincial Legislature. When his death made a by-election necessary his son, Walter, the corps Bandmaster (as his father had been) succeeded him.

Walter Dinsdale, a decorated R.C.A.F. night fighter pilot, was elected to represent Brandon in the Federal Parliament in 1951 and six years later became a Cabinet Minister in Prime Minister John Diefenbaker's government, holding the portfolio of Minister of Northern Affairs and National Resources. He can often be seen in his Bandmaster's uniform around the Parliament Buildings in Ottawa and is respected for his pronounced religious convictions.

Another Canadian to become a chief citizen was Bandmaster Stanley Collier, of Vancouver Temple, when he was elected Reeve (Mayor) of West Vancouver.

Order of the Founder

HIGH on the roll of those admitted to the Order of the Founder, The Salvation Army's Order of Merit, are the names of musicians. After Bandmasters Alfred W. Punchard (1937) and Herbert Twitchin (1939), the next to be so honoured was Bandmaster Sidney W. Cox, of Exeter Temple, who, when the award was made in 1942, had ' rendered sixty years' continuous service at Exeter Temple Corps, his fifty-five years as Deputy Bandmaster and Bandmaster being the longest term served in this office by any Salvationist '. When the Bandmaster was promoted to Glory in 1947 he had completed fifty-three years in that appointment, which is still believed to be an Army record. Others to earn this rare recognition are Bandmaster John W. Turner, of Adelaide, Australia (1956), Divisional Bandmaster Arthur J. Stevens, of Hawthorn, Australia (1949), Bandmaster George Marshall (1950), Bandmaster George Foster, of Cambridge, Massachusetts, U.S.A. (1951), Envoy (Divisional Bandmaster) Robert H. Palmer, of Perth, Western Australia (1952), Staff Bandmaster Norman McLeod, of Melbourne, Australia (1955) and Bandmaster Henry Kragh Jensen, of Copenhagen Temple, Denmark, 1962. The officers to receive the award in recognition of their services to Salvation Army music are Lieut.-Colonel Richard Slater (1923) and Colonel George Fuller (1942).

Professional musicians

IN contrast to the pioneer Army bandsmen, few of whom were educated, is the ever-growing coterie of highly qualified Salvationist professional musicians, including holders of degrees and diplomas from the various colleges of music. Bandmaster William Overton, of Lewisham, has for some years been the principal trumpet of the B.B.C. Symphony Orchestra and since 1960 has held the appointment of Professor of Trumpet at the Royal Academy of Music. He was the first Salvationist to win a trumpet scholarship to the Royal Schools of Music and, in 1934, was only the second Salvationist to gain the A.R.C.M. diploma, Eric Ball having been successful, in the theory of music, nine years before. The Bandmaster's colleague on trumpet in the symphony orchestra for some time was Wesley Woodage, who sat by his side in the band at Margate when they were both teenagers.

Mrs. Maisie Wiggins (née Ringham), the only woman Bandmaster in the British Territory, was the first student of the Royal Manchester College of Music to become an Associate of that college for trombone playing. After a period with the B.B.C. Midland Light Orchestra she joined the famous Hallé Orchestra, of which she was a member for ten years, as principal trombone for most of the time. With the orchestra she gave the first performance in England of ' Fantasia for trombone ' by Paul Creston, a work she later broadcast in the B.B.C. Third Programme. Maisie also recorded Erik Leidzén's ' Concertino for band and trombone ', written especially for her, with the International Staff Band, the composer conducting.

In the professional world Maisie, like all Salvationists, has been subject to good humoured banter but is respected for her principles. Her husband, Raymond, states: ' When Sir John Barbirolli first saw Maisie in uniform—she had gone to a Hallé rehearsal straight from a Salvation Army appointment—he kissed her on both cheeks. Another time, at the Albert Hall, Manchester, she was writing a letter during a break in rehearsal and realized someone was calling her name. Looking up she saw Sir John wearing an Army bandsman's cap; it had evidently been left in the hall after a festival and eventually found its way to the men's dressing-room.'

One of the first Salvationist-musicians to apply himself to diligent study was Dr. T. Freeman Black. Appointed Bandmaster at Sheffield Citadel at twenty-one, he sought to equip himself for the task of directing thirty-eight bandsmen and in the years 1908, 1910 and 1911 took senior honours at the Trinity College of Music, London, the certificates of the Royal Academy and Royal College of Music for advanced harmony and counterpoint, and the diplomas of A.Mus., L.C.M. and A.Mus., B.C.M., London. He composed the ' Sheffield ' march. When the family moved to Scotland, he became Bandmaster at Dundee II (now Dundee Central).

When his widowed mother was taken suddenly ill and died the same day, Black, then a lad, was so distressed at not being able to help her that he resolved to study medicine and become a doctor. Whilst employed on the engineering staff of the Dundee Water Works he gave up every available moment of his spare time to his studies. In 1915 Bandmaster Black answered the call for skilled engineers to help the war effort and upon demobilization in 1919 lost no time in continuing his medical education, qualifying as a physician and surgeon in the summer of 1923, three months under the prescribed minimum time.

The Bandmaster later devoted much time and study to dental surgery, gaining expert knowledge which qualified him to advise Army bandsmen in securing dentures that would enable them effectively to continue their playing. This advice came in for great demand and a series of articles on the subject, with diagrams, which were first published in *The Bandsman and Songster* in 1932, has been reprinted in booklet form. Dentists have expressed admiration of the Bandmaster's prescription.

Bandmaster Black's interest in musical affairs was by no means over in 1934, when he added to his F.T.C.L. diploma for cornet playing that of L.G.S.M. (Bandmaster), a newly founded examination of the Guildhall School of Music for brass band conducting. Many Salvationists followed the Bandmaster's example. When he was promoted to Glory in 1941 the letters M.B., Ch.B., F.T.C.L., L.G.S.M. and M.R.S.T. could be added to his name. He was also a Justice of the Peace for some years.

In 1954 Bandmaster Philip B. Catelinet gave the first performance of Vaughan Williams's ' Concerto for Tuba and Orchestra ' at London's Royal Festival Hall. Later that year the Bandmaster played the solo part in this work at a Royal Albert Hall Promenade Concert, which was broadcast. Bandmaster Catelinet is also a brilliant pianist, securing the L.R.A.M. diploma for solo performer at an early age, one of the first Salvationists to do so.

Pioneer soloists

OF all the outstanding pioneer instrumental soloists the mention of two will have to suffice: William Packham and ' Mudgee ' Robertson. Both were cornetists and both were noted for their extreme range.

Packham showed early promise as a musician and was Bandmaster at Eastbourne by the time he was sixteen. After seven years of leadership he began his travels in search of work, troubles in the building trade making this necessary. He became associated with bands at Johannesburg (South Africa), Dovercourt (Canada) and the New York Staff Band (U.S.A.) before settling in Cardiff (Wales), thus enabling him to claim the record of having served as a Bandmaster or bandsman in five different countries.

Bandsman Packham, it is said, could play the National Anthem in five octaves and, in addition, used to perform what was termed 'a wonderful feat'. Laying his cornet down on its side, bell on top with the mouthpiece and shank flat on and touching the table, he would kneel down and, putting his lips to the mouthpiece, without touching the cornet at all with his hands, play 'Robin Adair' in two flats, starting on top F—actually an octave higher than the normal pitch— and with perfect tonality.

Adjutant Tom Robertson, an Australian officer, also became a legend in his life-time. Converted after hearing the newly formed Army band march past Bathurst Jail, New South Wales, where he was serving a sentence of four months following a wild escapade while in drink, Robertson entered the Melbourne training home in 1889. When it was discovered that he was not the only cadet by that name the difficulty was overcome by prefacing his name with 'Mudgee', after his native peaceful little town on the western side of the Blue Mountains. He adopted the nickname for life. One evening, when a Lieutenant at a country corps, 'Mudgee' chanced to hear a cornet player with a travelling circus performing in an extraordinary wide range, encompassing several octaves.

'If he can do that, I can,' said 'Mudgee'; and he set to work learning to do the same. At last he was proficient and could play in five and a half octaves. A skilled instrumentalist of that day wrote:

> In performing this extraordinary, if not altogether unique feat, the full chromatic scale was played throughout the entire gamut, and alternative methods of fingering were used. The progressive cadences were taken steadily and expressively, the Adjutant sustaining a pure flute-like tone without the labouring, straining effort noticeable in some players when in the top registers. He was the only cornetist I have known who could play two cornets at the same time. This feat he performed by placing one mouthpiece on each side of his lips and blowing into both at the same time, fingering one instrument with each hand. He could also play the cornet in reverse, with the bell pointing backways over his shoulder. This he did by changing around the big slide on his old-style brass cornet, incidentally transforming a B-flat instrument into an E-flat. On open notes he could mimic a parrot or a magpie, the barking of a dog, or the roaring of a bull.

Colonel Percival Dale remembers: 'In addition to the skill "Mudgee" possessed as a player, he had considerable powers of showmanship. He would start to play standing on the floor and rise on to successive heights as he ascended to higher octaves, sometimes pretending to break down. Then in triumph, standing on a chair on the highest tier and after running one hand through his hair, as though in despair of ever reaching the top note, he would give a rendering that was flawless.' Another 'trick' was to play a clarinet solo on a section of a broom handle, with a gum leaf in his mouth to produce the weird undulations of that instrument.

An early Army musical personality was Brigadier Tom Plant. Becoming an officer in 1888, he spent practically all his career in the appointment of 'musical special', travelling continuously throughout the British Isles and in many overseas territories, conducting musical campaigns and persuading his audiences to make music in a number of novel ways. With no training, Plant acquired skill on many instruments, guitar, banjo, concertina, flute, and tubular bells among them, and his happy disposition and ability to sing a good song, usually his own composition, made him a popular guest at any corps. He made innumerable friends for the Army whilst holding musical meetings with the servicemen in France during the First World War.

Education

THANKS to modern educational facilities it is no longer unusual for a Salvationist to become a university undergraduate. Thirty years ago a list published in *The Bandsman and Songster* gave sixteen names of Salvationist graduates, nine of them active musicians. Among these were Bandsman Augustus J. Ward, Ph.D., B.A., then studying in Warsaw, Poland. For nearly thirty years Dr. Ward has been a Cambridge don and can often be seen leaving King's College in Salvation Army uniform to take his place with the comrades of Cambridge Band in an open-air meeting.

Recording

As long ago as 1896 the Trade Headquarters Band contributed to a phonograph recording. A *War Cry* report states: 'The Trade Headquarters Band then played the "Indian" march, which was received into the phonograph and repeated five minutes later, accurately and minutely, applause as well. It was most interesting and in every way a success. The financial and spiritual prospects of these machines are boundless.' The technicians, however, reckoned without the softness of the wax used and this historic recording did not remain a permanent production.

Six years later Regent Hall Band recorded several hymn tunes, including ' Onward, Christian soldiers ', and this was probably the first official band recording issued. In that year (1902) Bandmaster Herbert Twitchin was selected to make two recordings on the cornet, the first with Staff-Captain Harry Green at the piano and the second with the Bandmaster himself providing a left-hand pianoforte accompaniment. Many years afterward Bandmaster Twitchin recorded the first cornet solo to appear on a disc, ' I love Him better every day ', and later still—in 1935 when he was in his sixty-first year—he recorded ' Wondrous Love '.

The other noted London band of that time, Chalk Farm, made its first records in 1912—for Pathé Frère. There were four, two ten-inch and two twelve-inch, and they had to be used with a sapphire point, not a needle, beginning at the middle and working to the outside.

When the ' modern ' technique of gramophone recording, with wax discs and steel needles, became established, the International Staff Band pioneered the way in 1927 with the first Army record made by Columbia Records on the ' Regal ' label. The ' Flag of freedom ' and ' The Liberator ' marches and the selection, ' Banner of liberty ' (two sides), were the pieces chosen. For the sake of convenience the early recordings of this era were confined to the London area, the bands of Salvationist Publishing and Supplies, Ltd., Regent Hall and Chalk Farm joining the Staff Band to produce Army classics of the day. There would appear to be no large-scale attempts officially to organize band recordings in overseas territories between the two world wars.

In the years immediately following the end of the Second World War there was a noticeable stepping-up of Army record production, especially on an international level. The best sections from the provinces, conducting week-end campaigns in London, were requested to travel earlier in order to prepare a recording. By this means such bands as Kettering, Edinburgh Gorgie and Bristol Easton Road became available on permanent discs. Sweden, with its ' Festival ' productions, was soon in the field and before long bands in Australia, New Zealand and the U.S.A. were producing worthy recordings. When EP and LP became the vogue these countries were quick off the mark, the New York Staff Band, from 1955, setting an industrious and efficient example.

Although the International Staff Band cut its first LP disc in connection with its U.S.A. and Canadian tour of 1957 and was later heard

in that way when a recording was made of the band's festival in
Massey Hall, Toronto, it was not until 1960 that the first was made in
Britain. In the summer of that year the band recorded ten pieces,
among them 'Motondo', 'Heroes of the faith' and 'Songs of the
seasons'.

Broadcasting

IN December, 1922, Salisbury (England) Band Vocal Quartet made
history by broadcasting—probably the first Salvationist-musicians to
do so. A wireless pioneer possessing a special licence broadcast a short
programme from his home on the outskirts of the city. This was
received at the city hall, a building then used by the Salvationists
while their citadel was being renovated. 'Onward March' and
'Heavenly Mansions' were the songs selected, and a cornet solo was
played by Bandsman H. Clarke, an item which proved so popular that,
in response to numerous telephone calls from local radio amateurs with
receiving sets, a repeat rendering was given. The other history-making
bandsmen were Ernest Grant (later Mayor of Salisbury), Arthur Burt
and Norrie Allen.

On November 7th the following year Govan Band broadcast a
programme from Glasgow which is believed to be the first in Army
Band history. Bandmaster Arthur Dry received a shoal of letters
marking the success. One read: 'I am a Regent Hall bandsman
tucked away in a flat near Selfridge's (in Oxford Street) and it does seem
wonderful to be able to listen to you up in Scotland; also it was
a delightful change to hear some Army music in the phones!' A
Gravesend fan was more forthright: 'You have really beaten the
Londoners!' That was from a former Clydebank bandsman! A
month later Sheffield Citadel became the second band to broadcast
when a programme was played over the Sheffield Relay Station C.F.L.
Bandmaster Herbert Mountain played a trombone solo.

The first London band to play 'on the air' was Chalk Farm which,
during its Scottish tour of 1924, gave a programme 'broadcast by
wireless' from Aberdeen on Saturday, August 9th. This innovation
must have aroused the citizens, for next day, 'in response to captivated
listeners', the band again visited the broadcasting station and 'dis-
pensed the salvation message through music into homes far and near'.
Seven years later this band was the first to broadcast a programme over
the National wavelength of the B.B.C., although the International
Staff Band had participated in a number of Army meetings from the
old 2LO station. In 1927 Chalk Farm Band gave its first broadcast
abroad, from Berne, Switzerland.

With the development of radio and the setting-up of regional stations around the British Isles there were, in the early 1930s, greater opportunity for the better bands to be heard.

Following the broadcast of Cambridge Heath Band from London on Christmas Eve, 1935, the door was unexpectedly flung open and for the next two and a half years numerous British bands could be heard at regular intervals and by audiences far removed from the international centre. Chalk Farm Band was invited to give a programme over the newly organized Empire wavelength—between three and four o'clock in the morning and beamed mainly to Canada. The experiment was an unqualified success, Bandmaster Punchard receiving cables and messages not only from thrilled listeners in Canada but also from a member of the British Embassy in Washington, D.C., and a Bandmaster of an Army leper colony band in India. Later the band was the first to broadcast direct to Australia and India.

The Empire broadcasts opened up a new world to Salvation Army bandsmen. For the first time the unique fellowship was linked by direct contact. The playing of ' Maoriland ' by the cornet soloist of the Salvationist Publishing and Supplies Band was heard by its composer, Brigadier Henry Goffin, in New Zealand at one o'clock on a Monday morning after a hot Sunday. (It was deep winter in Britain.) Bandmaster Norman Audoire heard his march, ' Montreal Citadel ', played by his old band, Cambridge Heath, while he was ' specialing ' with his band in Toronto. At Earlscourt, Toronto, a wireless set was installed in the hall at ten o'clock one Sunday night so that a broadcast by the International Staff Band might be enjoyed. Colonel (later Commissioner) William R. Dalziel, the Chief Secretary, hurried from a week-end appointment to share the thrill with two former members of the I.S.B., Colonel James Hawkins and Brigadier Fred W. Beer. That broadcast was also heard by another former Staff Bandsman who was studying medicine at Yale University.

A Captain stationed at Flin Flon, North-West Canada, heard a Chalk Farm broadcast which inspired him to persevere with his band of eight players. At the Lagos training college only two cadets had ever heard a radio set when the principal placed one in the dining-hall to receive a broadcast from London. On an occasion when a broadcast coincided with a Montreal Citadel band practice the men eagerly followed the copies before them as the music came over the ether.

After Chalk Farm Band's broadcast to Australia not only were messages received from such centres as Brisbane and Melbourne, but bandsmen in New Zealand also made it known that they, too, had listened, going to great lengths to ensure a reasonable reception. ' We

P

were thrilled to the boot-laces,' reported the Wellington Citadel flugel horn player!

At the other side of the world regular broadcasts were arranged featuring Newton, Wellington Citadel and Dunedin Citadel Bands in New Zealand, and several Australian sections, especially Sydney Congress Hall Band. These programmes were heard by radio enthusiasts in India, China and across the Pacific. Two bandsmen at Grays, England, picked up a broadcast by the New York Staff Band, which could be heard from the Wayne, New York, Station on two evenings a week. Pittsburgh Divisional Staff Sextet, directed by Brigadier William Broughton, was responsible for a weekly feature.

In 1935 four records sent out from London became the first Salvation Army music to be heard ' over the air ' in Japan. A year later the Japanese Staff Band gave its first broadcast from Seoul, Korea. At the same time Army records were relayed from radio stations in Latvia and Estonia, thanks to the influence of Major (later Colonel) Alfred Lockyer, then in charge of Army work in those countries. All this activity was in addition to the Army meetings that were being regularly featured in many parts of the world.

The wide-ranging spiritual influence of those early international broadcasts was quickly felt. A visitor to the Cincinnati, Ohio, studio while a programme was being broadcast knelt by the side of the radio and claimed deliverance from the habit of smoking, which had interfered with his spiritual experience. When Cambridge Heath Band had a few moments to spare at the end of a programme the hymn tune, ' Beethoven ', was played as an ' extra '. A young woman who had been listening-in was debating whether to spend the Sunday evening at a cinema or go for a walk in the park when she heard the band strike up the old tune. It had been her favourite in days gone by, for she had been brought up in the Army, but in recent years she had grown indifferent to the claims of God. That night she was one of five seekers in the meeting at Camberwell, London.

A plane conveying supplies and passengers to a mining camp situated on the shores of a lake in Northern Ontario was compelled to make a forced landing and send out an SOS for assistance. While waiting, the passengers listened-in to a programme being broadcast by Dovercourt Band in Rochester, New York, with the result that a young man was convinced of his need of a Saviour. A Christian companion gladly explained the way of life and a soul was born anew.

A broadcast from London unexpectedly linked two brothers—sons of Commissioner William Eadie—who were separated from each other and from the band by thousands of miles. One was in Edmonton, Alberta, Canada, and the other in Oudtshoorn, South Africa. Without the other knowing, each wrote to London in appreciation of the programme.

In Great Britain the auditioning of a Salvation Army band became a weekly feature of broadcast programme planning. At all the regional studios the better bands in the area were heard and, if successful, placed on the list for future reference. Castleford Young People's Band was the first junior section to pass an audition and had almost given up hope of broadcasting when a sudden call came in March, 1939, for the boys to give a programme in Children's Hour on the Northern Regional wavelength. This was not, however, a world record, for by that time the band of the Boys' Home in Seoul, Korea, had been carrying out a weekly broadcast for some years.

In 1939 a new series of broadcasts was introduced from Radio Normandy, Clapton Congress Hall Band supplying the first programme on February 21st. An Army band could be heard for fifteen minutes every Tuesday and Thursday afternoon. This popular feature continued until the outbreak of war in the September of that year.

Although broadcasting in Britain has never returned to the dimension enjoyed in those adventurous days of the 1930s, there was a brief resurgence in June, 1948, when the International Staff Band launched a series of Sunday morning programmes under the title of ' With Flag Unfurled '. This ran for six weeks and the feature was repeated two years later, but such opportunities are now rare.

Many overseas territories, on the other hand, have enjoyed privileges never experienced in England. For more than thirty years Brantford (Ontario) Band, Canada, has conducted a Sunday morning broadcast from its hall consisting of hymn tunes, a vocal solo, a march or selection, and a five-minute address. The band then marches to its open-air meeting.

The great International Voice of the Andes hook-up enables millions in North and South America to hear the music of many Australian and New Zealand bands. Hilversum, Holland, has for thirty years been identified with Army programmes. Many bands from other countries have recorded music in the Christian Studios there for later broadcast across the continent of Europe. It is estimated that two million people hear Army music each week in Canada by means of the half-hour transcribed series, ' This is My Story '.

Television

THESE are early days in the history of television, but where opportunities have been given Salvationists have seized them to ' take the

message and fling it wide '. All over the U.S.A. the Salvation Army
officer is becoming a familiar figure on the home screen. With most
towns having their own television station, bands and instrumental
groups make frequent appearances. The New York Staff Band is in
great demand in a variety of ways, including appearing on such
popular programmes as ' Can you beat the band? ' and ' The Gary
Moore Show '. At Edmonton, Alberta, the informal programme by
corps musicians is much looked forward to; the Army's public
relations representative in the area is co-producer of religious programmes on this station. In St. John's, Newfoundland, Army bands
have played on the TV since 1958. Recent facilities in New Zealand
and Australia are opening up similar avenues in the Antipodes.
Wellington Citadel, in 1963, was the first band to appear on TV in
New Zealand.

Something new in television was carried out by Earlscourt Band,
and later the International Staff Band, in providing the music for the
successful feature, ' The Living Word ', shown extensively across the
U.S.A. and Canada during the past seven years. During almost a
week's filming at a studio in south London, the International Staff
Band recorded no fewer than fifty-two marches, selections and other
types of compositions to cover twenty-six instalments of the series.
The 16,000 feet of film were flown across the Atlantic and edited, then
to be linked with other features of the programme prepared in Canada.
When the band was in Toronto in 1962 further work of this kind was
undertaken.

What is thought to be a unique Army event took place at Leighton
Buzzard, England, during a Saturday afternoon open-air meeting in
February, 1960. While TV cameras whirled, the Divisional Com-
mander for North London, Lieut.-Colonel Edmund Taylor, presented
Bandmaster George Reeve with his certificate of retirement after
forty-eight years in that appointment and commissioned Bandmaster
Bramwell Evans to succeed him. Two nights later millions of viewers
saw the ceremony.

The influence of a father and his three teenage sons playing brass
instruments in the market-place at Salisbury has spread until a Salvation Army Band, playing in the Hollywood Bowl, can be heard by a
hundred million listeners across the North American continent and
may be seen by half of that number. The words spoken by William
Booth when presiding over a festival held during the 1904 International
Congress were not without vision:

> I want to fill the world with the music of heaven—the music that shall
> be the herald of salvation, the handmaiden of holiness, the trumpet call to
> duty, the evangel of Christianity and the servant of the living God. I want

music that says something to the mind and the heart through the ear. . . .
How is all this to be attained? Let sense and sound go hand in hand. If you
want this godly kind of music you must have godly men and women to
make it.

Salvationist-musicians in every land seek to carry out the Founder's
edict, and dare not forget his inspired saying which set the timeless
standard—

'SOUL-SAVING MUSIC IS THE MUSIC FOR ME.'

BIBLIOGRAPHY

BIBLIOGRAPHY

The War Cry

The Bandsman and Songster

The Musician

The Salvation Army Year Book

William Booth, by Harold Begbie (Macmillan)

Herbert Booth, by Ford C. Ottman (Jarrolds)

These Fifty Years, by Bramwell Booth (Cassell)

What hath God Wrought? by Arnold Brown (S.A. Canada)

The History of The Salvation Army, Vols. I and II, by Robert Sandall (Nelson)

The History of The Salvation Army, Vol. IV, by Arch R. Wiggins (Nelson)

Great Bands of America, by Alberta Powell Graham (Nelson)

Father of Salvation Army Music, by Arch R. Wiggins (S.P. & S., Ltd.)

The Triumph of Faith, by Arch R. Wiggins (S.P. & S., Ltd.)

Zulu Queen (Marianne Pawson), by Ruth Tracy (S.P. & S., Ltd.)

Fifty Years of Army Music, by J. Mackenzie Rogan (Methuen)

Fighting in Many Lands (S.P. & S., Ltd.)

The Brass Band Movement, by J. F. Russell and J. H. Elliott

INDEX

Adams, Lieut.-Colonel Bernard, 35, 37, 44, 57, 143, 167, 182, 203, 205
Alaska, 57, 58
Alexandra Palace, 195
Allan, Commissioner John J., 50, 73, 163, 181, 182, 199
Antigua, 66
Appleby, Staff-Captain Harry, 21, 27, 30 33, 39, 40, 46, 54, 115, 191, 196
Argentina, 62, 63
Assurance Headquarters Boys' Band, 44
Assurance Songsters, 45
Australia, 68–75, 142, 165, 184, 187, 212, 213, 215–217, 220, 222
Australia, visits to, 142, 143
Austria, visits to, 130, 131

Bahamas, 66
Ball, Eric, 34, 41, 42, 45, 157, 182, 210, 213
Bands Department (N.H.Q., London), 166–172
Bandsman and Songster, The, 177, 178
Barbados, 66
Belgium, 79–81, 183
Belgium, visits to, 111, 130–132
Bermuda, 61, 182
Black, Bandmaster T. Freeman, 213, 214
Booth, General Evangeline, 48, 162, 164, 191
Booth, Commandant Herbert, 9, 21, 39, 40, 70, 71, 145, 147, 148, 185, 196
Booth-Tucker, Commissioner Frederick de L., 51, 117, 118, 186
Brazil, 63–65
Bristow, Lieut.-Colonel Arthur, 157, 175
Britain, brass bands in, 4
Britain, visits to, 91, 133, 134, 140, 141, 180
British Guiana, 66
broadcasting, 45, 50, 53, 56, 66, 105, 110, 115, 118, 127, 135, 138, 168, 175, 190, 210, 213, 218–221
Buckingham Palace, 199–204
Burgess, Bandmaster Caleb, 20, 27, 31
Burma, 121

Canada, 54–61, 132, 137, 165, 179, 182, 187, 188, 211, 212, 220–222
Canada, visits to, 24–26, 50, 83, 102, 134–136, 138, 139, 205
Canadian Staff Band, 59, 60, 197
Carpenter, General George, 63, 72
Case, Captain Valentine, 15

Catelinet, Bandmaster Phil. B., 157, 182, 214
Central Africa, 112–114
Central America and West Indies, 65–67
Ceylon, 120, 121
Chalk Farm, 16, 18, 19, 80, 81, 102, 104, 105, 109, 118, 130, 131, 139, 153, 169, 194, 202, 203, 207, 210, 217–219
Chicago Staff Band, 52, 59, 136, 162, 180, 197
Chief Office Band, 44
China, 124, 125
churches, music in, 3, 4
civic and parliamentary affairs, 211, 212
Clapton Congress Hall, 16, 19, 20, 147, 178, 179, 207, 211
Coles, Colonel Bramwell, 34, 56, 59, 102, 138, 156, 157, 160, 164
composers' festivals, 198, 199
concertinas, 184, 185, 194–196
Condon, Captain Leslie, 158
Congo, 110, 111
Consett, 12, 13
convalescent home, 172
Costa Rica, 66
councils, 193, 194
Coutts, General Frederick, 37, 41, 110, 203 206
Crystal Palace, The, 19, 185, 195–197
Czechoslovakia, 87–89
Czechoslovakia, visits to, 130

Davey, Mrs. Captain Abram, 15
Denmark, 96, 97, 132, 134, 180, 184, 213
Denmark, visits to, 130, 132, 141, 142, 180, 205
drum and fife bands, 14, 110, 114, 117, 118, 128, 129, 149, 178, 180, 194
drums, 110, 120, 122, 185–189
Duggins, Commissioner Norman, 88, 89

Earlscourt, 56, 132, 204, 222
East Africa, 114–116, 187
Empress of Ireland, 60, 135, 197
Equatorial Africa, 111, 112
Estonia, 220

Finland, 103
Finland, visits to, 130, 134
France, 78, 79, 183
France, visits to, 92, 130–132, 134

Fry family, 1, 2, 5, 7–9, 12, 13, 30, 68, 145–148, 153, 185, 186
Fuller, Colonel George, 33, 37, 143, 156, 164, 203, 213

German Staff Band, 64, 84–87, 197
Germany, 84–86
Germany, visits to, 19, 130, 132–134, 141, 184
Ghana, 109, 110
Godfrey, Sir Dan, 209, 210
Goffin, Major Dean, 162, 168, 171, 182, 199
Goldsmith, Colonel Arthur, 29, 35, 37, 42, 88, 151, 153, 154, 157, 164, 188
Government circles, 194, 205, 206
guitars, 92, 98–100, 103, 104, 110, 111, 126
Gullidge, Bandmaster Arthur, 74

Hall, Henry, 157
Hawkes, Colonel Frederick, 22, 27, 28, 40, 41, 148–157, 176
Haynes, Captain Eliza ('Happy Eliza'), 7
Hill, Henry, 147, 148, 153
Holland, visits to, 19, 30
Home Office Band, 39, 46, 153, 196
Hong Kong, 125
Household Troops Band, The, 21–30, 39, 81, 133, 148, 176, 195, 196
Hull, 14, 147
Hungary, 89

Iceland, 96
India, 117–120, 186
Indonesia, 127–129
instrument-making, 172–175
International Music Board, 41, 45, 163–165
International Staff Band, 29–39, 41, 44–46, 82, 84, 90, 113, 119, 124, 125, 134–136, 153, 157, 158, 161, 163, 165, 177, 180, 187, 188, 193–195, 197, 198, 203–207, 209, 210, 217, 218, 221, 222

Jakeway, Colonel Albert, 38, 45, 88, 157, 158, 203
Jamaica, 65, 66
Japan, 121–124, 220
Junior Staff Band, 29, 31, 62, 153, 179

Kent March, The Great, 21
Kenya, 114, 115

Kitching, General Wilfred, 79, 88, 101, 102, 110, 111, 115, 127, 162, 167, 170, 181, 187, 199
Korea, 126, 127, 220, 221
Korea, visit to, 124

Latvia, 220
Leedham, George, 3
Leidzén, Erik, 101, 102, 138, 161–163, 180, 182
Life Guards, The Band of the, 21
London Band, 125, 143
Lyne, Bandmaster Jabez, 31

Malaysia, 126
Manchukuo, visit to, 124
Marshall, Bandmaster George, 88, 157, 160, 195, 199, 212
McMillan, Commissioner John, 72
Men's Social Work Headquarters Band, 42–45, 132, 154, 158, 167
Mitchell, Commissioner George, 31–33
music boards, 41, 45, 163–165
music camps, 109, 181–184
Music Editorial Department, 145–165
Musician, The, 177, 178

Netherlands, The, 81–83, 132–134, 138, 165, 221
Netherlands, visits to The, 111, 130, 134, 136, 141, 204, 205
New Zealand, 75–77, 142, 162, 165, 184, 217, 220, 222
New Zealand, visit to, 142
New York Staff Band, 46, 49–51, 67, 136, 137, 140, 141, 163, 180, 197, 211, 217, 222
Newfoundland, 57
Nigeria, 108, 109
Northwich, 12
Norway, 93–96, 161, 183, 184
Norway, visits to, 130, 136, 142, 204

Order of the Founder, 212, 213
Orsborn, General Albert, 124, 163, 183
Østby, Lieut.-Colonel Klaus, 93–95, 101, 160, 161, 166
Overton, Bandmaster William, 213

Pakistan, 120
Panama, 66
Payne, Captain Tom, 15
persecution, 24, 29, 55, 62, 70, 87, 89, 184, 190–192
Philippines, The, 126

Plant, Brigadier Tom, 194, 216
professional musicians, 213, 214
publishing of music, 145–165
Puerto Rico, 67
Punchard, Bandmaster Alfred W., 18, 19, 29, 130, 139, 164, 169–171, 202, 203, 210, 212, 219

Railton, Commissioner Geo. S., 24, 25, 47, 49, 189, 190
recording, 50, 190, 216–218
Regent Hall, 16–18, 44, 50, 174, 186, 194, 196, 199–202, 205–207, 217
Rhodesia, 112–114
Rhodesia, visit to, 112
Rich, Commissioner Chas., 27
Robertson, Adjutant Tom, 215, 216
'Rosehill' Band, 45, 46, 165
royal occasions, 198, 199, 204, 205; see Buckingham Palace

S.A.A.S. Bands, 44–46
St. Helena, 108
Salisbury, 1, 3, 5, 7, 8, 12, 186, 211, 218
Scotney, Bandmaster Harold, 69, 70
Shaw, George Bernard, 207–209
Sheard, Arthur (Trumpeter), 9–11, 16, 17
Singing, Speaking and Praying Brigade, 39, 147
Skinner, Lieut.-Colonel Charles, 43, 158
Slater, Lieut.-Colonel Richard, 12, 23, 27, 37, 146–148, 150–156, 159, 161, 163, 166, 179, 193, 196, 213
Söderström, Emil, 138, 161, 162, 180
Sousa, John Philip, 47–49
South Africa, 105–108
South Africa, visit to, 113
South America, 62–65
Southern Territory (U.S.A.) Staff Band, 53
S.P. & S. Band, 41, 42, 45, 165, 177, 217
Steadman-Allen, Captain Ray, 158

Stewart, Lieut.-Colonel William, 34, 35
Stockton, 3
string bands, 86, 87, 95–97, 100, 101, 103, 104, 149, 180, 183, 193
Sweden, 98–103, 132–134, 137–140, 165, 180, 183, 197, 217
Sweden, visits to, 130, 131, 130, 141–144, 180
Switzerland, 89–92, 132–134, 183, 218
Switzerland, visits to, 130, 131, 134, 136

tambourines, 189, 190, 196
Tanganyika, 115, 116
television, 50, 190, 211, 221, 222
timbrel bands, 54, 74, 75, 109, 119, 194, 196
Trade Headquarters Band, 40, 41, 153, 173, 216
Trinidad, 66
Twitchin, Bandmaster Herbert, 17, 159, 199–201, 212, 217

uniform, 175–177
United States of America, 47–53, 137, 141, 162, 165, 180, 181, 188, 194, 197, 212, 217, 220, 222
United States of America, visits to, 26, 56, 83, 102, 134, 135, 137–140
Uruguay, 62

Ward, Major Walter J., 45
Welsh Minstrel ('Welsh Tom'), 7, 9, 55
West Africa, 109, 110
Western Territory (U.S.A.) Staff Band, 53
Whitechapel, 15, 18
Wiggins (née Ringham), Mrs. Maisie, 213
Williams, Dr. Ralph Vaughan, 38, 210
women composers, 163

young people's bands, 178–181, 221
Yugoslavia, 89